TALKS WITH
SWAMI VIVEKANANDA

Advaita Ashrama
(PUBLICATION DEPARTMENT)
5 DEHI ENTALLY ROAD • KOLKATA 700 014

Published by
Swami Bodhasarananda
Adhyaksha, Advaita Ashrama
Mayavati, Champawat, Uttarakhand
from its Publication Department, Kolkata
Email: mail@advaitaashrama.org
Website: www.advaitaashrama.org

© *All Rights Reserved*
Second Edition, 1946
Sixteenth Impression, January 2010
3M3C

ISBN 978-81-7505-153-9

Printed in India at
Trio Process
Kolkata 700 014

PREFACE

Great persons are usually known to us through their lectures, writings or public activities. But it is always a rare privilege to come into intimate contact with them and study their lives and thoughts at close quarters. This is all the more true of spiritual geniuses. Those who have attained to a great spiritual height live in a different plane, as it were, from that of ours, and in spite of their endeavour to do good to the world and their great sympathy for the suffering humanity, none except those who have been directly touched by them succeed in taking full advantage of their lives and teachings. Spiritual giants are worshipped from a distance but the influence of their examples enters into the lives of only a fortunate few. All are not destined to have direct contact with spiritual personalities, hence the next best thing for ordinary people is to know their teachings, in which is hidden the inspiration of their lives. It is therefore that the teachings or recorded sayings of saints are so much in demand. A few sayings of Christ found in the Bible and a few words of Buddha that have been left to the world as a great legacy are giving spiritual sustenance to millions of people for thousands of years. It is but natural.

The meteoric success of Swami Vivekananda as a religious teacher in two hemispheres dazzles us. We are struck with awe and reverence when we read his writings or go through his recorded speeches. We feel he is talking to us from a dizzy height. We are bewildered by the thought of the gulf between his greatness and our smallness. But when one would come into direct touch with him, one would feel that the distance had vanished, and find in Swami Vivekananda a close friend or an intimate relation, eager to do the highest good for all. It is only when such relationship is established that you can know the real man. The disciples who recorded their conversations with Swami Vivekananda in the following pages, had the privilege not only of finding the Swami as a Guru, but of being very free with him. So we find, they were discussing all kinds of subjects with him. And as Swami Vivekananda while giving out his views was not trammelled by formality as is the case when one stands on a public platform, his words as found here have got special value. Here Swami Vivekananda gives directions about spiritual practice and meditation, talks of high philosophy, and in the next breath discusses the problems of national regeneration, social reform, educational ideals, and what not. Now and then we find how the large heart of that great giant bled for the sufferings of the poor and the needy. People in almost all walks of life will find guidance from these conversations.

The conversations took place in Bengali and were originally published in the *Udbodhan*—a Bengali monthly of the Ramakrishna Order. They were translated, at places abridged, and incorporated in *The Complete Works of Swami Vivekananda*. We bring them out in a handy book form, hoping they will be of immense help to a larger circle of the reading public. May our hopes be justified.

PUBLISHER

ADVAITA ASHRAMA
MAYAVATI, HIMALAYAS
The 12th January, 1939

CONTENTS

	PAGE
PREFACE	iii
CHAPTER I	(1—409)

Sec. I. *The first meeting with Swami Vivekananda—Mr. Narendranath Sen, Editor of the Mirror—Comparison between the English and the American—The future result of preaching religion in foreign countries—The relative value of politics and religion—A preacher of cow-protection—Man is to be saved first* 1

Sec. II. *Rebellion against nature, the sign of consciousness—The same is true of nations—The cause of India's degradation—Need for self-confidence—Men or money?—The way to Self-realization—The Krishna of Kurukshetra—Need for the development of Rajas* 13

Sec. III. *Talking with some Pandits in Sanskrit—What is civilization—Characteristics of Indian civilization—*

	PAGE
Samadhi—Who is the real teacher—Hereditary Gurus—Sri Ramakrishna	25
Sec. IV. The Birthday anniversary of Sri Ramakrishna at Dakshineswar—Need of religious festivals—Swami Vivekananda did not preach sectarianism	33
Sec. V. Initiating the disciple—Origin of the sacred thread—The problem of virtue and vice—When is the Self realized	41
Sec. VI. Starting the Ramakrishna Mission—Did Swami Vivekananda differ from Sri Ramakrishna—Swami Vivekananda's attitude towards Sri Ramakrishna—The Law of grace—Girish Chandra Ghosh	49
Sec. VII. Solar Eclipse—Nature of meditation—Practical hints on meditation—Need for renunciation	62
Sec. VIII. Female education—Mahakali Pathashala—Women in India and the West—Early marriage—Right type of female education—Spread of education	68

Sec. IX. Rig-Veda—Max Müller—The theory of creation—Swami Vivekananda's great heart—Need for the

CONTENTS

	PAGE
study of scriptures—Service of living beings	78
Sec. X. *The ideal of Sannyasa—Buddha and the institution of Sannyasa—Meeting the criticism against Sannyasa—Who is a real Sannyasin*	91
Sec. XI. *Consecration of the temple of Sri Ramakrishna*	105
Sec. XII. *Guru Govind Singh—Psychic powers*	108
Sec. XIII. *Tithipuja of Sri Ramakrishna—Investing some non-Brahmin devotees with holy thread—Girish Chandra Ghosh—Karma-Yoga or unselfish work—Its aim and utility*	117
Sec. XIV. *Installation of Sri Ramakrishna at Belur Math—Shankaracharya—Buddha—Cause of the downfall of Buddhism—Influence of pilgrimage—Different methods of worship*	127
Sec. XV. *In a reminiscent mood—His psychic powers—American men and women—Opposition from the bigoted Christians—Self-surrender and inertia*	

CONTENTS

PAGE

—Nag Mahashaya 140

Sec. XVI. *Swami Vivekananda's experiences at Amarnath and Kshir Bhavani—Hearing a divine voice—Existence of ghosts and spirits—Swami Vivekananda's experience of a disembodied spirit* 150

Sec. XVII. *Composing a Sanskrit hymn—About Bengali language and style—"Be fearless"—Need for the study of scriptures—Result of Self-realization* 156

Sec. XVIII. *Swami Vivekananda's experience of Nirvikalpa Samadhi—Extraordinary power of Avataras* ... 166

Sec. XIX. *Need for faith in oneself—Service and business—So-called educated people—Masses—Their future* 174

Sec. XX. *At the Zoological Garden at Alipur—Darwin, Theory of Evolution and Patanjali—Need for physical strength* 185

Sec. XXI. *Swami Vivekananda's future plan about Belur Math—Work and*

CONTENTS

PAGE

meditation—Nescience—Brahman and the world of matter 195

Sec. XXII. *The Bengali monthly 'Udbodhan'—Its future policy* 210

Sec. XXIII. *India wants not lecturing but work—The crying problem in India is poverty—Young Sannyasins to be trained both as secular and spiritual teachers and workers for the masses—Exhortations to young men to work for others* 217

Sec. XXIV. *Reconciliation of Jnana and Bhakti—Sat-Chit-Ananda—How sectarianism originates—Bring in Shraddha and the worship of Shakti and Avataras—The ideal of the hero we want now, not the Madhura-bhava—Sri Ramakrishna—Avataras* 225

Sec. XXV. *Brahman and differentiation—Personal realization of oneness—Supreme Bliss is the goal of all—Think always, I am Brahman—Discrimination and renunciation are the means—Be fearless* 235

CONTENTS

Sec. XXVI. *Renunciation of Kamakanchana—God's mercy falls on those who struggle for realization—Unconditional mercy and Brahman are one* ... 244

Sec. XXVII. *The doctrine of Ahimsa and meat-eating—The Sattva, Rajas and Tamas in man—Discrimination of food and spirituality—'Ahara'—The three defects in food—Don't-touchism and caste-prejudices—Plan of restoring the old Chaturvarna and the laws of the Rishis* ... 250

Sec. XXVIII. *Cause of India's degradation—Ancient Vedic customs must be remodelled according to the need of the society and the times—New Smriti to be compiled* ... 259

Sec. XXIX. *Auspiciousness of time and place—Work and Self-realization—Karma-yoga—India wants manifestation of Rajas—Bright future for the country* ... 267

Sec. XXX. *Laws of Brahmacharya—New Order of Sannyasins—Wanted Karma-yoga as taught in the Gita* ... 277

CONTENTS

PAGE

Sec. XXXI. *Meeting with Nag Mahashaya* 280

Sec. XXXII. *Brahman, Ishvara, Jiva and Avidya—Renunciation and Self-realization—How to control the mind—Atman as the object of meditation—Jnana, Bhakti, Karma and Yoga—The doctrine of incarnation of God—Exhortation for Self-realization—Work of a Jnani* 287

Sec. XXXIII. *On art—Difference between Indian and Western arts—Seal of the Ramakrishna Mission, its significance—Plan of the Ramakrishna temple* 303

Sec. XXXIV. *A power working through Swami Vivekananda—Reminiscence of East Bengal and the visit to Nag Mahashaya's house—Renunciation and not the observance of external forms is the test of spiritual progress—Firm determination needed to realize the Self* 312

Sec. XXXV. *Plan of the future Math for women—Soul has no sex—Women have equal opportunity for realizing the Brahman—Religion to be the centre of female education—Definition of good work—Work and knowledge*   323

Sec. XXXVI. *Swami Vivekananda's wonderful memory—His opinion about Bharatchandra and Michael Madhusudan Dutt, two Bengali poets* ... 337

Sec. XXXVII. *Why Atman is not perceived though so very near—On Self-realization all questionings cease—Mother Kali* 343

Sec. XXXVIII. *Wanted a sturdy band of young men ready to sacrifice all for others—Manliness should be the ideal—Remedy against low spirits and weakness of mind—Work for others—No individual liberation before the salvation of all—Influence of thoughts* 349

Sec. XXXIX. *Swami Vivekananda's plan to celebrate Durga Puja at Belur Math—His visit to the temple at kalighat* 360

Sec. XL. *The last birthday anniversary of Sri Ramakrishna that Swami Vivek-*

PAGE

ananda saw—Swami Vivekananda's idea as to how the celebration should take place—How far a Guru can help—What is meant by grace—Swami Vivekananda's vision of Sri Ramakrishna 363

Sec. XLI. *Swami Vivekananda's love and sympathy for the poor—"Don't-touchism"—Who serves Jiva serves God indeed* 371

Sec. XLII. *Life at the Belur Math in early days—Swami Vivekananda's reminiscence of Baranagore Math—Rigours of monastic vow* 376

Sec. XLIII. *On meditation—How to awaken the Kundalini—How to have concentration—Directions about spiritual practice* 384

Sec. XLIV. *About disciples of Sri Ramakrishna* 390

Sec. XLV. *Different grades of devotees of Sri Ramakrishna—Different interpretation of the teachings of Sri Ramakrishna—Future of the message of Sri Ramakrishna* 395

xvi CONTENTS

PAGE

Sec. XLVI. *Denationalisation and national degradation—Directions about spiritual practice* 403

CHAPTER II ... ... (410—469)

Sec. I. *Educative value of royal Durbars—Freedom and discipline—Swami Vivekananda's catholicity—Test of civilization* 410

Sec. II. *The picture of Sri Krishna, the preacher of the Gita—What is meant by 'Karma' in the Gita—Egoism and self-surrender—Problem of evil—The value of sincerity—Origin of image worship—Tantrikism—Harmony of Yogas—Reverence for women* ... 414

Sec. III. *Reminiscence—The problem of famines in India, and self-sarrificing workers—East and West—Is it Sattva or Tamas—A nation of mendicants—The "give and take" policy—Tell a man his defects directly but praise his virtues before others—Vivekananda everyone may become—Unbroken Brahmacharya is the secret of power—Samadhi and work* 424

CONTENTS xvii

PAGE

Sec. IV. *Reminiscences—Pranayama—Thought-reading—Knowledge of previous births* 440

Sec. V. *The art and science of music, Eastern and Western* 443

Sec. VI. *The old institution of living with the Guru—The present University system—Lack of Shraddha—We have a national history—Western science coupled with Vedanta—The so-called higher education—The need of technical education and education on national lines—The story of Satyakama—Mere book-learning and education under Tyagis—Sri Ramakrishna and the Pandits—Establishment of Maths with Sadhus in charge of colleges—Text-books for boys to be compiled—Stop early marriage—Plan of sending unmarried graduates to Japan—The secret of Japan's greatness —Art, Asiatic and European—Art and utility—Styles of dress—The food question and poverty* 447

Sec. VII. *The discrimination of the four castes according to Jati and Guna—*

CONTENTS

	PAGE
Brahmanas and Kshatriyas in the West—The Kula-Guru system in Bengal	465

CHAPTER III ... ... (470—495)

Sec. I. *The loss of Shraddha in India and need of its revival—Men we want —Real social reform* 470

Sec. II. *Reconciliation of Jnana Yoga and Bhakti Yoga—God in good and in evil too—Use makes a thing good or evil—Karma—Creation—God— Maya* 474

Sec. III. *Intermarriage among subdivisions of a Varna—Against early marriage—The education that India needs —Brahmacharya* 481

Sec. IV. *Madhura-bhava—Prema— Namakirtana—Its danger—Bhakti tempered with Jnana—A curious dream* 488

CHAPTER IV ... ... (496—500)
Think of death always and new life will come within—Work for others— God, the last refuge 496

TALKS WITH SWAMI VIVEKANANDA

CHAPTER I

(From the Diary of a Disciple*)

I

THE FIRST MEETING WITH SWAMI VIVEKANANDA —MR. NARENDRANATH SEN, EDITOR OF THE *MIRROR*—COMPARISON BETWEEN THE ENGLISH AND THE AMERICAN—THE FUTURE RESULT OF PREACHING RELIGION IN FOREIGN COUNTRIES— THE RELATIVE VALUE OF POLITICS AND RELIGION —A PREACHER OF COW-PROTECTION—MAN IS TO BE SAVED FIRST.

[Place : *Calcutta, the house of the late Babu Priyanath Mukhopadhyaya, Baghbazar. Year : 1897.*]

It is three or four days since Swamiji has set his foot in Calcutta after his first return from the West. The joy of the devotees of Sri Ramakrishna knows no bounds at enjoying his holy presence after a long time. And the

---

* The disciple is Babu Saratchandra Chakravarty. He has brought out his records in a Bengali book named *Swâmi-Shishya-Samvâda*.

well-to-do among them are considering themselves blessed to warmly invite Swamiji to their own houses. This afternoon Swamiji had an invitation to the house of Srijut Priyanath Mukhopadhyaya, a devotee of Sri Ramakrishna, at Rajballabhpara in Baghbazar. Receiving this news, many devotees assembled to-day in his house.

The disciple also, informed of it through indirect sources, reached the house of Mr. Mukherjee at about 2-30 p.m. He had not yet made his acquaintance with Swamiji. So this was to be his first meeting with the Swami.

On the disciple's reaching there, Swami Turiyananda took him to Swamiji and introduced him. After his return to the Belur Math, the Swami had already heard about him, having read a Hymn on Sri Ramakrishna composed by the disciple. Swamiji also had come to know that the disciple used to visit Nâg Mahâshaya, a foremost devotee of Sri Ramakrishna.*

When the disciple prostrated himself before him and took his seat, Swamiji addressed him in Sanskrit and asked him about Nag Maha-

---

* Durga Charan Nag, the great saint and perfected soul, living as a householder, who wonderfully reflected in his life—in many of its phases—the greatness of the Master, Sri Ramakrishna.

shaya and his health, and while referring to his superhuman renunciation, his unbounded love for God and his humility, he said,

वयं तत्त्वान्वेषात् हताः मधुकर त्वं खलु कृती ।†

"We are undone by our vain quest after reality; while, O bee, you are indeed blessed with success!" He then asked the disciple to send these words to Nag Mahashaya. Afterwards, finding it rather inconvenient to talk to the disciple in the crowd, he called him and Swami Turiyananda to a small room to the west, and, addressing himself to the disciple, began to recite these words from Vivekachudâmani :

मा भैष्ठ विद्वन् तव नास्त्यपायः
संसारसिन्धोस्तरणेऽस्त्युपायः ।
येनैव याता यतयोऽस्य पारं
तमेव मार्गं तव निर्दिशामि ॥

"O wise one, fear not; you have not to perish. Means there are for crossing the ocean of this round of birth and death. I shall show you the same way by which holy men of

† Words addressed by King Dushyanta to the bee which was teasing Sakuntalâ by plunging at her face. —Kâlidâsa's Sakuntala.

renunciation have crossed this ocean." He then asked him to read Âchârya Shankara's work named Vivekachudâmani.

At these words, the disciple went on musing within himself. Was the Swami in this way hinting at the desirability of his own formal initiation ? The disciple was at that time a staunch orthodox man in his ways, and a Vedantin. He had not yet settled his mind as regards the adoption of a Guru and was a devoted advocate of Varnâshrama, or caste ordinances.

While various topics were going on, a man came in and announced that Mr. Narendranath Sen, the Editor of the Mirror, had come for an interview with Swamiji. Swamiji asked the bearer of this news to show him into that small room. Narendra Babu came and taking a seat there opened various topics about England and America. In answer to his questions Swamiji said, "Nowhere in the world is to be found another nation like the Americans, so generous, broad-minded, hospitable and so sincerely eager to accept new ideas." "Whatever work," he went on, "has been done in America has not been done through my power. The people of America have accepted the ideas of Vedanta, because they are so good-hearted." Referring to England he said, "There is no nation in the world so conservative as the English. They do not like so easily to accept any new idea, but if through perseverance they can be once made to understand any idea, they will never give it up by any means. Such firm determination you will find in no other nation. This is why they occupy the foremost position in the world in power and civilisation."

Then declaring that if qualified preachers could be had there was greater likelihood of the Vedanta work being permanently established in England than in America, he continued, "I have only laid the foundation of the work. If future preachers follow my path, a good deal of work may be done in time."

Narendra Babu asked, "What future prospect is there for us in preaching religion in this way?"

Swamiji said, "In our country there is only this religion of Vedanta. Compared with the Western civilisation, it may be said, we have hardly got anything else. But by the preaching of this universal religion of Vedanta, a religion which gives equal rights to acquire spirituality to men of all creeds and all paths of religious practice, the civilised West would come to know what a wonderful degree of spirituality once developed in India and how that is still existing. By the study of this religion, the Western nations will have increasing regard and sympathy for us—already these have grown to some extent. In this way, if we have their real sympathy and regard, we would learn from them the sciences bearing on our material life, thereby qualifying ourselves better for the struggle of existence. On the other hand by learning this Vedanta from us, they will be enabled to secure their own spiritual welfare."

Narendra Babu asked, "Is there any hope of our political progress in this kind of interchange?" Swamiji said, "They (the Western nations) are the children of the great hero Virochana!* Their power makes the five elements play like puppets in their hands. If you people believe that we shall in case of conflict with them gain freedom by applying those material forces, you are profoundly mistaken. Just as a little piece of stone figures before the Himalayas, so we differ from them

---

* In ancient Indian tradition Virochana was the first great king of the Asuras, possessing supernatural powers. Recent investigations in Assyrian mythology prove the existence of a tradition in Assyrian history about such a king, called Berosus in certain ancient genealogies.

in point of skill in the use of those forces. Do you know what my idea is? By preaching the profound secrets of the Vedanta religion in the Western world, we shall attract the sympathy and regard of these mighty nations, maintaining for ever the position of their teacher in spiritual matters, and they will remain our teachers in all material concerns. The day when, surrendering the spiritual into their hands, our countrymen would sit at the feet of the West to learn religion, that day indeed the nationality of this fallen nation will be dead and gone for good. Nothing will come of crying day and night before them, 'Give me this or give me that.' When there will grow a link of sympathy and regard between both nations by this give-and-take intercourse, there will be then no need for these noisy cries. They will do everything of their own accord. I believe that by this cultivation of religion and the wider diffusion of Vedanta, both this country and the West will gain enormously. To me the pursuit of politics is a secondary means in comparison with this. I shall lay down my life to practically carry out this belief. If you believe in any other way of accomplishing the good of India, well, you may go on working your own way."

Narendra Babu shortly left, expressing his unqualified agreement with Swamiji's ideas. The disciple, hearing the above words from Swamiji, astonishingly contemplated his luminous features with steadfast gaze.

When Narendra Babu had departed, an enthusiastic preacher belonging to the society for the protection of cows came for an interview with Swamiji. He was dressed almost like a Sannyâsin, if not fully so—with a GERUA turban tied on the head; he was evidently an upcountry Indian. At the announcement of this preacher of cow-protection Swamiji came out to the parlour room. The preacher saluted Swamiji and presented him with a picture of the mother-cow. Swamiji took that in his hand and making it over to one standing by, commenced the following conversation with the preacher:—

Swamiji:—What is the object of your society?

Preacher:—We protect the mother-cows of our country from the hands of the butcher. Cow-infirmaries have been founded in some places where the diseased, decrepit mother-cows or those bought from the butchers are provided for.

Swamiji:—That is very good indeed. What

is the source of your income ?

Preacher :—The work of the society is carried on only by gifts kindly made by great men like you.

Swamiji :—What amount of money have you now laid by ?

Preacher :—The Marwari traders' community are the special supporters of this work. They have given a big amount for this good cause.

Swamiji :—A terrible famine has now broken out in Central India. The India Government has published a death-roll of nine lakhs of starved people. Has your society done anything to render help in this time of famine ?

Preacher :—We do not help during famine or other distresses. This society has been established only for the protection of mother-cows.

Swamiji :—During a famine when lakhs of people, your own brothers and sisters, have fallen into the jaws of death, you have not thought it your duty, though having the means, to help them in that terrible calamity with food ?

Preacher :—No. This famine broke out as a result of men's Karma, their sins. It is a case of 'like Karma, like fruit.'

Hearing the words of the preacher, sparks

of fire, as it were, scintillated out of Swamiji's large eyes; his face became flushed. But he suppressed his feeling and said, "Those associations which do not feel sympathy for men, and even seeing their own brothers dying from starvation do not give them a handful of rice to save their lives, while giving away piles of food to save birds and beasts, I have not the least sympathy for them, and I do not believe that society derives any good from them. If you make a plea of Karma by saying that men die through their Karma, then it becomes a settled fact that it is useless to try or struggle for anything in this world; and your work for the protection of animals is no exception. With regard to your cause also, it can be said—the mother-cows through their own Karma fall into the hands of the butchers and die, and we need not do anything in the matter."

The preacher was a little abashed and said, "Yes, what you say is true, but the Shâstras say that the cow is our mother."

Swamiji smilingly said, "Yes, that the cow is our mother, I understand; who else could give birth to *such* accomplished children?"

The upcountry preacher did not speak further on the subject; perhaps he could not understand the point of Swamiji's poignant ridicule. He told Swamiji that he was begging something of him for the objects of the society.

Swamiji :—I am a Sannyâsin, a fakir. Where shall I find money enough to help you? But if ever I get money in my possession, I shall first spend that in the service of man. Man is first to be saved; he must be given food, education and spirituality. If any money is left after doing all these, then only something would be given to your society.

At these words, the preacher went away after saluting Swamiji. Then Swamiji began to speak to us : "What words these, forsooth! Says he that men are dying by reason of their Karma, so what avails doing any kindness to them! This is decisive proof that the country has gone to rack and ruin! Do you see how much abused the Karma theory of your Hinduism has been? Those who are men and yet have no feeling in the heart for man, well, are such to be counted as men at all?" While speaking these words, Swamiji's whole body seemed to shiver in anguish and grief.

Then, while smoking, Swamiji said to the disciple, "Well, see me again."

Disciple :—Where will you be staying, sir? Perhaps you might put up in some rich man's house. Will he allow me there?

Swamiji :—At present, I shall be living either at the Alambazar Math or at the garden-house of Gopal Lal Seal at Cossipore. You may come to either place.

Disciple :—Sir, I very much wish to speak with you in solitude.

Swamiji :—All right. Come one night. We shall speak plenty of Vedanta.

Disciple :—Sir, I have heard that some Europeans and Americans have come with you. Will they not get offended at my dress or my talk ?

Swamiji :—Why, they are also men, and moreover, they are devoted to the Vedanta religion. They will be glad to converse with you.

Disciple :—Sir, Vedanta speaks of some distinctive qualifications for its aspirants ; how could these come out in your Western disciples ? The Shâstras say—he who has studied the Vedas and the Vedanta, who has formally expiated his sins, who has performed all the daily and occasional duties enjoined by the scriptures, who is self-restrained in his food and general conduct, and specially he who is accomplished in the four special Sâdhanâs (preliminary disciplines), he alone has a right to the practice of Vedanta. Your Western disciples are in the first place non-Brahmins, and then they are lax in point of proper food and dress; how could they understand the system of Vedanta?

Swamiji:—When you speak with them you will know at once whether they have understood Vedanta or not.

Swamiji, perhaps, could now see that the disciple was rigidly devoted to the external observances of orthodox Hinduism. Swamiji then, surrounded by some devotees of Sri Ramakrishna, went over to the house of Srijut Balaram Basu at Baghbazar. The disciple bought the book Vivekachudâmani at Bat-tala and went towards his own home at Darjipara.

II

REBELLION AGAINST NATURE, THE SIGN OF CONSCIOUSNESS—THE SAME IS TRUE OF NATIONS—THE CAUSE OF INDIA'S DEGRADATION—NEED FOR SELF-CONFIDENCE—MEN OR MONEY?—THE WAY TO SELF-REALISATION—THE KRISHNA OF KURUKSHETRA—NEED FOR THE DEVELOPMENT OF RAJAS.

[Place: *On the way from Calcutta to Cossipore and in the garden of the late Gopal Lal Seal.* Year: *1897.*]

To-day Swamiji was taking rest at noon in

the house of Srijut Girish Chandra Ghosh.*
The disciple reaching there saluted him and
found that Swamiji was just ready to go to the
garden-house of Gopal Lal Seal. A carriage
was waiting outside. He said to the disciple,
"Well, come with me." The disciple agreeing,
Swamiji got up with him into the carriage, and
it started. When it drove up the Chitpur road,
on seeing the Ganges, Swamiji broke forth in
a chant, self-involved : गंगातरंग-रमणीय-जटाकलाप' ।
etc.† The disciple listened in silent wonder
to that wave of music, when after a short while,
seeing a railway engine going towards the Chitpur
hydraulic bridge, Swamiji said to the
disciple, "Look how it goes majestically like a
lion!" The disciple replied, "But that is inert
matter. Behind it there is the intelligence of
man working, and hence it moves. In moving
thus, what credit is there for it?"

Swamiji :—Well, say then, what is the sign
of consciousness?

Disciple :—Why, sir, that indeed is conscious
which acts through intelligence.

Swamiji :—Everything is conscious which

---

* The famous actor and dramatist of Bengal and a foremost devotee of Sri Ramakrishna.
† From Vyâsa's Hymn to Vishwanâtha, meaning "whose matted locks look charming with the waves of the Ganges playing among them."

rebels against nature : there, consciousness is manifested. Just try to kill a little ant, even it will once resist to save its life. Where there is struggle, where there is rebellion, there is the sign of life, there consciousness is manifested.

Disciple :—Sir, can that test be applied also in the case of man and of nations ?

Swamiji :—Just read the history of the world and see whether it applies or not. You will find that excepting yours it holds good in the case of all other nations. It is you only who are in this world lying prostrate to-day like inert matter. You have been hypnotised. From very old times, others have been telling you that you are weak, that you have no power, and you also, accepting that, have for about a thousand years gone on thinking, "We are wretched, we are good for nothing." (Pointing to his own body, he said) This body also is born of the soil of your country ; but I never thought like that. And hence you see how, through His will, even those who always think us low and weak, have done and are still doing me divine honour. If you can think that infinite power, infinite knowledge and indomitable energy lie within you and if you can bring out that power, you also can become like me.

Disciple :—Where is the capacity in us for

thinking that way, sir? Where is the teacher or preceptor who from our childhood can speak thus before us and make us understand? What we have heard and have learnt from all is that the object of having an education nowadays is to secure some good job.

Swamiji :—For that reason is it that we have come forward with quite another precept and example. Learn that truth from us, understand it and realise it; and then spread that idea broadcast, in cities, in towns and in villages. Go and preach to all, "Arise, awake, sleep no more; within each of you there is the power to remove all wants and all miseries. Believe this, and that power will be manifested." Teach this to all and with that, spread among the masses in plain language the central truths of science, philosophy, history and geography. I have a plan to open a centre with the unmarried youths; first of all I shall teach them, and then carry on the work through them.

Disciple :—But that requires a good deal of money. Where will you get this money?

Swamiji :—What do you talk! Isn't it man that makes money? Where did you ever hear money making man? If you can make your thoughts and words perfectly at one, if you can, I say, make yourself one in speech and action, money will pour in at your feet of itself, like water.

Disciple :—Well, sir, I take it for granted that money will come, and you will begin that good work. But what will that matter ? Before this, also, many great men carried out many good deeds. But where are they now ? To be sure, the same fate awaits the work which you are going to start. Then, what is the good of such an endeavour ?

Swamiji :—He who always speculates as to what awaits him in future, accomplishes nothing whatsoever. What you have understood as true and good, just do that at once. What's the good of calculating what may or may not befall in future ? The span of life is so, so short— and can anything be accomplished in it if you go on forecasting and computing results ? God is the only dispenser of results ; leave it to Him to do all that. What have you got to do with it ? Don't look that way, but go on working.

While he was thus going on, the cab reached the garden-house. Many people from Calcutta came to the garden that day to see Swamiji. Swamiji got down from the carriage, took his seat in the room, and began conversation with them all. Mr. Goodwin, a Western disciple of Swamiji, was standing near by, like the embodiment of service, as it were. The disciple had already made his acquaintance; so he came to Mr. Goodwin and both engaged in a variety of talk about Swamiji.

In the evening Swamiji called the disciple and asked him, "Have you got the *Kathopanishad* by heart ?"

Disciple :—No, sir, I have only read it with Shankara's commentary.

Swamiji :—Among the Upanishads, one finds no other book so beautiful as this. I wish you would all get it by heart. What will it do only to read it ? Rather try to bring into your life the faith, the courage, the discrimination and the renunciation of Nachiketa.

Disciple :—Give your blessings please, that I may realize these.

Swamiji :—You have heard of Sri Ramakrishna's words, haven't you ? He used to say, "The breeze of mercy is already blowing, do you only hoist the sail." Can anybody, my boy, thrust Realization upon another ? One's destiny is in one's own hands—the Guru only makes this much understood. Through the power of the seed itself the tree grows, the air and water are only aids.

Disciple :—There is, sir, the necessity also of extraneous help.

Swamiji :—Yes, there is. But you should know that if there be no substance within, no amount of outside help will avail anything. Yet there come a time for everyone to realize the Self. For everyone is Brahman. The distinction of higher and lower is only in the degree of manifestation of that Brahman. In time, everyone will have perfect manifestation. Hence the Shâstras say—"कालेनात्मनि विन्दति" —"In time, That is realized in one's self."

Disciple :—When, alas, will that happen, sir ? From the Shâstras we hear how many births we have had to pass in ignorance!

Swamiji :—What's the fear ? When you have come here this time, the goal shall be attained in this life. Liberation or Samâdhi— all this consists in simply doing away with the obstacles to the manifestation of Brahman. Otherwise the Self is always shining forth like the sun. The cloud of ignorance has only veiled It. Remove the cloud and the Sun will manifest. Then you get into the state of "भिद्यते हृदय ग्रन्थिः" (the knots of the heart are torn asunder) etc. The various paths that you find, all advise you to remove the obstacles on the way. The way by which one realizes the Self, is the way which he preached to all. But the goal of all is the knowledge of the Self, the realization of this Self. To it all men, all beings have equal right. This is the view acceptable to all.

Disciple :—Sir, when I read or hear these words of the Shâstras, the thought that the Self has not yet been realized makes the heart very disconsolate.

Swamiji :—This is what is called longing. The more it grows the more will the cloud of obstacles be dispelled, and stronger will faith be established. Gradually the Self will be realized like a fruit on the palm of one's hand. This realization alone is the soul of religion. Everyone can go on abiding by some observances and formalities. Everyone can fulfil certain injunctions and prohibitions, but how few have this longing for realization! This intense longing—becoming mad after realizing God or getting the knowledge of the Self—is real spirituality. The irresistible madness which the Gopis had for the Lord, Sri Krishna, yea, it is intense longing like that which is necessary for the realization of the Self! Even in the Gopis' mind there was a slight distinction of man and woman. But in real Self-knowledge, there is not the slightest distinction of sex.

While speaking thus, Swamiji introduced the subject of *Gita-Govindam* and continued saying :—

Jayadeva was the last poet in Sanskrit literature, though he often cared more for the jingling of words than for depth of sentiment. But just see, how the poet has shown the culmination of love and longing in the Shloka "पतति पतत्रे" etc.* Such love indeed is necessary for Self-realization. There must be fretting and pining within the heart. Now from His playful life at Vrindavan come to the Krishna of Kurukshetra, and see how that also is fascinating—how amidst all that horrible din and uproar of fighting Krishna remains calm, balanced and peaceful. Aye, on the very battlefield, He is speaking the Gitâ to Arjuna and getting him on to fight, which is the Dharma of a Kshatriya! Himself an agent to bring about this terrible warfare, Sri Krishna remains unattached to action,—He did not take up arms! To whichsoever phase of it you look, you will find the character of Sri Krishna perfect. As if He was the embodiment of knowledge, work, devotion, power of concentration and everything! In the present age, this aspect of

* पतति पतत्रे विचलति पत्रे शङ्कितभवदुपयानम् ।
रचयति शयनं सचकितनयनं पश्यति तव पन्थानम् ॥

"At the flying of a bird or the stirring of a leaf, he fancies you are coming; he arranges your bed with eyes all alert looking towards the way you would come."

Sri Krishna should be specially studied. Only contemplating the Krishna of Vrindavan with His flute, won't do nowadays,—that will not bring salvation to humanity. Now is needed the worship of Sri Krishna uttering forth the lion-roar of the Gita, of Râma with His bow and arrows, of Mahâvira, of Mother Kali. Then only will the people grow strong by going to work with great energy and will. I have considered the matter most carefully and come to the conclusion, that of those who profess and talk of religion nowadays in this country, the majority are full of morbidity—crack-brained or fanatic. Without development of an abundance of Rajas, you have hopes neither in this world, nor in the next. The whole country is enveloped in intense Tamas; and naturally the result is—servitude in this life and hell in the next."

Disciple :—Do you expect in view of the Rajas in the Westerners that they will gradually become Sâttvika ?

Swamiji :—Certainly. Possessed of a plenitude of Rajas, they have now reached the culmination of Bhoga or enjoyment. Do you think that it is not they, but you, who are going to achieve Yoga,—you who hang about for the sake of your bellies ? At the sight of their highly refined enjoyment, the delineation in *Megha-*

dutam- विद्युद्दन्तं ललितवसनाः etc.*—comes to my mind. And your Bhoga consists in lying on a ragged bed in a muggy room, multiplying progeny every year like a hog —Begetting a band of famished beggars and slaves! Hence do I say, let people be made energetic and active in nature by the stimulation of Rajas. Work, work, work, नान्यः पन्था विद्यतेऽयनाय —there is no other path of liberation but this.

Disciple :—Sir, did our forefathers possess this kind of Rajas ?

Swamiji :—Why, did they not ? Does not history tell us that they established colonies in many countries, and sent preachers of religion to Tibet, China, Sumâtra and even to far-off

---

* विद्युद्दन्तं ललितवसनाः सेन्द्रचापं सचित्राः
सङ्गीताय प्रहतमुरजाः स्निग्धगम्भीरघोषम् ।
अन्तस्तोयं मणिमयभुवस्तुङ्गमभ्रं लिहाग्राः
प्रासादास्त्वां तुलयितुमलं यत्र तैस्तैर्विशेषैः ॥

"The mansions of that city may well be compared with you, O cloud, for there is correspondence in features : while flashes of lightning play within you, they have charmingly attired damsels moving within them ; while you have the rainbow, they have their paintings ; you have your deep, rolling rumble, they have their drums sounding forth music ; you contain pellucid water within you, they have their interior bedecked with transparent gems ; you soar so high, their roofs also kiss the sky.' Kâlidâsa thus introduces his description of the enjoyments of Alakâpuri. So the reference here is not only to the first verse quoted, but also to the whole description which follows.

Japan ? Do you think there is any other means of achieving progress except through Rajas ?

As conversation thus went on, night approached; and meanwhile Miss Müller came there. She was an English lady, having great reverence for Swamiji. Swamiji introduced the disciple to her, and after a short talk Miss Müller went upstairs.

Swamiji :—See, to what a heroic nation they belong! How far-off is her home, and she is the daughter of a rich man—yet how long a way has she come, only with the hope of realizing the spiritual ideal!

Disciple :—Yes, sir, but your works are stranger still! How so many Western ladies and gentlemen are always eager to serve you! For this age, it is very strange indeed!

Swamiji :—If this body lasts, you will see many more things. If I can get some young men of heart and energy, I shall revolutionize the whole country. There are a few in Madras. But I have more hope in Bengal. Such clear brains are to be found scarcely in any other country. But they have no strength in their muscles. The brain and muscles must develop simultaneously. Iron nerves with an intelligent brain—and the whole world is at your feet.

Word was brought that supper was ready

for Swamiji. He said to the disciple, "Come and have a look at my food." While going on with the supper, he said, "It is not good to take much fatty or oily substance. *Roti* is better than *luchi*. *Luchi* is the food of the sick. Take fish and meat and fresh vegetables, but sweets sparingly." While thus talking, he enquired, "Well, how many *rotis* have I taken? Am I to take more?" He did not remember how much he took, and did not feel even if he yet had any appetite. The sense of body faded away so much while he was talking!

He finished after taking a little more. The disciple also took leave and went back to Calcutta. Getting no cab for hire, he had to walk, and while walking he thought over in his mind how soon again he could come the next day to see Swamiji.

III

TALKING WITH SOME PANDITS IN SANSKRIT—
WHAT IS CIVILIZATION—CHARACTERISTICS OF
INDIAN CIVILIZATION—SAMADHI—WHO IS THE REAL
TEACHER—HEREDITARY GURUS—SRI RAMAKRISHNA.

[Place : *Cossipore; at the garden of the late Gopal Lal Seal.* Year : 1897.]

After his first return from the West, Swamiji

resided for a few days at the garden of the late Gopal Lal Seal at Cossipore. Some well-known Pandits living at Barabazar, Calcutta, came to the garden one day, with a view to hold a disputation with him. The disciple was present there on the occasion.

All the Pandits that came there could speak in Sanskrit fluently. They came and greeting Swamiji who sat surrounded by a circle of visitors, began their conversation in Sankskrit. Swamiji also responded to them in melodious Sanskrit. The disciple cannot remember now the subject on which the Pandits argued with him that day. But this much he remembers that the Pandits, almost all in one strident voice, were rapping out to Swamiji in Sanskrit subtle questions of philosophy and he, in a dignified serious mood, was giving out to them calmly his own well-argued conclusions about those questions.

In the discussion with the Pandits Swamiji represented the side of the Siddhânta or conclusions to be established, while the Pandits represented that of the Purvapaksha, or objections to be raised. The disciple remembers that, while arguing, Swamiji wrongly used in one place the word *Asti* instead of *Swasti*, which made the Pandits laugh out. At this Swamiji

at once submitted :
—"I am but a servant of the Pandits, please excuse this mistake." The Pandits also were charmed at this humility of Swamiji. After a long dispute the Pandits at last admitted that the conclusions of the Siddhânta side were adequate, and preparing to depart, they made their greetings to Swamiji.

After the Pandits had left, the disciple learnt from Swamiji that these Pandits who took the side of the Purvapaksha were well versed in the Purva-Mimâmsâ Shâstras. Swamiji advocated the philosophy of the Uttara-Mimâmsâ or Vedanta and proved to them the superiority of the path of knowledge, and they were obliged to accept his conclusions.

About the way the Pandits laughed at Swamiji, picking up one grammatical mistake, he said that this error of his was due to the fact of his not having spoken in Sanskrit for many years together. He did not blame the Pandits a bit for all that. But he pointed out in this conection, that in the West it would imply a great incivility on the part of an opponent to point out any such slip in language, deviating from the real issue of dispute. A civilized society in such cases would accept the idea, taking no notice of the language. "But in your country, all the fighting is going on over the husk, nobody searches for the kernel within." So saying, Swamiji began to talk with the disciple in Sanskrit. The disciple also gave answers in broken Sanskrit. Yet he praised him for the sake of encouragement. From that day, at the request of Swamiji, the disciple used to speak with him in Sanskrit off and on.

In reply to the question : what is civilization, Swamiji said that day, "The more advanced a society or nation is in spirituality, the more is that society or nation civilized. No nation can be said to have become civilized, only because it has succeded in increasing the comforts of material life by bringing into use lots of machinery and things of that sort. The present-day civilization of the West is multiplying day by day only the wants and distresses of men. On the other hand, the ancient Indian civilization, by showing people the way to spiritual advancement, doubtless succeeded, if not in removing once for all, at least in lessening, in a great measure, the material needs of men. In the present age, it is to bring into coalition both these civilizations that Bhagavân Sri Ramakrishna was born. In this age, as on the one hand people have to be intensely practical, so on the other hand they have to acquire deep spiritual knowledge." Swamiji made us clearly understand that day that from such interaction of the Indian civilization with that of the West would dawn on the world a new era. In the course of dilating upon this, he happened to remark in one place, "Well, another thing. People there in the West think that the more a man is religious, the more demure he must be in his outward bearing—no word about anything else from his lips! As the priests in the West would on the one hand be struck with wonder at my liberal religious discourses, they would be as much puzzled on the other hand when they found me, after such discourses, talking frivolities with my friends. Sometimes they would speak out to my face: 'Swami, you are a priest, you should not be joking and laughing in this way like ordinary men. Such levity does not look well in you.' To which I would reply, 'We are children of bliss, why should we look morose and sombre?' But I doubt if they could rightly catch the drift of my words."

That day Swamiji also spoke many things about Bhâva Samâdhi and Nirvikalpa Samâdhi. These are produced below as far as possible:—

Suppose a man is cultivating that type of devotion to God which Hanumân represents. The more intense the attitude becomes, the more will the pose and demeanour of that aspirant, nay even his physical configuration, be cast in that mould. It is in this way that transmutation of species takes place. Taking up any such emotional attitude the worshipper becomes gradually shaped into the very form of his ideal. The ultimate stage of any such sentiment is called Bhâva Samâdhi. While the aspirant in the path of Jnâna pursuing the process of *"neti, neti"*, "not this, not this", such as "I am not the body, nor the mind, nor the intellect" and so on, attains to the Nirvikalpa Samâdhi when he is established in absolute consciousness. It requires striving through many births to reach perfection or the ultimate stage with regard to a single one of these devotional attitudes. But Sri Ramakrishna the king of the realm of spiritual sentiment, perfected himself in no less than eighteen different forms of devotion! He also used to say that his body would not have endured, had he not held himself on to this play of spiritual sentiment."

The disciple asked that day, 'Sir, what sort of food did you use to take in the West?"

Swamiji :—The same as they take there. We are Sannyâsins and nothing can take away our caste!

On the subject of how he would work in

future in this country, Swamiji said that day that starting two centres, one in Madras and another in Calcutta, he would rear up a new type of Sannyâsins for the good of all men in all its phases. He further said that by a destructive method no progress either for the society or for the country could be achieved. In all ages and times progress has been effected by the constructive process, that is, by giving a new mould to old methods and customs. Every religious preacher in India, during the past ages, worked in that line. Only the religion of Bhagavân Buddha was destructive. Hence that religion has been extirpated from India.

The disciple remembers that while thus speaking on, he remarked, "If the Brahman is manifested in one man, thousands of men advance, finding their way out in that light. Only the knowers of Brahman are the spiritual teachers of mankind. This is corroborated by all scriptures and by reason too. It is only the selfish Brâhmins who have introduced into this country the system of hereditary Gurus, which is against the Vedas and against the Shâstras. Hence it is that even through their spiritual practice men do not now succeed in perfecting themselves or in realizing Brahman. To remove all this corruption in religion, the Lord has incarnated Himself on earth in the present age in the person of Sri Ramakrishna. The universal teachings that he offered, if spread all over the world, will do good to humanity and the world. Not for many a century past has India produced so great, so wonderful, a teacher of religious synthesis."

A brother-disciple of Swamiji at that time asked him, "Why did not you publicly preach Sri Ramakrishna as an Avatâra in the West?"

Swamiji :—They make much flourish and fuss over their science and philosophy. Hence, unless you first knock to pieces their intellectual conceit through reasoning, scientific argument and philosophy, you cannot build anything there. Those who finding themselves off their moorings through their utmost intellectual reasoning would approach me in a real spirit of truth-seeking, to them alone, I would speak of Sri Ramakrishna. If, otherwise, I had forthwith spoken of the doctrine of incarnation, they might have said, "Oh, you do not say anything new—why, we have our Lord Jesus for all that!"

After thus spending some three or four delightful hours, the disciple came back to Calcutta that day along with the other visitors.

IV

THE BIRTHDAY ANNIVERSARY OF SRI RAMA-
KRISHNA AT DAKSHINESWAR—NEED OF RELIGIOUS
FESTIVALS—SWAMI VIVEKANANDA DID NOT PREACH
SECTARIANISM.

[Place : *The Kali-temple at Dakshineswar and the Alambazar Math.* Year : *1897, March.*]

When Swamiji returned from England for the first time, the Ramakrishna Math was located at Alambazar. The birthday anniversary of Bhagavân Sri Ramakrishna was being celebrated this year at the Kali-temple of Rani Râsmani at Dakshineswar. Swamiji with some of his brother-disciples reached there from the Alambazar Math at about nine or ten A.M. He was bare-footed, with a yellow turban on his head. Crowds of people were waiting to see and hear him. In the temple of Mother Kali, Swamiji prostrated himself before the Mother of the Universe, and thousands of heads, following him, bent low. Then after prostrating himself before Radhakantaji he came into the room which Sri Ramakrishna had used to occupy. There was not the least breathing space in the room.

Two European ladies who accompanied

Swamiji to India attended the festival. Swamiji took them along with himself to show them the holy Panchavati and the Vilwa tree.* Though the disciple was not yet quite familiar with Swamiji, he followed him, and presented him with the copy of a Sanskrit Ode about the Utsav composed by himself. Swamiji read it while walking towards the Panchavati. And on the way he once looked aside towards the disciple and said, "Yes, it's done well. Attempt others like it."

The householder devotees of Sri Ramakrishna happened to be assembled on one side of the Panchavati, among whom was Babu Girish Chandra Ghosh. Swamiji accompanied by a throng came to Girish Babu and saluted him, saying, "Hallo! here is Mr. Ghosh." Girish Babu returned his salutation with folded palms. Reminding Girish Babu of the old days Swamiji said, "Think of it, Mr. Ghosh—from those days to these, what a transition!" Girish Babu endorsed Swamiji's sentiment and said, "Yes, that is true; but yet the mind longs to see more of it." After a short conversation, Swamiji proceeded towards the Vilwa tree situated on

* Panchavati is a grove of five special trees arranged and grown to serve purposes of spiritual practice. The Vilwa is also a holy tree of that sort.

the north-east of the Panchavati.

Now a huge crowd stood in keen expectancy to hear a lecture from Swamiji. But though he tried his utmost, Swamiji could not speak louder than the noise and clamour of the people. Hence he had to give up attempting a lecture and left with the two European ladies to show them sites connected with Sri Ramakrishna's spiritual practices and introduce them to particular devotees and followers of the Master.

After 3 P.M. Swamiji said to the disciple, "Fetch me a cab, please; I must go to the Math now." The disciple brought one accordingly. Swamiji himself sat on one side and asked Swami Niranjanananda and the disciple to sit on the other and they drove towards the Alambazar Math. On the way, Swamiji said to the disciple, "It won't do to live on abstract ideas merely. These festivals and the like are also necessary; for then only, these ideas would spread gradually among the masses. You see, the Hindus have got their festivals throughout the year, and the secret of it is to infuse the great ideals of religion gradually into the minds of the people. It has also its drawback, though. For people in general miss their inner significance and become so much engrossed in externals that no sooner are these festivities over than they become their old selves again. Hence it is true that all these form the outer covering of religion, which in a way hide real spirituality and self-knowledge.

"But there are those who cannot at all understand in the abstract what 'religion' is or what the 'Self' is, and they try to realise spirituality gradually through these festivals and ceremonies. Just take this festival celebrated today; those that attended it will at least once think of Sri Ramakrishna. The thought will occur to their minds as to who he was in whose name such a great crowd assembled and why so many people came at all in his name. And those who will not feel that much even, will come once in a year to see all the devotional dancing and singing, or at least to partake of the sacred food-offerings, and will also have a look at the devotees of Sri Ramakrishna. This will rather benefit them than do any harm."

Disciple :—But, sir, suppose somebody thinks these festivals and ceremonies to be the only thing essential, can he possibly advance any further ? They will gradually come to be commonplace observances, like the worship in our country of *Shasthi, Mangalchandi* and the like. People are found to observe these rites till death, but where do we find even one among them rising through such observances to the knowledge of Brahman?

Swamiji :—Why? In India so many spiritual heroes were born, and did they not make them the means of scaling the heights of greatness? When by persevering in practice through these props they gained a vision of the Self, they ceased to be keen on them. Yet, for the preservation of social balance even great men of the type of Incarnations follow these observances.

Disciple :—Yes, they may observe these for appearance only. But when to a knower of the Self even this world itself becomes unreal like magic, is it possible for him to recognise these external observances as true?

Swamiji :—Why not? Is not our idea of truth also a relative one, varying in relation to time, place and person? Hence all observances have their utility, relatively to the varying qualifications in men. It is just as Sri Ramakrishna used to say, that the mother cooks *polâo* and *kâliâ* (rich dishes) for one son, and *sago* for another.

Now the disciple understood at last and kept quiet. Meanwhile the carriage arrived at the Alambazar Math. The disciple followed

Swamiji into the Math where Swamiji, being thirsty, drank some water. Then putting off his coat, he rested recumbent on the blanket spread on the floor. Swami Niranjanananda, seated by his side, said, "We never had such a great crowd in any year's Utsav before! As if the whole of Calcutta flocked there!"

Swamiji :—It was quite natural; stranger things will happen hereafter.

Disciple :—Sir, in every religious sect are found to exist external festivals of some kind or other. But there is no amity between one sect and another in this matter. Even in the case of such a liberal religion as that of Mohammed, I have found in Dacca that the *Shias* and *Sunnis* go to loggerheads with each other.

Swamiji :—That is incidental more or less wherever you have sects. But do you know what the ruling sentiment amongst us is ?— non-sectarianism. Our Lord was born to point that out. He would accept all forms, but would say withal that, looked at from the standpoint of the knowledge of Brahman, they were only like illusory Mâyâ.

Disciple :—Sir, I can't understand your point. Sometimes it seems to me that by thus celebrating these festivals you are also inaugurating another sect round the name of Sri Ramakrishna. I have heard it from the lips of Nâg Mahâshay that Sri Ramakrishna did not belong to any sect. He used to pay great respect to all creeds such as the Shâktas, the Vaishnavas, the Brahmos, the Mohammedans and the Christians.

Swamiji :—How do you know that we do not also hold in as great esteem all the religious creeds?

So saying, Swamiji called out in evident amusement to Swami Niranjanananda. "Only think what this Bângâl* is saying!"

Disciple :—Kindly make me understand, sir, what you mean.

Swamiji :—Well, you have, to be sure, read my lectures. But where have I built on Sri Ramakrishna's name? It is only the pure Upanishadic religion that I have gone about preaching in the world.

Disciple :—That's true, indeed. But what I find by being familiar with you is that you have surrendered yourself, body and soul, to Ramakrishna. If you have understood Sri Ramakrishna to be the Lord Himself, why not give it

---

* This term as used of people hailing from East Bengal is too often supposed to have a ring of derision. But in the case of the disciple, it very easily and naturally grew to be a term of peculiar endearment. —Ed.

out to the people at large ?

Swamiji :—Well, I do preach what I have understood. And if you have found the Advaitic principles of Vedanta to be the truest religion, then why don't you go out and preach it to all men ?

Disciple :—But I must realize, before I can preach it to others. I have only studied Advaitism in books.

Swamiji :—Good; realize first and then preach. Now, therefore, you have no right to say anything of the beliefs each man tries to live by. For you also proceed now only by putting your faith on some such beliefs.

Disciple :—True, I am also living now by believing in something ; but I have the Shâstras for my authority. I do not accept any faith opposed to the Shâstras.

Swamiji :—What do you mean by the Shâstras ? If the Upanishads are authority, why not the Bible or the Zend-avesta equally so ?

Disciple :—Granted these scriptures are also good authority, they are not however, as old as the Vedas. And nowhere, moreover, is the theory of the Atman better established than in the Vedas.

Swamiji :—Supposing I admit that contention of yours, what right have you to maintain that truth can be found nowhere except in the Vedas?

Disciple:—Yes, truth may also exist in all the scriptures other than the Vedas, and I don't say anything to the contrary. But as for me, I choose to abide by the teachings of the Upanishads, for I have very great faith in them.

Swamiji:—Quite welcome to do that, but if somebody else has 'very great' faith in any other set of doctrines, surely you should allow him to abide by that. You will discover that in the long run both he and yourself will arrive at the same goal. For haven't you read in the Mahimna-stotram— त्वमसि पयसामर्णव इव —"Thou art as the ocean to the rivers falling into it?"

V

INITIATING THE DISCIPLE—ORIGIN OF THE SACRED THREAD—THE PROBLEM OF VIRTUE AND VICE—WHEN IS THE SELF REALIZED.

[Place: *Alambazar Math*. Year: *1897, May*.]

It was the 19th Vaishakh of the year 1303 B.S. Swamiji had agreed to initiate the disciple today. So early in the morning he reached the Alambazar Math. Seeing the disciple Swamiji jocosely said, "Well, you are to be 'sacrificed' today, are you not ?"

After this remark to the disciple, Swamiji with a smile resumed his talk with others about American subjects. And in due relevancy came along such topics also as how one-pointed in devotion one has to be in order to build up a spiritual life, how firm faith and strong devotion to the Guru have to be kept up, how deep reliance has to be placed on the words of the Guru, and how even one's life has to be laid down for his sake. Then putting some questions to the disciple, Swamiji began to test his heart : "Well, are you ready to do my bidding to your utmost, whatever it be and whenever it may come ? If I ask you to plunge into the Ganges or to jump from the roof of a house, meaning it all for your good, could you do even that without any hesitation ? Just think of it even now, otherwise don't rush forward on the spur of the moment to accept me as your Guru." And the disciple nodded assent to all questions of the kind.

Swamiji then continued : "The real Guru is he who leads you beyond this Mâyâ of endless birth and death—who graciously destroys all the griefs and maladies of the soul. The disciple of old used to repair to the hermitage of the Guru, fuel in hand, and the Guru, after ascertaining his competence, would teach him the Vedas after initiation, fastening round his waist the threefold filament of *munja,* a kind of grass, as the emblem of his vow to keep his body, mind and speech in control. With the help of this girdle, the disciple used to tie up his *Kaupina.* Later on the custom of wearing the sacred thread superseded this girdle of *munja* grass."

Disciple :—Would you, then, say, sir, that the use of the holy thread we have adopted is not really a Vedic custom ?

Swamiji :—Nowhere is there mention of thread being so used in the Vedas. The modern author of Smritis, Raghunandan Bhattâchârya, also puts it thus : "At this stage,* the sacrificial girdle should be put on." Neither in Gobhila's Grihya-sutras do we find any mention of the girdle made of thread. In the Shâstras, this first Vedic Samskâra (purification ceremony) before the Guru has been called the Upanayana ; but see, to what a sad pass our country has been brought! Straying away from the true path of the Shâstras, the country

---

* Referring, that is to say, to some steps in the Vedic ceremony of a Brâhmana's initiation.

has been overwhelmed with usages and observances orginating in particular localities, or popular opinion, or with the womenfolk! That's why I ask you to proceed along the path of the Shâstras as in olden times. Have faith within yourselves and thereby bring it back into the country. Plant in your heart the faith of Nachiketa. Even go off to the world of Yama like him. Yes, if to know the secrets of the Atman, to liberate your soul, to reach the true solution of the mystery of birth and death, you have to go to the very jaws of death and realize the truth thereby, well, go there with an undaunted heart. It is fear alone that is death. You have to go beyond all fear. So from this day be fearless. Off at once, to lay down your life for your own liberation and for the good of others. What good is it carrying along a load of bones and flesh! Initiated into the *mantra* of extreme self-sacrifice for the sake of God, go, lay down for others this body of flesh and bones like the Muni Dadhichi! Those alone, say the Shâstras, are the real Gurus, who have studied the Vedas and the Vedanta, who are knowers of the Brahman, who are able to lead others beyond to fearlessness; when such are at hand, get yourself initiated, "no speculation in such a case." Do you know what has become of this principle now?—"like the blind leading the blind"!

* * *

The initiation ceremony was duly gone through in the chapel. After this Swamiji spoke out: "Give me the Guru-dakshinâ."* The disciple replied, "Oh, what shall I give." On this Swamiji suggested, "Well, fetch any fruit from the store-room." So the disciple ran for the store-room and came back into the chapel with ten or twelve lichis. These Swamiji took from his hand and ate up one by one, saying, "Now, your Guru-dakshina is made."

A member of the Math, Brahmachâri (afterwards Swami) Suddhananda, also had his initiation from Swamiji on this occasion.

Swamiji then had his dinner and went to take a short rest.

After the siesta he came and sat in the hall of the upper story. The disciple finding this opportunity asked, "Sir, how and whence came the ideas of virtue and vice?"

Swamiji:—It is from the idea of the manifold that these have evolved. The more a man advances towards oneness, the more the ideas of

---

* i.e., the special gift which a disciple has to make to his Guru as the symbol of the mutual relation being consummated.

"I" and "you" subside, ideas from which all these pairs of opposites such as virtue and vice have originated. When the idea that so-and-so is different from me comes to the mind, all other ideas of distinction begin to manifest, while with the complete realization of oneness, no more grief or illusion remains for man. तत्र को मोहः कः शोक एकत्वमनुपश्यतः—"For him who sees oneness, where is there any grief or any delusion?" Sin may be said to be the feeling of every kind of weakness. From this weakness springs jealousy, malice and so forth. Hence weakness is sin. The Self within is always shining forth resplendent. Turning away from that people say "I," "I," "I," with their attention held up by this material body, this queer cage of flesh and bones. This is the root of all weakness. From that habit only, the relative outlook on life has emerged in this world. The absolute Truth lies beyond that duality.

Disciple:—Well, is then all this relative experience not true?

Swamiji:—As long as this idea of "I" remains, it is true. And the instant the realization of "I" as the Atman comes, this world of relative existence becomes false. What people speak of as sin is the result of weakness—is but another form of the egoistic idea—"I am the body." When the mind gets steadfast in the truth—"I am the Self," then you go beyond merit and demerit, virtue and vice. Sri Ramakrishna used to say, "When the 'I' dies, all trouble is at an end."

Disciple :—Sir, this "I" has a most tenacious life. It is very difficult to kill it.

Swamiji :—Yes, in one sense, it is very difficult, but in another sense, it is quite easy. Can you tell me where this "I" exists ? How can you speak of anything being killed, which never exists at all ? Man only remains hypnotised with the false idea of an ego. When this ghost is off from us all dreams vanish, and then it is found that the one Self only exists from the highest Being to a blade of grass. This will have to be known, to be realized. All practice or worship is only for taking off this veil. When that will go, you will find that the Sun of Absolute Knowledge is shining in its own lustre. For, the Atman only is self-luminous and has to be realized by Itself. How can that, which can be experienced only by itself, be known with the help of any other thing ? Hence the Shruti says, विज्ञातारमरे केन विजानीयात्— "well, through what means is that to be known which is the Knower ?" Whatever you know, you know through the instrumentality of your mind.

But mind is something material. It is active only because there is the pure Self behind it. So, how can you know that Self through your mind ? But this only becomes known, after all, that the mind cannot reach the pure Self, no, nor even the intellect. Our relative knowledge ends just there. Then, when the mind is free from activity or functioning, it vanishes and the Self is revealed. This state has been described by the commentator Shankara as अपरोक्षानुभूतिः or supersensuous perception.

Disciple :—But, sir, the mind itself is the "I." If that mind is gone, then the "I" also cannot remain.

Swamiji :—Yes, the state that comes then, is the real nature of the ego. The "I" that remains then, is omnipresent, all-pervading, the Self of all. Just as the Ghatâkâsha,* when the jar is broken, becomes the Mahâkâsha—for with the destruction of the jar the enclosed space is not destroyed. The puny "I" which you were thinking of as confined in the body becomes spread out and is thus realized in the form of the all-pervading "I" or the Self. Hence,

---

* Ghatâkâsha and Mahâkâsha are the technical terms used in Vedanta. They mean, the space enclosed by the jar and the omnipresent sky. According to Vedanta, the two are one and the same, only the former is limited by the Upâdhi (adjunct) of the Ghata or jar.

what matters it to the real "I" or the Self, whether the mind remains or is destroyed? What I say you will realize in course of time. काळेनात्मनि विदन्ति, —"It is realized within oneself in due time." As you go with Shravana and Manana (proper hearing and proper thinking), you will fully understand it in due time and then you will go beyond mind. Then there will be no room for any such question.

Hearing all this, the disciple remained quiet on his seat, and Swamiji, as he gently smoked, continued: "How many Shâstras have been written to explain this simple thing, and yet men fail to understand it! How they are wasting this precious human life on the fleeting pleasures of some silver coins and the frail beauty of women! Wonderful is the influence of Mahâmâya! Mother! O Mother!"

VI

STARTING THE RAMAKRISHNA MISSION—DID SWAMI VIVEKANANDA DIFFER FROM SRI RAMAKRISHNA—SWAMI VIVEKANANDA'S ATTITUDE TOWARDS SRI RAMAKRISHNA—THE LAW OF GRACE—GIRISH CHANDRA GHOSH.

[Place : *Baghbazar, Calcutta.* Year : *1897.*]

Swamiji has been staying for some days at

the house of the late Balaram Babu. At his wish, a large number of devotees of Sri Ramakrishna have assembled at the house at 3 P.M. (on May 1, 1897.) Swami Yogananda is amongst those present here. The object of Swamiji is to form an association. When all present had taken their seats, Swamiji proceeded to speak as follows:

"The conviction has grown in my mind after all my travels in various lands that no great cause can succeed without an organization. In a country like ours, however, it does not seem quite practicable to me to start an organization at once with a democratic basis or work by general voting. People in the West are more educated in this respect, and less jealous of one another than ourselves. They have learnt to respect merit. Take for instance my case. I was just an insignificant man there, and yet see how cordially they received and entertained me. When with the spread of education the masses in our country will grow more sympathetic and liberal, when they will learn to have their thoughts expanded beyond the limits of sect or party, then it will be possible to work on the democratic basis of organization. For this reason it is necessary to have a dictator for this society. Everybody should obey him, and then in time we may work on the principle of general voting.

"Let this association be named after him in whose name, indeed, we have embraced the monastic life, with whom as your Ideal in life you all toil on the field of work from your station in family-life, within twenty years of whose passing away a wonderful diffusion of his holy name and extraordinary life has taken place both in the East and the West. We are the servants of the Lord. Be you all helpers in this cause.

When Srijut Girish Chandra Ghosh and all other householder disciples present had approved of the above proposal, the future programme of this society of Sri Ramakrishna was taken up for discussion. The society was named the Ramakrishna Mission.

Swamiji himself became the general President of the Mission and other office-bearers also were elected. The rule was laid down that the association should hold meetings at the house of Balaram Babu every Sunday at 4 P.M. Needless to say that Swamiji used to attend these meetings whenever convenient.

When the meeting had broken up and the members departed, addressing Swami Yogananda, Swamiji said: "So the work is now begun this way; let us see how far it succeeds by the will of Sri Ramakrishna."

Swami Yogananda :—You are doing these things with Western methods. Should you say Sri Ramakrishna left us any such instructions?

Swamiji :—Well, how do you know that all this is not on Sri Ramakrishna's lines? He had an infinite breadth of feeling, and dare you shut him up within your own limited views of life? I will break down these limits and scatter broadcast over the earth his boundless inspiration. He never instructed me to introduce any rites of his own worship. We have to realise the teachings he has left us about religious practice and devotion, concentration and meditation and such higher ideas and truths, and then preach these to all men. The infinite number of faiths are only so many paths. I haven't been born to found one more sect in a world already teeming with sects. We have been blessed with obtaining refuge at the feet of the Master, and we are born to carry his message to the dwellers of the three worlds.

Swami Yogananda uttered no word of dissent and so Swamiji continued : Time and again have I received in this life marks of his grace. He stands behind and gets all this work done by me. When lying helpless under a tree in an agony of hunger, when I had not even a scrap of cloth for *kaupin*, when I was resolved on travelling penniless round the world, even then help came in all ways by the grace of Sri Ramakrishna. And again when crowds jostled with one another in the streets of Chicago to have a sight of this Vivekananda, then also, just because I had his grace, I could digest without difficulty all that honour—a hundredth part of which would have been enough to turn mad any ordinary man; because I had his grace, and by his will, victory followed everywhere. Now I must conclude by doing something in this country. So casting all doubt away, please help my work; and you will find everything fulfilled by his will.

Swami Yogananda :—Yes, whatever you will, shall be fulfilled; and are we not all ever obedient to you? Now and then I do clearly see how Sri Ramakrishna is getting all these things done through you. And yet, to speak plainly, some misgiving rises at intervals, for as we saw it, his way of doing things was different. So I question myself : "Are we sure that we are not going astray from Sri Ramakrishna's teachings?" And so I take the opposing attitude and warn you.

Swamiji :—You see, the fact is that Sri

Ramakrishna is not exactly what the ordinary followers have comprehended him to be. He had infinite moods and phases. Even if you might form an idea of the limits of Brahmajnâna, the knowledge of the Absolute, you could not have any idea of the unfathomable depths of his mind! Thousands of Vivekanandas may spring forth through one gracious glance of his eyes! But instead of doing that, he has chosen to get things done this time through me as his single instrument, and what can I do in this matter, you see?

Saying this, Swamiji left to attend to something else waiting for him, and Swami Yogananda went on praising Swamiji's versatile gifts.

Meanwhile Swamiji returned and asked the disciple, "Do the people in your part of the country know much of Sri Ramakrishna?"

Disciple:—Only one man, Nâg Mahâshaya, came to Sri Ramakrishna from our part of Bengal; it is from him that many came to hear of him and had their curiosity excited to know more. But that Sri Ramakrishna was the Incarnation of God, the people there have not yet come to know, and some would not believe it even if told so.

Swamiji:—Do you think it is an easy matter to believe so? We who had actual dealings with him in every respect, we who heard of that fact again and again from his own lips, we who lived and stayed with him for twenty-four hours of the day,—even we have doubts about it coming on us off and on! So what to speak of others!

Disciple :—Did Sri Ramakrishna out of his own lips ever say that he was God, the all-perfect Brahman ?

Swamiji :—Yes, he did so many times. And he said this to all of us. One day while he was staying at the Cossipore garden, his body in imminent danger of falling off for ever, by the side of his bed I was saying in my mind, "Well, now if you can declare that you are God, then only will I believe you are really God Himself." It was only two days before he passed away. Immediately, he looked up towards me all on a sudden and said, "He who was Râma, He who was Krishna, verily is He now Rama krishna in this body. And that not merely from the standpoint of your Vedanta!"* At this I was struck dumb. Even we haven't had yet the perfect faith, after hearing it again and again from the holy lips of our Lord himself

---

* In the Sense that a knower of Brahman may declare his identity with any being, such as Manu and so forth. Vide the *Vedanta-Sutras* I. i. 30.

—our minds still get disturbed now and then with doubt and despair—and so, what shall we speak of others being slow to believe? It is indeed a very difficult matter to be able to declare and believe a man with a body like ours to be God Himself. We may just go to the length of declaring him to be a "perfected one," or a "knower of Brahman." Well, it matters nothing, whatever you may call him or think of him, a saint or a knower of Brahman, or anything. But take it from me, never did come to this earth such an all-perfect man as Sri Ramakrishna! In the utter darkness of the world this great man is like the shining pillar of illumination in this age! And by his light alone will man now cross the ocean of Samsâra!

Disciple:—To me it seems, sir, that true faith comes only after actually seeing or hearing something. Mathur Babu,† I have heard, actually saw so many things about Sri Ramakrishna, and thus had that wonderful faith in him.

Swamiji:—He who believes not, believes not even after seeing, and thinks that it is all hallucination, or dream and so on. The great transfiguration of Krishna, the Vishwarupa (form-

---

† Son-in-law of Rani Rasmani, the foundress of the Temple at Dakshineswar.

universal), was seen alike by Duryodhana and by Arjuna. But only Arjuna believed, while Duryodhana took it to be magic! Unless He makes us understand, nothing can be stated or understood. Somebody comes to the fullest faith even without seeing or hearing, while somebody else remains plunged in doubt even after witnessing with his own eyes various extraordinary powers for twelve years! The secret of it all is His grace! But then one must persevere, so that the grace may be received.

Disciple:—Is there, sir, any law of grace?

Swamiji:—Yes and no.

Disciple:—How is that?

Swamiji:—Those who are pure always in body, mind and speech, who have strong devotion, who discriminate between the real and the unreal, who persevere in meditation and contemplation—upon them alone the grace of the Lord descends. The Lord, however, is beyond all natural laws—is not under any rules and regulations, or just as Sri Ramakrishna used to say, He has the child's nature—and that's why we find some failing to get any response even after calling on Him for millions of births, while some one else whom we regard as a sinful or penitent man, or a disbeliever, would have Illumination in a flash! On the latter the

Lord perhaps lavishes His grace quite unsolicited! You may argue that this man had good merits stored up from previous life, but the mystery is really difficult to understand. Sri Ramakrishna used to say sometimes, "Do rely on Him; be like the dry leaf at the mercy of the wind" and again he would say, "The wind of His grace is always blowing; what you need to do is to unfurl your sail."

Disciple :—But, sir, this is a most tremendous statement. No reasoning, I see, can stand here.

Swamiji :—Ah, all reasoning and arguing is within the limit of the realm of Mâyâ; it lies within the categories of space, time and causation. But He is beyond these categories. We speak of His law, still He is beyond all law. He creates, or becomes, all that we speak of as laws of nature and yet He is outside of them all. He on whom His grace descends, in a moment goes beyond all law. For this reason there is no condition in grace. It is as His play or sport. All this creation of the universe is like His play, लोकवत् लीलाकैवल्यम् —"It is the pure delight of sport as in the case of men."[*] Is it not possible for Him who creates and destroys the universe as if in play to grant salvation by grace to the

[*] *Vedanta-Sutras* II. i. 33.

greatest sinner ? But then it is just His pleasure, His play, to get somebody through the practice of spiritual discipline and somebody else without it.

Disciple :—Sir, I can't understand this.

Swamiji :—And you needn't. Only get your mind to cling to Him as far as you can. For then only the great magic of this world will break of itself. But then, you must persevere. You must take off your mind from lust and lucre, must discriminate always, between the real and the unreal—must settle down into the mood of bodilessness with the brooding thought that you are not this body, and must always have the realization that you are the all-pervading Atman. This persevering practice is called Purushakâra (self-exertion—as distinguished from grace). By such self-exertion will come true reliance on Him, and that is the goal of human achievement.

After a pause Swamiji resumed : "Had you not been receiving His grace, why else would you come here at all ? Sri Ramakrishna used to say, 'Those who have had the grace of God cannot but come here. Wherever they might be, whatever they might be doing, they are sure to be affected by words or sentiments uttered from here'.* Just take your own case—do you think it is possible without the grace of God to have the blessed company of Nâg Mahâshaya, a man who rose to spiritual perfection through the strength of divine grace and came to know fully what this grace really means ? अनेकजन्मसंसि द्धस्ततो याति परां गतिम् "One attains the highest stage after being perfected by the practice of repeated births' (Gita vi. 45). It is only by virtue of great religious merit acquired through many births that one comes across a great soul like him. All the characteristics of the highest type of Bhakti, spoken of in the scriptures, have manifested themselves in Nâg Mahâshaya. It is only in him that we actually see fulfilled the widely quoted text, तृणादपि सुनीचेन † Blessed indeed is your East Bengal to have been hallowed by the touch of Nâg Mahâshaya's feet!"

While speaking thus, Swamiji rose to pay a visit to the great poet, Babu Girish Chandra Ghosh. Swami Yogananda and the disciple followed him. Reaching Girish Babu's place, Swamiji seated himself and said : "You see,

---

* With his egoism perfectly merged in the consciousness of the Mother, the use of the word 'here' by Sri Ramakrishna would often stand for the ordinary reference to self. By 'here' is evidently meant this centre of the Mother's self-revelation.—Ed.

† "Lowlier far than the lowly stalk of grass."

G. C., the impulse is constantly coming nowadays to my mind to do this and to do that, to scatter broadcast on earth the message of Sri Ramakrishna and so on. But I pause again to reflect, lest all this give rise to another sect in India. So I have to work with a good deal of caution. Sometimes I think, what if a sect does grow up. But then again the thought comes— no. Sri Ramakrishna never disturbed anybody's own spiritual outlook; he always looked at the inner sameness. Often do I restrain myself with this thought. Now, what do you say?"

Girish Babu :—What can I say to this? You are the instrument in his hand. You have to do just what he would have you do. I don't trouble myself over the detail. But I see that the power of the Lord is getting things done by you. I see it clear as daylight.

Swamiji :—But I think we do things according to our own will. Yet, that in misfortunes and adversities, in times of want and poverty, he reveals himself to us and guides us along the true path—this I have been able to realize. But alas, I still fail to comprehend in any way the greatness of his power.

Girish Babu :—Yes, he said, "If you undersand it to the full, everything will at once vanish. Who will work then, or who will be made to work?"

After this the talk drifted on to America. And Swamiji grew warm on this subject and went on describing the wonderful wealth of the country, the virtues and defects of men and women there, their luxury and so on.

VII

SOLAR ECLIPSE—NATURE OF MEDITATION—PRACTICAL HINTS ON MEDITATION—NEED FOR RENUNCIATION.

[Place : *Calcutta.* Year : *1897.*]

For some days past, Swamiji has been staying at Balaram Bose's house, Baghbazar. There will be a total eclipse of the sun today. The disciple is to cook for Swamiji this morning and on his presenting himself, Swamiji said, "Well, the cooking must be in the East Bengal style; and we must finish our dinner before the eclipse comes."

The inner apartments of the house were all unoccupied now. So the disciple went inside into the kitchen and started cooking. Swamiji also was looking in now and then with a word of encouragement and sometimes with a joke, as, "Take care, the soup* must be after

* The Bengali expression has a peculiar pronunciation in East Bengal which gives the point of the joke.

the East Bengal fashion."

The cooking had been almost completed, when Swamiji came in after his bath and sat down for dinner, putting up his own seat and plate. "Do bring in anything finished, quick," he said, "I can't wait, I'm burning with hunger!" While eating, Swamiji was pleased with the curry with bitters and remarked, "Never have I enjoyed such a nice thing! But none of the things is so hot as your soup." "It's just after the style of the Burdwan District," said Swamiji tasting the sour preparation. He then brought his dinner to a close and after washing sat on the bedstead inside the room. While having his after-dinner smoke, Swamiji remarked to the disciple, "Whoever cannot cook well cannot become a good Sâdhu; unless the mind is pure, good tasteful cooking is not possible."

Soon after this, the sound of bells and conch-shells etc., rose from all quarters, when Swamiji said, "Now that the eclipse has begun, let me sleep, and you please massage my feet!" Gradually the eclipse covered the whole of the sun's disc and all around fell the darkness of dusk.

While there were fifteen or twenty minutes left for the eclipse to pass off, Swamiji rose from his siesta, and after washing, jocosely said while taking a smoke, "Well, people say that whatever one does during an eclipse, one gets that millionfold in future; so I thought that the Mother, Mahâmâyâ, did not ordain that this body might have good sleep, and if I could get some sleep during the eclipse, I might have plenty of it in future. But it all failed, for I slept only for fifteen minutes at the most."

After this, at the behest of Swamiji some short speeches were made. There was yet an hour left before dusk. When all had assembled in the parlour Swamiji told them to put him any question they liked.

Swami Suddhananda asked, "What is the real nature of meditation, sir?"

Swamiji:—Meditation is the focussing of the mind on some object. If the mind acquires concentration on one object, it can be so concentrated on any object whatsoever.

Disciple:—Mention is made in the scriptures of two kinds of meditation—one having some object and the other objectless. What is meant by all that, and which of the two is the higher one?

Swamiji:—First, the practice of meditation has to proceed with some one object before the mind. Once I used to concentrate my mind on some black point. Ultimately, during those days, I could not see the point any more, nor notice that the point was before me at all—the mind used to be no more—no wave of functioning would rise, as if it were all an ocean without any breath of air. In that state I used to experience glimpses of supersensuous truth. So I think, the practice of meditation even with some trifling external object leads to mental concentration. But it is true that the mind very easily attains calmness when one practices meditation with anything on which one's mind is most apt to settle down. This is the reason why we have in this country so much worship of the images of gods and goddesses. And what wonderful art developed from such worship! But no more of that now. The fact however is that the objects of meditation can never be the same in the case of all men. People have proclaimed and preached to others only those external objects to which they held on to become perfected in meditation. Oblivious of the fact, later on, that these objects are aids to the attainment of perfect mental calmness, men have extolled them beyond everything else. They have wholly concerned themselves with the means, getting comparatively unmindful of the end. The real aim is to make the mind functionless, but this cannot be got at unless one becomes absorbed in some object.

Disciple :—But if the mind becomes completely engrossed and identified with some object, how can it give us the consciousness of Brahman ?

Swamiji :—Yes, though the mind at first assumes the form of the object, yet later on the consciousness of that object vanishes. Then only the experience of pure "isness" remains.

Disciple :—Well, sir, how is it that desires rise even after mental concentration is acquired ?

Swamiji :—Those are the outcome of previous Samskâras (deep-rooted impressions or tendencies). When Buddha was on the point of merging in Samâdhi (superconsciousness), Mâra made his appearance. There was really no Mâra extraneous to the mind; it was only the external reflection of the mind's previous Samskâras.

Disciple :—But one hears of various fearful experiences prior to the attainment of perfection. Are they all mental projections ?

Swamiji :—What else but that ? The aspiring soul, of course, does not make out at that time that all these are external manifestations of his own mind. But all the same, there is nothing outside of it. Even what you see as this world does not exist outside. It is all a mental projection. When the mind becomes functionless, it reflects the Brahman-consciousness. Then the vision of all spheres of existence may supervene—यं यं लोकं मनसा संविभाति—"Whatsoever sphere one may call up in mind." Whatsoever is resolved on becomes realized at once. He who, even on attaining this state of unfalsified self-determination, preserves his watchfulness and is free from the bondage of desire, verily attains to the knowledge of Brahman. But he who loses his balance after reaching this state, gets the manifold powers but falls off from the supreme goal.

So saying, Swamiji began to repeat "Shiva, Shiva", and then continued: "There is no way, none whatsoever, to the solution of the profound mystery of this life except through renunciation. Renunciation, renunciation and renunciation—let this be the one motto of your lives. सर्वं वस्तु भयान्वितं भुवि नृणां वैराग्यमेवाभयम्—'For men, all things on earth are infected with fear, Vairâgyam alone constitutes fearlessness.'"

VIII

FEMALE EDUCATION—MAHAKALI PATHSHALA—WOMEN IN INDIA AND THE WEST—EARLY MARRIAGE—RIGHT TYPE OF FEMALE EDUCATION—SPREAD OF EDUCATION.

[Place: *Calcutta*. Time: *1897, March or April.*]

Today the disciple came to meet Swamiji at Baghbazar, but found him ready for a visiting engagement. "Well, come along with me," were the words with which Swamiji accosted him as he went downstairs, and the disciple followed. They then put themselves into a hired cab which proceeded southwards.

Disciple:—Sir, where are you going to visit, please?

Swamiji:—Well, come with me and you will see.

Thus keeping back the destination from the disciple, Swamiji opened the following conversation as the carriage reached the Beadon Street: one does not find any real endeavour in your country to get the women educated. You, the men, are educating youselves to develop your manhood, but what are you doing to educate and advance those who share all your happiness and misery, who lay down their lives to serve you in your homes?

Disciple :—Why, sir, just see how many schools and colleges have sprung up nowadays for our women, and how many of them are getting degrees of B.A. and M.A.

Swamiji :—But all that is in the Western style. How many schools have been started on your own national lines, in the spirit of your own religious ordinances? But alas, such a system does not obtain even among the men of your country, what to speak of women! It is seen from the official statistics that only three or four per cent of the people in India are educated, and not even one per cent of the women.

Otherwise, how could the country come to such a fallen condition? How can there be any progress of the country without the spread of education, the dawning of knowledge? Even no real effort or exertion in the cause is visible among the few in your country who are the promise of the future, you who have received the blessings of education. But know for certain that absolutely nothing can be done to improve the state of things, unless there is spread of education first among the women and the masses. And so I have it in my mind to train up some Brahmachâris and Brahmachârinis, the former of whom will eventually take the vow of Sannyâsa and try to carry the light of education among the masses, from village to village, throughout the country, while the latter will do the same among women. But the whole work must be done in the style of our own country. Just as centres have to be started for men, so also centres have to be started for teaching women. Brahmachârinis of education and character should take up the task of teaching at these different centres. History and the Purânas, housekeeping and the arts, the duties of home-life and principles that make for the development of an ideal character, have to be taught with the help of modern science, and the women students must be trained up in ethical and spiritual life. We must see to their growing up as ideal matrons of home in time. The children of such mothers will make further progress in the virtues that distinguish themselves. It is only in the homes of educated and pious mothers that great men are born. And you have reduced your women to something like manufacturing machines; alas, for heaven's sake, is this the outcome of your education? The uplift of the women, the awakening of the masses, must come first, and then only can any real good come about for the country, for India.

Near Chorebagan Swamiji gave it out to the disciple that the foundress of the Mahâkâli Pâthshâla, the Tapaswini Mâtâji (ascetic mother), had invited him to visit her institution. When our carriage stopped at its destination, three or four gentlemen greeted Swamiji and showed him up to the first floor. There the Tapaswini mother received him standing. Presently she escorted him into one of the classes, where all the maidens stood up in greeting. At a word from Mâtâji all of them commenced reciting the Sanskrit meditation of Lord Shiva with proper intonation. Then they demonstrated at the instance of the mother how they were taught the ceremonies of worship in their school. After watching all this with much delight and interest, Swamiji proceeded to visit the other classes. After this Mâtâji sent for some particular girl and asked her to explain before Swamiji the first verse of the third canto of Kâlidâsa's Raghuvamsa, which she did in Sanskrit. Swamiji expressed his great appreciation of the measure of success Mâtâji had attained by her perseverance and application in the cause of diffusing education among women. In reply, she said with much humility, "In my service to my students, I look upon them as the Divine Mother; well, in starting the school I have neither fame nor any other object in view."

Being asked by Mâtâji, Swamiji recorded his opinion about the institution in the Visitors' Book, the last line of which was : "The movement is in the right direction."

After saluting Mâtâji, Swamiji went back to his carriage, which then proceeded towards Baghbazar, while the following conversation took place between Swamiji and the disciple.

Swamiji :—How far is the birthplace of this venerable lady! She has renounced everything of her worldly life, and yet how diligent in the service of humanity! Had she not been a woman, could she ever have undertaken the teaching of women in the way she is doing ? What I saw here was all good, but that some male householders should be pitchforked as teachers is a thing I cannot approve of. The duty of teaching in the school ought to devolve in every respect on educated widows and Brahmachârinis. It is good to avoid in this country any association of men with women's schools.

Disciple :—But, sir, how would you get now in this country learned and virtuous women like Gârgi, Khanâ or Lilâvati ?

Swamiji :—Do you think women of the type don't exist now in the country ? Still on this sacred soil of India, this land of Sitâ and Sâvitri, among women may be found such character, such spirit of service, such affection, compassion, contentment and reverence, as I could not find anywhere else in the world! In the West, the women did not very often seem to me to be women at all, they appeared to be quite the replicas of men! Driving vehicles, drudging in offices, attending schools, doing professorial duties! In India alone the sight of feminine modesty and reserve soothes the eye! With such materials of great promise, you could not, alas, work out their uplift! You did not try to infuse the light of knowledge into them! For if they get the right sort of education, they may well turn out to be the ideal women in the world.

Disciple :—Do you think, sir, the same consummation would be reached through the way Mâtâji is educating her students? These students would soon grow up and get married and would presently shade into the likeness of all other women of the common run. So I think, if these girls might be made to adopt Brahmacharya, then only could they devote their lives to the cause of the country's progress and attain to the high ideals preached in our sacred books.

Swamiji :—Yes, everything will come about in time. Such educated men are not yet born in this country, who can keep their girls unmarried without fear of social punishment. Just see how before the girls exceed the age of twelve or thirteen, people hasten to give them away in marriage out of this fear of their social equals. Only the other day, when the Age of Consent Bill was being passed, the leaders of society massed together millions of men to send up the cry, "We don't want the Bill." Had this been in any other country, far from getting up meetings to send forth a cry like that, people would have hidden their heads under their roofs in shame, that such a calumny could yet stain their society.

Disciple :—But, sir, I don't think the ancient lawgivers supported this custom of early marriage without any rhyme or reason. There must be some secret meaning in this attitude of theirs.

Swamiji :—Well, what might have been this secret meaning, please ?

Disciple :—Take it, for instance, in the first place that if the girls are marired at an early age, they may come over to their husbands' homes to learn the particular ways and usages of the family from the early years of their life.

They may acquire adequate skill in the duties of the household under the guidance of their their parents-in-law. In the homes of their own parents, on the other hand, there is the likelihood of grown-up daughters going astray. But married early, they have no chance of thus going wrong, and over and above this, such feminine virtues as modesty, reserve, fortitude and diligence are apt to develop in them.

Swamiji :—In favour of the other side of the question, again, it may be argued that early marriage leads to premature child-bearing, which accounts for most of our women dying early; their progeny also, being of low vitality, go to swell the ranks of our country's beggars! For if the physique of the parents be not strong and healthy, how can strong and healthy children be born at all? Married a little later and bred in culture, our mothers will give birth to children who would be able to achieve real good of the country. The reason why you have so many widows in every home lies here, in this custom of early marriage. If the number of early marriages declines, that of widows is bound to follow suit.

Disciple :—But, sir, it seems to me, if our women are married late in life, they are apt to be less mindful of their household duties. I have heard that the mothers-in-law in Calcutta very often do all the cooking, while the educated daughters-in-law sit idle with red paint round their feet! But in our East Bengal such a thing is never allowed to take place.

Swamiji :—But everywhere under the sun you find the same blending of the good and the bad. In my opinion society in every country shapes itself out of its own initiative. So we need not trouble our heads prematurely about such reforms as the abolition of early marriage, the remarriage of widows and so on. Our part of the duty lies in imparting true education to all men and women in society. As an outcome of that education, they will of themselves be able to know what is good for them and what is bad, and will spontaneously eschew the latter. It will not be then necessary to pull down or set up anything in society by coercion.

Disciple :—What sort of education, do you think, is suited to our women?

Swamiji :—Religion, arts, science, housekeeping, cooking, sewing, hygiene—the simple essential points in these subjects ought to be taught to our women. It is not good to let them touch novels and fiction. The Mahâkâli Pâthshâla is to a great extent moving in the right direction. But only teaching rites of worship won't do; their education must be an eye-opener in all matters. Ideal characters must always be presented before the view of the girls to imbue them with a devotion to lofty principles of selflessness. The noble examples of Sitâ, Sâvitri, Damayanti, Lilâvati, Khanâ, and Mirâ should be brought home to their minds and they should be inspired to mould their own lives in the light of these.

Our cab now reached the house of the late Babu Balaram Bose at Baghbazar. Swamiji alighted from it and went upstairs. There he recounted the whole of his experience at the Mahâkâli Pâthshâla to those who had assembled there to see him.

Then while discussing what the members of the newly formed Ramakrishna Mission should do, Swamiji proceeded to establish by various arguments the supreme importance of the "gift of learning" and the "gift of knowledge."* Turning to the disciple he said, "Educate, educate, नान्यः पन्था विद्यतेऽयनाय —'than this there is no other way.'" And referring in banter to the party who do not favour educational propaganda, he said, "Well, don't go into the party of Prahlâdas!" Asked as to the

---

* The allusion here is to the classification of various gifts, mentioned by Manu.

meaning of the expression he replied, "Oh, haven't you heard? Tears rushed out of the eyes of Prahlâda at the very sight of the first letter 'Ka' of the alphabet as it reminded him of Krishna, so how could any studies be proceeded with? But then the tears in Prahlâda's eyes were tears of love, while your fools affect tears in fright! Many of the devotees are also like that." All of those present burst out laughing on hearing this, and Swami Yogananda said to Swamiji, "Well, once you have the urge within towards anything to be done, you won't have any peace until you see the utmost done about it. Now what you have a mind to have done, shall be done no doubt."

IX

RIG-VEDA—MAX MULLER—THE THEORY OF CREATION—SWAMI VIVEKANANDA'S GREAT HEART—NEED FOR THE STUDY OF SCRIPTURES—SERVICE OF LIVING BEINGS.

[Place : *Calcutta.* Year : *1897.*]

For the last ten days, the disciple had been studying Sâyana's commentary on the Rig-veda with Swamiji, who was staying then at the house of the late Babu Balaram Bose at Baghbazar. Max Müller's volumes on Rig-veda had been brought from a wealthy friend's private library. Swamiji was correcting the disciple every now and then and giving him the true pronunciation or construction as necessary. Sometimes while explaining the arguments of Sâyana to establish the eternity of the Vedas, Swamiji was praising very highly the commentator's wonderful ingenuity; sometimes again while arguing out the deeper significance of the doctrine, he was putting forward a difference in view and indulging in an innocent squib at Sâyana.

While our study had proceeded thus for a while, Swamiji raised the topic about Max Müller and continued thus : Well, do you know, my impression is that it is Sâyana who is born again as Max Müller to revive his own commentary on the Vedas ? I have had this notion for long. It became confirmed in my mind. it seems, after I had seen Max Müller. Even here in this country, you don't find a scholar so persevering, and so firmly grounded in the Vedas and the Vedanta. Over and above this, what a deep, unfathomable respect for Sri Ramakrishna ! Do you know, he believes in his Divine Incarnation ! And what great hospitality towards me when I was his guest ! Seeing the old man and his lady, it seemed to me that they were living their home-life like another Vashishtha and Arundhati! At the time of parting with me, tears came into the eyes of the old man.

Disciple :—But, sir, if Sâyana himself became Max Müller, then why was he born as a *mlechchha* instead of being born in the sacred land of India?

Swamiji :—The feeling and the distinction that I am an Aryan and the other is a *mlechchha*, come from ignorance. But what are Varnâshrama and caste divisions to one who is the commentator of the Vedas, the shining embodiment of knowledge? To him they are wholy meaningles, and he can assume human birth wherever he likes for doing good to mankind. Specially, if he did not choose to be born in a land which excelled both in learning and wealth, where would he secure the large expenses for publishing such stupendous volumes? Didn't you hear that the East India Company paid nine lakhs of rupees in cash to have the Rig-veda published! Even this money was not enough. Hundreds of Vedic Pandits had to be employed in this country on monthly stipends. Has anybody seen in this age here, in this country such profound yearning for knowledge, such prodigious investment of money for the sake of light and learning? Max Müller himself has written it in his preface, that for twenty-five years he prepared only the manuscripts. Then the printing took another twenty years! It is not possible for an ordinary man to drudge for forty-five years of his life with one publication. Just think of it! Is it an idle fancy of mine to say he is Sâyana himself?

After this talk about Max Müller the reading of the Vedas was resumed. Now Swamiji began variously to support the view of Sâyana that creation proceeded out of the Vedas. He said: "Veda means the sum total of eternal truths; the Vedic Rishis experienced those truths; they can be experienced only by seers of the supersensuous and not by common men like us. That is why in the Vedas the term Rishi means the seer of the truth of the Mantras, and not any Brahmana with the holy thread hanging down the neck. The division of society into castes came about later on. Veda is of the nature of Shabda or of idea. It is but the sum total of ideas. Shabda, according to the old Vedic meaning of the term, is the subtle idea, which reveals itself by taking the gross form later on. So owing to the dissolution of the creation, the subtle seeds of the future creation become involved in the Veda. Accordingly, in the Purânas you find that during the first Divine Incarnation, the Minâvatâra, the Veda is first made manifest. In this Incarnation the Veda is first revealed, the other creative manifestations began to follow. Or in other words, all the created objects began to come into concrete being out of the Shabdas, or ideas, in the Veda. For in Shabda, or idea, all gross objects have their subtle forms. Creation had proceeded in the same way in all previous cycles or Kalpas. This you find in the Sandhyâ Mantra of the Vedas : सूर्याचन्द्रमसौ धाता यथापूर्वमकल्पयत् पृथिवीं दिवं चान्तरिक्षमथो स्वः —"The sun, the moon, the earth, the atmosphere, the heaven, the upper spheres, all, the Creator projected in the same manner and process as in previous cycles.' Do you understand ?"

Disciple :—But, sir, how in the absence of an actual concrete object can the Shabda or idea be applied and for what ? And how are the names to be given at all ?

Swamiji :—Yes, that is what on first thought seems to be the difficulty. But just think of this. Supposing this jug breaks into pieces, does the idea of a jug become null and void ? No. Because, the jug is the gross effect, while the idea, "jug," is the subtle state, or the Shabda-state, of the jug. In the same way, the Shabda State of every object is its Subtle State, and the things we see, hear, touch, or perceive in any manner, are the gross manifestations of entities in the subtle, or Shabda state. Just as we may speak of the effect and its cause. Even when the whole creation is annihilated, the Shabda, as the consciousness of the universe or the subtle reality of all concrete things, exists in Brahman as the cause. At the point of creative manifestation, this sum total of causal entities vibrates into activity, as it were, and as being the sonant, material substance of it all, the eternal, primal sound of "Om" continues to come out of itself. And then from the causal totality, comes out first the subtle image, or Shabda-form, of each particular thing and then its gross manifestation. Now that causal Shabda, or world-consciousness, is Brahman and it is the Veda. This is the purport of Sâyana. Do you now understand?

Disciple:—No, sir, I can't clearly comprehend it.

Swamiji:—Well, you understand, I suppose, that even if all the jugs in the universe were to be destroyed, the idea, or Shabda, "jug," would still exist. So if the universe be destroyed—I mean if all the things going to make up the universe be smashed to atoms—why should not the ideas, or Shabdas, representing all of them in consciousness be still existing? And why cannot a second creation be supposed to come out of them in time?

Disciple:—But, sir, if one cries out "jug," "jug," that does not cause any jug to be produced!

Swamiji:—No, nothing is produced if you or I cry out like that; but a jug must be revealed if the idea of it rises in the Brahman which is perfect in its creative determinations. When we see even those established in the practice of religion (Sâdhakas) bringing about by will-power things otherwise impossible to happen, what to speak of Brahman with perfect creativeness of will? At the point of creation Brahman becomes manifest as Shabda (Idea), and then assumes the form of "Nâda," or "Om". At the next stage, the particular Shabdas, or ideas, that variously existed in former cycles, such as Bhuh, Bhuvah, Swah, cow, man, etc., begin to come out of that "Om". As soon as these ideas appear in Brahman endowed with perfect will, the corresponding concrete things also appear, and gradually the diversified universe becomes manifest. Do you now understand how Shabda is the source of creation?

Disciple:—Yes, I just form some idea of it, but there is no clear comprehension in the mind.

Swamiji:—Well, clear comprehension, inward realization, is no small matter my son. When the mind proceeds towards self-absorption in Brahman, it passes through all these stages one by one to reach the absolute (Nirvikalpa) state at last. In the process of entering into Samâdhi, first the universe appears as one mass of ideas; then the whole thing loses itself in a profound "Om". Then even that melts away, even that seems to be between being and non-being. That is the experience of the eternal Nâda. And then the mind becomes lost in the Reality of Brahman, and then it is done! All is peace!

The disciple sat mute, thinking that none could express and explain it in the way Swamiji was doing, unless the whole thing were matter of one's own experience!

Swamiji then resumed the subject: Great men like Avatâras, in coming back from Samâdhi to the realm of "I" and "mine," first experience the unmanifest Nâda, which by degress grows distinct and appears as Om, and then from Omkâra, the subtle form of the universe as a mass of ideas becomes experienced, and last, the material universe, comes into perception. But ordinary Sâdhakas somehow reach beyond Nâda through immense practice, and when once they attain to the direct realization of Brahman, they cannot again come back to the lower plane of material perception. They melt away in Brahman,— क्षीरे नीरवत्—"like water in milk."

When all this talk on the theory of creation was going on, the great dramatist, Babu Girish Chandra Ghosh, appeared on the scene. Swamiji gave him his courteous greetings and continued his lessons to the disciple.

Shabdas are again divided into two classes, the Vedic Shabdas and those in common human use. I found this position in the Nyâya book called *"Shabdashaktiprakâshikâ"*. There the arguments no doubt indicate great power of thought, but, oh, the terminology confounds the brain!

Now turning to Girish Babu Swamiji said: "What do you say, G. C.? Well, you do not care to study all this, you pass your days with your adoration of this and that god, eh?"

Girish Babu:—What shall I study, brother? I have neither time nor understanding enough to pry into all that. But this time, with Sri Ramakrishna's grace, I shall pass by with greetings to your Vedas and Vedanta, and take one leap to the far beyond! He gets you through all these studies, because he wants to get many a thing done by you. But we have no need of them.

Saying this, Girish Babu again and again touched the big Rig-veda volumes with his head, uttering, "All victory to Ramakrishna in the form of the Veda!"

Swamiji was now in a sort of deep reverie, when Girish Babu suddenly called out to him and said: 'Well, hear me, please. A good deal of study you have made in the Vedas and Vedanta, but say, did you find anywhere in them any way for us out of all these profound miseries in the country, all these wailings of grief, all this starvation, all these crimes of adultery and the many horrible sins?'

Saying this he painted over and over again the horrid pictures of society. Swamiji remained perfectly quiet and speechless, while at the thought of the sorrows and miseries of his fellowmen, tears began to flow out of his eyes, and seemingly to hide his feelings from us, he rose and left the room.

Meanwhile, addressing the disciple, Girish Babu said: "Did you see, Bângâl? What a great loving heart! I don't honour your

Swamiji simply for being a Pandit versed in the Vedas; but I honour him for that great heart of his which just made him retire weeping at the sorrows of his fellow-beings."

The disciple and Girish Babu then went on conversing with each other, the latter proving that knowledge and love were ultimately the same.

In the meantime, Swamiji returned and asked the disciple, "Well, what was all this talk going on between you?" The disciple said, "Sir, we were talking about the Vedas, and the wonder of it is that our Girish Babu has not studied these books, but has grasped the ultimate truths with clean precision!"

Swamiji :—All truths reveal themselves to him who has got real devotion to the Guru; he has hardly any need of studies. But such devotion and faith are very rare in this world. He who possesses those in the measure of our friend here, need not study the Shâstras. But he who rushes forward to imitate him, will only bring about his own ruin. Always follow his advice, but never attempt to imitate his ways.

Disciple :—Yes, sir.

Swamiji :—No saying ditto merely! Do grasp clearly the words I say. Don't nod assent like a fool to everything said. Don't put im-

plicit faith, even if *I* declare something. First
clearly grasp and then accept. Sri Ramakrishna
always used to insist on my accepting every
word of his only after clear comprehension of
it. Walk on your path only, with what sound
principle, clear reasoning and scripture all declare as true. Thus by constant reflection, the
intellect will become clear, and then only can
Brahman be reflected therein. Do you understand ?

Disciple :—Yes, sir, I do. But the brain
gets puzzled with the different views of different
men. This very moment I was being told by
Girish Babu, "What will you do with all this
studying ?" And then you come and say,
"Reflect on what you hear and read about."
So what exactly am I to do ?

Swamiji :—Both what he and I have advised
you are true. The only difference is that the
advice of both has been given from different
standpoints. There is a stage of spiritual life
where all reasonings are hushed— मूकास्वादनवत्—
"like some delicious taste enjoyed by the dumb."
And there is another mode of spiritual life in
which one has to realize the Truth through the
pursuit of scriptural learning, through studying
and teaching. You have to proceed through
studies and reflection, that is *your* way to realiza-

tion. Do you see?

Receiving such a mandate from Swamiji, the disciple in his folly took it to imply Girish Babu's discomfiture, and so turning towards him said, "Do you hear, sir? Swamiji's advice to me plainly is just to study and reflect on the Vedas and Vedanta."

Girish Babu :—Well, *you* go on doing so; with Swamiji's blessings, you will, indeed, succeed in that way.

Swami Sadananda arrived there at that moment, and seeing him, Swamiji at once said, "Do you know, my heart is sorely troubled by the picture of our country's miseries G. C. was depicting just now; well, can you do anything for our country?"

Sadananda :—Mahâraj, let the mandate once go forth; your slave is ready.

Swamiji :—First, on a pretty small scale, start a relief-centre, where the poor and the distressed may obtain relief and the diseased may be nursed. Helpless people having none to look after them will be relieved and served there, irrespective of creed or colour, do you see?

Sadananda :—Just as you command, sir.

Swamiji :—There is no greater Dharma than this service of living beings. If this Dharma can be practised in the real spirit, then— मुक्तिः करफलायते —"liberation comes as a fruit on the very palm of one's hand."

Addressing Girish Babu now, Swamiji said, "Do you know, Girish Babu, it occurs to me that even if a thousand births have to be taken in order to relieve the sorrows of the world, surely I will take them. If by my doing that, even a single soul may have a little bit of his grief relieved, why, I will do it. Well, what avails it all to have only one's own liberation? All men should be taken along with oneself on that way. Can you say why a feeling like this comes up foremost in my mind?"

Girish Babu :—Ah, otherwise why should Sri Ramakrishna declare you to be greater than all others in spiritual competence!

Saying this, Girish Babu took leave of us all to go elsewhere on some business.

X

THE IDEAL OF SANNYASA—BUDDHA AND THE INSTITUTION OF SANNYASA—MEETING THE CRITICISM AGAINST SANNYASA—WHO IS A REAL SANNYASIN.

[Place : *The Alambazar Math.* Year : *1897*.]

After Swamiji's first return to Calcutta from

the West, he always used to place before the zealous young men who visited him the lofty ideals of renunciation, and anyone expressing his desire of accepting Sannyâsa would receive from him great encouragement and kindness. So, inspired by his enthusiasm some young men of great good fortune gave up their wordly life in those days and became initiated by him into Sannyâsa. The disciple was present at the Alambazar Math the day the first four of this batch were given Sannyâsa by Swamiji.

Often has the disciple heard it from the Sannyâsins of the Math that Swamiji was repeatedly requested by his brother-monks not to admit one particular candidate into Sannyâsa, whereupon Swamiji replied "Ah, if even *we* shrink from working out the salvation of the sinful, the heavy-laden, the humiliated, and the afflicted in soul, who else are to take care of them in this world? No, don't you please stand against me in this matter." So Swamiji's strong opinion triumphed, and always the refuge of the helpless, he resolved out of his great love to give him Sannyâsa.

The disciple had been staying at the Math for the last two days, when Swamiji called him and said : "Well, you belong to the priestly class ; tomorrow you get them to perform their

Shrâddha, and the next day I shall give them Sannyâsa. So get yourself ready by consulting the books of ceremonials today." The disciple bowed to this mandate of Swamiji, and the ceremony was duly gone through.

But the disciple became very much depressed at the thought of the great sternness of Sannyâsa. Swamiji detecting his mental agitation asked him: "Well, I see, you feel some dread in your mind at all this experience, is it not so?" And when the disciple confessed it to be so, Swamiji said: "From this day these four are dead to the world, and new bodies, new thoughts, new garments will be theirs from tomorrow—and shining in the glory of Brahman they will live like flaming fire! न कर्मणा न प्रजया धनेन त्यागेनैके अमृतत्वमानशुः —'Not by work, nor by progeny, nor by wealth, but by renunciation alone some attained Immortality.'"

After the ceremony, the four Brahmachârins bowed at the feet of Swamiji. He blessed them and said, "You have the enthusiasm to embrace the loftiest vow of human life; blessed indeed is your birth, blessed your family, blessed the mothers who held you in their womb! कुलं पवित्रं जननी कृतार्थी —'The whole family-line becomes hallowed, the mother achieves her highest!'"

That day after supper Swamiji talked of the

ideal of Sannyâsa alone. To the zealous candidates for Sannyâsa, he said : "The real aim of Sannyâsa is—आत्मनो मोक्षार्थं जगद्धिताय च—'For the highest freedom of the self and the good of the world.' Without having Sannyâsa none can really be a knower of Brahman—this is what the Vedas and the Vedanta proclaim. Don't listen to the words of those who say, 'We shall both live the worldly life and be knowers of Brahman.' That is the flattering self-consolation of crypto-pleasure-seekers. He who has the slightest desire for worldly pleasures, even a shred of some such craving, will feel frightened at the thought of the path you are going to tread; so, to give himself some consolation he goes about preaching that impossible creed of harmonising Bhoga and Tyâga. That is all the raving of lunatics, the frothings of the demented —idle theories contrary to the scriptures, contrary to the Vedas. No freedom without renunciation. Highest love for God can never be achieved without renunciation. Renunciation is the word— नान्यः पन्था विद्यते अयनाय 'There no other way than this.' Even the Gita says, काम्यानां कर्मणां न्यासं संन्यासं कवयो विदुः 'The sages know Sannyâsa to be the giving up of all work that has desire for its end.'

"Nobody attains Freedom without shaking

TALKS WITH SWAMI VIVEKANANDA

off the coils of worldly worries. The very fact that somebody lives the worldly life proves that he is tied down to it as the bond-slave of some craving or other. Why otherwise will he cling to that life at all? He is the slave either of lust or of gold, of position or of fame, of learning or of scholarship. It is only after freeing oneself from all this thraldom that one can get on along the way of Freedom. Let people argue as loud as they please, I have got this conviction that unless all these bonds are given up, unless the monastic life is embraced, none is going to be saved, no attainment of Brahmajnâna is possible."

Disciple :—Do you mean, sir, that merely taking up Sannyâsa will lead one to the goal?

Swamiji :—Whether the goal is attained or not is not the point before us now. But until you get out of this wheel of Samsâra, until the slavery of desire is shaken off, you can't attain either Bhakti or Mukti. To the knower of Brahman, supernatural powers or prosperity are mere trivialities.

Disciple :—Sir, is there any special time for Sannyâsa, and are there different kinds of it?

Swamiji :—There is no special time prescribed for a life of Sannyâsa. The Shruti says : यदहरेव विरजेत् तदहरेव प्रव्रजेत् —"Directly the spirit of renunciation comes, you should take up Sannyâsa." The *Yogavâshishtha* also says:

युवैव धर्मशीलः स्यात् अनित्यं खलु जीवितम् ।
को हि जानाति कस्याद्य मृत्युकालो भविष्यति ॥

"Owing to life itself being frail and uncertain, one should be devoted to religion even in one's youth. For who knows when one's body may fall off?" The Shâstras are found to speak of four kinds of Sannyâsa: (1) Vidwat, (2) Vividishâ, (3) Markata, (4) Âtura. The awakening of real renunciation all at once and the consequent giving up of the world through Sannyâsa is something that never happens unless there are strong Samskâras, or tendencies, developed from previous birth. And this is called the Vidwat Sannyâsa. Vividishâ Sannyâsa is the case of one who out of a strong yearning for knowledge of the Self through the pursuit of scriptural study and practice, goes to the man of realization and from him embraces Sannyâsa to give himself up to those pursuits. Markata Sannyâsa is the case of a man who is driven out of the world by some of its chastisements such as the death of a relative or the like, and then takes up Sannyâsa, though in such a case the renouncing spirit does not endure long. Sri Ramakrishna used to say of it: With this kind of renunciation one hastens away to the upcountry and then happens to get hold of a nice job; and then eventually perhaps arranges to get his wife brought over to him or perhaps takes to a new one! And last, there is another kind of Sannyâsa which the Shâstras prescribe for a man who is lying on his deathbed, the hope of whose life has been given up. For then, if he dies, he dies with the holiest of vows upon him, and in his next birth the merit of it will accrue to him. And in case he recovers, he shall not go back to his old life again but live the rest of his days in the noble endeavour after Brahmajnâna. Swami Shivananda gave this kind of Sannyâsa to your uncle. The poor man died but through that initiation he will come to a new birth of higher excellence. After all, there is no other way to the knowledge of the Self but through Sannyâsa.

Disciple :—What then, sir, will be the fate of the householders?

Swamiji :—Why, through the merit of good Karma, they shall have this renunciation in some future birth of theirs. And directly this renunciation comes, there is an end of all troubles—with no further delay he gets across this mystery of life and death. But then all rules have their exceptions. A few men, one or two, may be seen to attain the highest freedom by the true fulfilment of the householder's Dharma, as we have amongst us Nâg Mahâshaya, for instance.

Disciple :—Sir, even the Upanishads etc., do not clearly teach about renunciation and Sannyâsa.

Swamiji :—What do you talk like a madman! Renunciation is the very soul of the Upanishads. Illumination born of discriminative reflection is the ultimate aim of Upanishadic knowledge. My belief, however, is that it was since the time of Buddha that the monastic vow was preached more thoroughly all over India, and renunciation, the giving up of sense-enjoyment, was recognised as the highest aim of religious life. And Hinduism has absorbed into itself this Buddhistic spirit of renunciation. Never was a great man of such renunciation born in this world as Buddha.

Disciple :—Do you then mean, sir, that before Buddha's advent there was very little of the spirit of renunciation in the country, and there were hardly any Sannyâsins at all?

Swamiji :—Who says that? The monastic institution was there, but the generality of people did not recognise it as the goal of life; there was no such staunch spirit for it, there was no such firmness in spiritual discrimination.

So even when Buddha betook himself to so many Yogis and Sâdhus, nowhere did he acquire the peace he wanted. And then to realize the Highest he fell back on his own exertions, and seated on a spot with the famous words, इहासने शुष्यतु मे शरीरं—"Let my body wither away on this seat," etc., rose from it only after becoming the Buddha, the Illumined One. All the many Maths that you now see in India occupied by monks were once in the possession of Buddhism. The Hindus have only made them their own now by modifying them in their own fashion. Really speaking, the institution of Sannyâsa originated with Buddha; it was he who breathed life into the dead bones of this institution.

Swami Ramakrishnananda, a brother-disciple of Swamiji, interposed, "But the ancient law books and Purânas are good authority that all the four Ashramas had existed in India before Buddha was born." Swamiji replied, "Most of the Purânas, the codes of Manu and others, as well as much of the Mahâbhârata form but recent literature. Bhagavân Buddha was much earlier than all that." "On that supposition," rejoined Swami Ramakrishnananda, "discussions about Buddhism would be found in the Vedas, Upanishads, the law-books, Puranas, and the like. But since such discussions are not found in these ancient books, how can you say that Buddha antedated them all? In a few old Purânas, of course, accounts of the Buddhistic doctrine are partially given, but from these, it can't be concluded that the scriptures of the Hindus such as the law-books and Purânas are of recent date."

Swamiji :—Please read history,* and you will find that Hinduism has become so great only by absorbing all the ideas of Buddha.

S. Ramakrishnananda :—It seems to me that Buddha has only left revivified the great Hindu ideas, by thoroughly practising in his life such principles as renunciation, non-attachment and so on.

Swamiji :—But this position can't be proved. For we don't get any history before Buddha was born. If we accept history only as authority, we have to admit that in the midst of the profound darkness of the ancient times, Buddha only shines forth as a figure radiant with the

---

* Evidently, during the argumentation, Swamiji was taking his stand on the conclusions of modern historical studies, thereby giving his encouragement and support to such new efforts and methods. But we know from one of his letters to Swami Swarupananda that Swamiji broke off later on from the position of these modern scholars and worked out the pre-Buddhistic origin of much of modern Hinduism, which these scholars are still fond of tracing to Buddhistic sources.—Ed.

light of knowledge.

Now the topic of Sannyâsa was resumed and Swamiji said: "Wheresoever might lie the origin of Sannyâsa, the goal of human life is to become a knower of Brahman by embracing this vow of renunciation. The supreme end is to enter the life of Sannyâsa. They alone are blessed indeed, who have broken off from worldly life through a spirit of renunciation."

Disciple:—But many people are of opinion nowadays, sir, that with the increase of wandering monks in the country, much harm has been done to its material progress. They assert it on the ground that these monks idly roam about depending on householders for their living, that these are of no help to the cause of social and national advancement.

Swamiji:—But will you explain to me first what is meant by the term material or secular advancement?

Disciple:—Yes; it is to do as people in the West are doing by securing the necessaries of life through education, and promoting through science such objects in life as commerce, industry, communications, and so on.

Swamiji:—But can all these be ever brought about, if real Rajas is not awakened in man? Wandering all over India, nowhere I found this

Rajas manifesting itself. It is all Tamas and Tamas! The masses lie engulfed in Tamas, and only among the monks could I find this Rajas and Sattva. These people are like the backbone of the country. The real Sannyâsin is a teacher of householders. It is with the light and teaching obtained from them that householders of old triumphed many a time in the battles of life. The householders give food and clothing to the Sâdhus only in return for their invaluable teachings. Had there been no such mutual exchange in India, her people would have become extinct like the American Indians by this time. It is because the householders still give a few morsels of food to the Sâdhus that they are yet able to keep their foothold on the path of progress. The Sannyâsins are not idle. They are really the fountainhead of all activity. The householders see lofty ideals carried into practice in the lives of the Sâdhus and accept from them such noble ideas; and this it is that has up till now enabled them to fight their battle of life from the sphere of Karma. The example of holy Sâdhus makes them work out holy ideas in life and imbibe real energy for work. The Sannyâsins inspire the householders in all noble causes by embodying in their lives the highest principle of giving up everything for the sake of God and the good of the world, and as a return the householders give them a few doles of food. And the very disposition and capacity to grow that food develops in the people because of the blessings and good wishes of the all-renouncing monks. It is because of their failure to understand the deeper issues that people blame the monastic institution. Whatever may be the case in other countries, in this land the bark of householders' life does not sink only because the Sannyâsins are at its helm.

Disciple:—But, sir, how many monks are to be found who are truly devoted to the good of men?

Swamiji:—Ah, quite enough if one great Sannyâsin like Sri Ramakrishna comes in a thousand years! For a thousand years after his advent, people may well guide themselves by those ideas and ideals he leaves behind. It is only because this monastic institution exists in the country that men of his greatness are born here. There are defects, more or less, in all the institutions of life. But what is the reason that in spite of its faults, this noble institution stands yet supreme over all the other institutions of life? It is because the true Sannyâsins forego even their own liberation and live simply for doing good to the world. If you don't feel grateful to such a noble institution, fie on you again and again!

While speaking these words, Swamiji's countenance became aglow. And before the eyes of the disciple he shone as the very embodiment of Sannyâsa.

Then, as if realizing deep within his soul the greatness of this institution, self-absorbed, he broke forth in sweetest symphony :—

वेदान्तवाक्येषु सदा रमन्तो
भिक्षान्नमात्रेण च तुष्टिमन्तः ।
अशोकमन्तःकरणे चरन्तः
कौपीनवन्तः खलु भाग्यवन्तः ॥

"Brooding blissfully in mind over the texts of the Vedanta, quite contented with food obtained as alms and wandering forth with a heart untouched by any feeling of grief, thrice happy are the Sannyâsins, with only their loin-cloth for dress."

Resuming the talk, he went on : "For the good of the many, for the happiness of the many, is the Sannyâsin born. His life is all vain, indeed, who, embracing Sannyâsa, forgets this ideal. The Sannyâsin, verily, is born into this world to lay down his life for others, to stop the bitter cries of men, to wipe the tears of the widow, to bring peace to the soul of the bereaved mother, to equip the ignorant masses for the struggle for existence, to accomplish the secular and spiritual well-being of all through the diffusion of spiritual teachings and to arouse the sleeping lion of Brahman in all by throwing in the light of knowledge." Addressing then his brothers of the Order, he said, "Our life is आत्मनो मोक्षार्थं जगद्धिताय च— for the sake of our self-liberation as well as for the good of the world.' So what are you sitting idle for ? Arise, awake; wake up yourselves, and awaken others. Achieve the consummation of human life before you pass off—'Arise, awake, and stop not till the goal is reached!'"

XI

CONSECRATION OF THE TEMPLE OF SRI RAMAKRISHNA.

[Place : *The house of the late Babu Nabagopal Ghosh, Ramkrishnapur, Howrah.* Time : *6th February, 1898.*]

Today the festival of installing the image of Sri Ramakrishna was to come off at the residence of Babu Nabagopal Ghosh of Ramkrishnapur, Howrah. The Sannyâsins of the Math and the householder devotees of Sri Ramakrishna had all been invited there.

Swamiji with party reached the bathing ghat at Ramkrishnapur. He was dressed in the simplest garb of ochre with turban on his head and was barefooted. On both sides of the road were standing multitudes of people to see him. Swamiji commenced singing the famous Nativity Hymn on Sri Ramakrishna—"Who art Thou laid on the lap of a poor Brahmin mother," etc., and headed a procession, himself playing on the Khol.* All the devotees assembled there followed, joining in the chorus.

Shortly after the procession reached its destination, Swamiji went upstairs to see the chapel. The chapel was floored with marble. In the centre was the throne and upon it was the porcelain image of Sri Ramakrishna. The arrangement of materials was perfect and Swamiji was much pleased to see it.

The wife of Nabagopal Babu prostrated herself before Swamiji with the other female members of the house and then took to fanning him. Hearing Swamiji speaking highly of every arrangement she addressed him and said, "What have we got to entitle us to the privilege of worshipping Thâkur?—A poor home and poor

* A kind of Indian drum elongated and narrow at both ends.

means! Do bless us please by installing him here out of your own kindness!"

In reply to this, Swamiji jocosely said: "Your Thakur never had in his fourteen generations such a marble-floored house to live in! He had his birth in that rural thatched cottage and lived his days on indifferent means. And if he does not live here so excellently served, where else should he live?" Swamiji's words made everybody laugh out.

Now, with his body rubbed with ashes and gracing the seat of the priest, Swamiji himself conducted the worship, with Swami Prakashananda to assist him. After the worship was over, Swamiji while still in the worship-room composed extempore this Mantra for prostration before Bhagavân Sri Ramakrishna:

स्थापकाय च धर्मस्य सर्व धर्मस्वरूपिणे ।
अवतारवरिष्ठाय रामकृष्णाय ते नमः ।

"I bow down to Ramakrishna, who established *the* religion, embodying in himself the reality of all religions and being thus the foremost of divine Incarnations."

All prostrated before Sri Ramakrishna with this Mantra.

In the evening Swamiji returned to Baghbazar.

XII

GURU GOVIND SINGH—PSYCHIC POWERS.

[Place : *Balaram Babu's residence, Calcutta.*
Year : *1898.*]

Swamiji had been staying during the last two days at Balaram Babu's residence at Baghbazar. He was taking a short stroll on the roof of the house, and the disciple with four or five others was in attendance. While walking to and fro, Swamiji took up the story of Guru Govind Singh, and with his great eloquence touched upon the various points in his life— how the revival of the Sikh sect was brought about by his great renunciation, austerities, fortitude, and life-consecrating labours—how by his initiation he re-Hinduised Mohammedan converts and took them back into the Sikh community—and how on the banks of the Narmada* he brought his wonderful life to a close. Speaking of the great power that used to be infused in those days into the initiates of Guru Govind, Swamiji recited a popular *dohâ* (couplet) of the Sikhs :

सवा लाख पर एक चढ़ांऊ ।
जब गुरुगोविन्द नाम सुनांऊ ॥

* According to Historical records Guru Govind Singh was Killed in 1708, at Nanded on the banks of the Godavari.-*Ed.*

The meaning is—when Guru Govind gives the Name, i.e., the initiation, a single man becomes strong enough to triumph over a lakh and a quarter of his foes. Each disciple, deriving from his inspiration a real spiritual devotion, had his soul filled with such wonderful heroism! While holding forth thus on the glories of religion, Swamiji's eyes dilating with enthusiasm seemed to be emitting fire, and his hearers, dumb-stricken and looking at his face, kept watching the wonderful sight.

After a while the disciple said : "Sir, it was very remarkable that Guru Govind could unite both Hindus and Mussalmans within the fold of his religion and lead them both towards the same end. In Indian history, no other example of this can be found."

Swamiji :—Men can never be united unless there is a bond of common interest. You can never unite people merely by getting up meetings, societies and lectures, if their interests be not one and the same. Guru Govind made it understood everywhere that the men of his age, be they Hindus or Mussalmans, were living under a régime of profound injustice and oppression. He did not create any common interest, he only pointed it out to the masses. And so both Hindus and Mussalmans followed him. He was a great worshipper of Shakti. Yes, in Indian history, such an example is indeed very rare.

Finding then that it was getting late into the night, Swamiji came down with others into the parlour on the first floor, where the following conversation on the subject of miracles took place.

Swamiji said, "It is possible to acquire miraculous powers by some little degree of mental concentration," and turning to the disciple he asked, "Well, should you like to learn thought-reading? I can teach that to you in four or five days."

Disciple:—Of what avail will it be to me, sir?

Swamiji:—Why, you will be able to know others' minds.

Disciple:—Will that help my attainment of the knowledge of Brahman?

Swamiji:—Not a bit.

Disciple:—Then I have no need to learn that science. But, sir, I would very much like to hear about what you have yourself seen of the manifestation of such psychic powers.

Swamiji:—Once when travelling in the Himalayas I had to take up my abode for a night in a village of the hill-people. Hearing the beating of drums in the village some time after nightfall, I came to know upon enquiring of my host that one of the villagers had been possessed by a Devatâ or good spirit. To meet his importunate wishes and to satisfy my own curiosity, we went out to see what the matter really was. Reaching the spot, I found a great concourse of people. A tall man with long, bushy hair was pointed out to me and I was told that person had got the Devatâ on him. I noticed an axe being heated in fire close by the man, and after a while, I found the red-hot thing being seized and applied to parts of his body and also to his hair! But wonder of wonders, no part of his body or hair thus branded with the red-hot axe was found to be burnt, and there was no expression of any pain in his face! I stood mute with surprise. The headman of the village, meanwhile, came up to me and said, "Mahârâj, please exorcise this man out of your mercy." I felt myself in a nice fix, but moved to do something, I had to go near the possessed man. Once there, I felt a strong impulse to examine the axe rather closely, but the instant I touched it, I burnt my fingers, although the thing had been cooled down to blackness. The smarting made me restless and all my theories about the axe phenomenon were spirited away from my mind! However, smarting with the burn, I placed my hand on the head of the man and repeated for a short while the Japa. It was a matter of surprise to find that the man came round in ten or twelve minutes. Then, oh, the gushing reverence the villagers showed to me! I was taken to be some wonderful man! But, all the same, I couldn't make any head or tail of the whole business. So without a word one way or the other, I returned with my host to his hut. It was about midnight, and I went to bed. But what with the smarting burn in the hand and the impenetrable puzzle of the whole affair, I couldn't have any sleep that night. Thinking of the burning axe failing to harm living human flesh, it occurred again and again to my mind, "There are more things in heaven and earth, Horatio, than are dreamt of in your philosophy."

Disciple :—But, could you later on ever explain the mystery, sir?

Swamiji :—No. The event came back to me in passing just now, and so I related it to you.

He then resumed, "But Sri Ramakrishna used to disparage these supernatural powers; his teaching was that one cannot attain to the

Supreme Truth if the mind is diverted to the manifestation of these powers. The human mind, however, is so weak that, not to speak of householders, even ninety per cent of the Sâdhus happen to be votaries of these powers. In the West, men are lost in wonderment if they come across such miracles. It is only because Sri Ramakrishna has mercifully made us understand the evil of these powers as being hindrances to real spirituality that we are able to take them at their proper value. Haven't you noticed how for that reason the children of Sri Ramakrishna pay no heed to them?"

Swami Yogananda said to Swamiji at this moment, "Well, why don't you narrate to our Bângâl* that incident of yours in Madras when you met the famous ghost-tamer?"

At the earnest entreaty of the disciple Swamiji was persuaded to give the following account of his experience :

Once while I was putting up at Manmatha Babu's† place, I dreamt one night that my mother had died. My mind became much distracted. Not to speak of corresponding with anybody at home, I used to send no letters in

* i.e. the disciple.
† Babu Manmatha Nath Bhattacharya, M.A., late Accountant General, Madras.

those days even to our Math. The dream being disclosed to Manmatha, he sent a wire to Calcutta to ascertain facts about the matter. For the dream had made my mind uneasy on the one hand, and on the other, our Madras friends, with all arrangements ready, were insisting on my departing for America immediately, and I felt rather unwilling to leave before getting any news of my mother. So Manmatha who discerned this state of my mind suggested our repairing to a man living some way off from town, who having acquired mystic powers over spirits could tell fortunes and read the past and the future of a man's life. So at Manmatha's request and to get rid of my mental suspense, I agreed to go to this man. Covering the distance partly by railway and partly on foot, we four of us— Manmatha, Alasinga, myself and another— managed to reach the place, and what met our eyes there was a man with a ghoulish, haggard, soot-black appearance, sitting close to a cremation ground. His attendants used some jargon of South Indian dialect to explain to us that this was the man with perfect power over the ghosts. At first the man took absolutely no notice of us, and then, when we were about to retire from the place, he made a request for us to wait. Our Alasinga was acting as the interpreter and he explained the request to us. Next, the man commenced drawing some figures with a pencil, and presently I found him getting perfectly still in mental concentration. Then he began to give out my name, my genealogy, the history of my long line of forefathers and said that Sri Ramakrishna was keeping close to me all through my wanderings, intimating also to me good news about my mother. He also foretold that I would have to go very soon to far-off lands for preaching religion. Getting good news thus about my mother, we all travelled back to town, and after arrival there received by wire from Calcutta the assurance of mother's doing well.

Turning to Swami Yogananda, Swamiji remarked, "Everything that the man had foretold came to be fulfilled to the letter, call it some fortuitous concurrence or anything you will."

Swami Yogananda said in reply, "It was because you would not believe all this before that this experience was necessary for you."

Swamiji :—Well, I am not a fool to believe anything and everything without direct proof. And coming into this realm of Mahâmâyâ, oh, the many magic mysteries I have come across alongside this bigger magic conjuration of a universe! Mâyâ, it is all Mâyâ! Goodness! What rubbish we have been talking so long this day! By thinking constantly of ghosts, men become ghosts themselves, while whoever repeats day and night, knowingly or unknowingly—"I am the eternal, pure, free, self-illumined Atman,"—verily becomes the knower of Brahman.

Saying this, Swamiji affectionately turned to the disciple and said, "Don't allow all that worthless nonsense to occupy your mind. Always discriminate between the real and the unreal, and devote yourself heart and soul to the attempt to realize the Atman. There is nothing higher than this knowledge of the Atman; all else is Mâyâ, mere jugglery. The Atman is the one unchangeable Truth. This I have come to understand, and that is why I try to bring it home to you all. एकमेवाद्वयं ब्रह्म नेह नानास्ति किञ्चन —'One Brahman there is without a second, there is nothing manifold in existence.'"

All this conversation continued up to eleven o'clock at night. After that, his meal being finished, Swamiji retired for rest. The disciple bowed down at his feet to bid him good-bye. Swamiji asked, "Are you not coming tomorrow?"

Disciple :—Yes, sir, I am coming, to be sure.

TALKS WITH SWAMI VIVEKANANDA 117

The mind longs so much to meet you at least once before the day is out.

Swamiji :—So good-night now, it is getting very late.

XIII

TITHIPUJA OF SRI RAMAKRISHNA—INVESTING SOME NON-BRAHMIN DEVOTEES WITH HOLY THREAD —GIRISH CHANDRA GHOSH—KARMA-YOGA OR UNSELFISH WORK—ITS AIM AND UTILITY.

[Place : *Belur, the rented Math premises.*
Year : *1898.*]

Swamiji was staying at the time at the rented garden-house of Nilambar Babu where the Math had been removed from Alambazar. Arrangements had been made for Sri Ramakrishna's Tithipujâ (Nativity) on a grand scale.

On the morning of the auspicious day, Swamiji personally inspected the preliminaries of the worship. The inspection over, Swamiji asked the disciple, "Well, you have brought the holy threads, I hope?"

Disciple :—Yes, sir, I have. Everything is ready, as you desired. But sir, I can't make out why so many holy threads are in requisition.

Swamiji :—Every Dwijâti* (twice-born) has a right to investiture with the holy thread. The Vedas themselves are authority in this matter. Whoever will come here on the sacred birthday of Sri Ramakrishna, I shall invest him with the holy thread. These people have fallen from their true status, and the scriptures say that after proper expiation those fallen in the way earn the right to investiture with the holy thread. This is the great day of Sri Ramakrishna's nativity, and men will be purified by taking his name. So the assembled devotees are to be invested with the holy thread today; do you now understand ?

Disciple :—I have collected, sir, quite a good number of holy threads according to your instructions, and after the worship I shall with your permission invest the Bhaktas with them.

Swamiji :—To the Bhaktas who are not Brâhmins, give this Mantra of Gâyatri (here Swamiji communicated to the disciple the special Gâyatris for them). By degrees all the people of the land have to be lifted to the position of Brahmins, not to speak of the Bhaktas of Sri Ramakrishna. Each Hindu, I say, is a brother to every other, and it is we who have degraded

---

* The Brâhmins, Kshatriyas and the Vaishyas are all Dwijâtis.

them by our outcry, "Don't touch," "don't touch!" And so the whole country has been plunged to the utmost depths of meanness, cowardice and ignorance. These men have to be uplifted; words of hope and faith have to be proclaimed to them. We have to tell them, "You are also men like us and you have all the rights that we have." Do you understand?

Disciple :—Yes, sir, it should be so.

Swamiji :—Now, ask those who will take the holy thread to finish their bath in the Ganges. Then after prostrations before Sri Ramakrishna, they will have their investiture.

About forty to fifty Bhaktas then duly received the Gâyatri from the disciple and were invested with the holy thread. When receiving them Swamiji's face beamed with profound delight. A little after this, Srijut Girish Chandra Ghosh arrived at the Math from Calcutta.

Now arrangements for music were made at the desire of Swamiji, and Sannyâsins of the Math decorated Swamiji as a Yogin.

Swamiji now chanted with the sweetest intonation, to the accompaniment of the Tanpurâ, the Sanskrit hymn beginning with कूजन्त रामरामेति "repeating in a low tone the name of Râma etc.," and when the chanting came to a close, he went on repeating with exquisite charm the holy words, "Ram, Ram, Sri Ram, Ram." His eyes were half-closed and the natural sublimity of his countenance seemed today to have deepened a hundredfold. Everybody remained spell-bound for over half-an-hour.

After the chanting of Sri Rama's name, Swamiji continued to sing a song of Tulsidâs on Sri Ramachandra in the same intoxicated strain of mind. Then other music followed.

After this, Swamiji suddenly took to putting off all the decorations he had on his person and began to dress Girish Babu with them. Then he declared Paramahamsadeva used to say, our brother is the incarnation of Bhairava.* There's no distinction between him and us. Girish Babu sat speechless all the time. A piece of Gerûa cloth was also brought, and he was draped in it and uttered no word of remonstrance. For he had merged his self fully today in the wishes of his brother-disciples. Swamiji now said: "Well, G. C., you are to speak to us today about Thâkur. And all of you (turning all round himself) sit quiet and attentive." Even then, Girish Babu sat motionless, voiceless like marble, absolutely lost in joy. And when at last he opened his lips, he did so to say, "Ah, what can this humble self speak of our Lord of

* Divine companion of Shiva.

unbounded mercy! Verily in this alone I realize that mercy that to me, this lowly creature, He has extended the privilege of sitting and mixing on the same footing with you, Sannyâsins, pure from your childhood, who have renounced all lust and lucre." While speaking thus, the words choked in his throat and he could not speak anything more.

After this, some pieces of Hindi music were rendered by Swamiji. The devotees were now called to partake of refreshments. After refreshment Swamiji came and took his seat in the parlour on the ground floor, and all the many visitors sat round him. Accosting a householder friend who had his investiture with the holy thread that day Swamiji said: "Really you all belong to the twice-born castes, only it is long since you lost your status. From this day again you become the twice-born. Repeat the Gâyatri at least a hundred times daily, won't you?" The householder expressed his assent.

Meanwhile Srijut Mahendranath Gupta (Master Mahashaya or M.) appeared on the scene. Swamiji cordially received him and made him take his seat. "Master Mahashaya," said Swamiji, "this is the anniversary of Sri Ramakrishna's birthday. So you shall have to relate to us something about him." Master

Mahashaya bent his head down smilingly in reply.

Just now it was announced that Swami Akhandananda had come from Murshidabad with two *pântuâs** which weighed one maund and a half! All of us hurried out to see these prodigious *pântuâs*. When they were shown to Swamiji, he said, "Take them up to the chapel for offering."

Making Swami Akhandananda the subject of his remarks, Swamiji said to the disciple, "Mark you, what a great hero he is in work! Of fear, death and the like he has no cognisance— doggedly going on doing his own work—'work for the welfare of the many, for the happiness of the many.'"

Disciple :—Sir, that power must have come to him as the result of a good deal of austerities.

Swamiji :—True, power comes of austerities ; but again, working for the sake of others itself constitutes Tapasyâ (practice of austerity). The Karmayogins regard work itself as a part of Tapasyâ. As on the one hand the practice of Tapasyâ intensifies altruistic feelings in the devotee and actuates him to unselfish work, so

---
* A sweetmeat usually about two inches in length, made mostly of fresh cheese fried in ghee and put in syrup.

also the pursuit of work for the sake of others carries the worker to the last fruition of Tapasyâ, namely the purification of the heart, and leads him thus to the realization of the supreme Atman.

Disciple :—But, sir, how few of us can work wholeheartedly for the sake of others from the very outset! How difficult it is for such broadmindedness to come at all as will make men sacrifice the desire for their own happiness and devote their lives for others!

Swamiji :—And how many have their minds going after Tapasyâ? With the attraction for lust and lucre working the other way, how many long for the realization of God? In fact, disinterested work is quite as difficult as Tapasyâ. So you have no right to say anything against those who go in for work in the cause of others. If you find Tapasyâ to be to your liking, well, go on with it. Another may find work as congenial to himself, and you have no right to make a prohibition in his case. You seem to have the settled idea in your mind that work is no Tapasyâ at all!

Disciple :—Yes, sir, before this I used to mean quite a different thing by Tapasyâ.

Swamiji :—As by continuing our religious practices we gradually develop a certain determined tendency for it, so by performing disinterested work over and over again, even unwillingly, we gradually find the will merging itself in it. The inclination to work for others develops in this way, do you see ? Just do some such work even though unwillingly, and then see if the actual fruit of Tapasyâ is realized within or not. As the outcome of work for the sake of others, the angularities of the mind get smoothened down and men are gradually prepared for sincere self-sacrifice for the good of others.

Disciple :—But, sir, what is the necessity at all for doing good to others ?

Swamiji :—Well, it is necessary for one's own good. We become forgetful of the ego when we think of the body as dedicated to the service of others—the body with which most complacently we identify the ego. And in the long run comes the consciousness of disembodiedness. The more intently you think of the well-being of others, the more oblivious of self you become. In this way, as gradually your heart gets purified by work, you will come to feel the truth that your own Self is pervading all beings and all things. Thus it is that doing good to others constitutes a way, a means of revealing one's own Self or Atman. Know this also to be one of the spiritual practices, a discipline for God-realization. Its aim also is Self-realization. Exactly as that aim is attained by Jnâna (knowledge), Bhakti (devotion) and so on, so also by work for the sake of others.

Disciple :—But, sir, if I am to keep thinking of others day and night, when shall I contemplate on the Atman? If I rest wholly occupied with something particular and relative, how can I realize the Atman which is Absolute?

Swamiji :—The highest aim of all disciplines, all spiritual paths, is the attainment of the knowledge of Atman. If you, by being devoted to the service of others and by getting your heart purified by such work, attain to the vision of all beings as the Self, what else remains to be attained in the way of Self-realization? Would you say that Self-realization is the state of existing as inert matter, as this wall or as this piece of wood, for instance?

Disciple :—Though that is not the meaning, yet what the scriptures speak of as the withdrawal of the Self into Its real nature, consists in the arresting of all mind-functions and all work.

Swamiji :—Yes, this Samâdhi of which the

scriptures speak is a state not at all easy to attain. When very rarely it appears in somebody, it does not last for long; so what will he keep himself occupied with? Thus it is that after realizing that state described in the scriptures, the saint sees the Self in all beings and in that consciousness devotes himself to service, so that any Karma that was yet left to be worked out through the body, may exhaust itself. It is this state which has been described by the authors of Shâstras as Jivanmukti, "Freedom while living."

Disciple :—So after all it comes about, sir, that unless this state of Jivanmukti is attained, work for the sake of others can never be pursued in the truest sense of the term.

Swamiji :—Yes, that is what the Shâstras say, but they also say that work or service for the good of others leads to this state of Jivanmukti. Otherwise, there would be no need on the part of the Shâstras to teach us a separate path of religious practice called the Karma-Yoga.

The disciple now understood the point and became silent, and Swamiji giving up the topic, commenced rendering in a voice of superhuman sweetness the song composed by Babu Girish Ch. Ghosh to commemorate Sri Ramakrishna's Nativity :—

"Who art Thou lying on the lap of the poor Brahmin mother," etc.

XIV

INSTALLATION OF SRI RAMAKRISHNA AT BELUR MATH—SHANKARACHARYA—BUDDHA—CAUSE OF THE DOWNFALL OF BUDDHISM—INFLUENCE OF PILGRIMAGE—DIFFRENT METHODS OF WORSHIP.

[Place : *The rented Math premises at Belur.* Year : *1898.*]

Today Swamiji is to perform a sacrifice and install Sri Ramakrishna on the site of the new Math. The disciple has been staying at the Math since the night before, with a view to witnessing the installation ceremony.

In the morning Swamiji had his bath in the Ganga and entered the worship-room. Then he made offerings to the consecrated Padukâ of Sri Ramakrishna and fell to meditation.

Meditation and worship over, preparations were now made for going to the new Math premises. Swamiji himself took on his right shoulder the ashes of Sri Ramakrishna's body preserved in a copper casket, and led the van. The disciple in company of the other Sannyâsins brought up the rear. There was the music of bells and conches. On his way Swamiji said to the disciple: "Sri Ramakrishna said to me, 'Wherever you will take me on your shoulders, there I will go and stay, be it under a tree or in a hut.' It is therefore that I am myself carrying him on my shoulders to the new Math grounds. Know it for certain that Sri Ramakrishna will keep his seat fixed there, for the welfare of the many, for a long time to come."

Disciple:—When was it that he said this to you?

Swamiji:—(Pointing to the Sâdhus of the Math) Didn't you hear from them? It was at the Cossipore garden.

Disciple:—I see. It was on this occasion, I suppose, that the split took place between Sri Ramakrishna's Sannyâsin and householder disciples regarding the privilege of serving him?

Swamiji:—Yes, but not exactly a "split"— it was only a misunderstanding, that's all. Rest assured that among those that are Sri Ramakrishna's devotees, and have *truly* obtained his grace, there is no sect or schism, there *cannot* be—be they householders or Sannyâsins. As to that kind of slight misunderstanding, do you know what it was due to? Well, each devotee colours Sri Ramakrishna in the light of his own understanding and each forms his own idea of him from his peculiar standpoint. He was, as it were, a great Sun, and each one of us is eyeing him, as it were, through a different kind of coloured glass, and coming to look upon that one Sun as parti-coloured. Of course, it is quite true that this leads to schism in course of time. But then, such schisms rarely occur in the lifetime of those who are fortunate enough to have come in direct contact with an Avatâra. The effulgence of that Personality, who takes pleasure only in his Self, dazzles their eyes, and sweeps away pride, egotism, and narrow-mindedness from heir minds. Consequently they find no opportunity to create sects and party factions. They are content to offer him their heart's worship, each in his own fashion.

Disciple :—Sir, do the devotees of the Avatâra, then, view him differently notwithstanding their knowing him to be God, and does this lead the succeeding generations of their followers to limit themselves within narrow bounds and form various little sects?

Swamiji :—Quite so. Hence sects are bound to form in course of time. Look, for instance, how the followers of Chaitanya Deva have been divided into two or three hundred sects; and those of Jesus hold thousands of creeds. But all those sects without exception follow

Chaitanya Deva or Jesus and none else.

Disciple :—Then, perhaps, Sri Ramakrishna's followers, too, will be divided in course of time into various sects?

Swamiji :—Well, of course. But then this Math that we are building will harmonize all creeds, all standpoints. Just as Sri Ramakrishna held highly liberal views, this Math, too, will be a centre for propagating similar ideas. The blazing lights of universal harmony that will emanate from here will flood the whole world.

While all this was going on, the party reached the Math premises. Swamiji took the casket down from his shoulder, placed it on the carpet spread on the ground and bowed before it touching the ground with his forehead. Others too followed suit.

Then Swamiji again sat for worship. After going through the Pujâ he lighted the sacrificial fire, made oblations to it, and himself cooking *pâyasa* (milk-rice with sugar) with the help of his brother-disciples, offered it to Sri Ramakrishna. Probably also he initiated certain householders on the spot that day. All this ceremony being done, Swamiji cordially addressed the assembled gentlemen and said : "Pray today all of you heart and soul to the holy feet of Sri Ramakrishna, that the great Avatâra of this cycle that he is, he may, for the welfare of the many, and for the happiness of the many— बहुजनहिताय बहुजनसुखाय —reside in this holy spot from this day for a great length of time, and ever continue to make it the unique centre of harmony amongst all religions." Everyone prayed like that with folded palms. Swamiji next called the disciple and said : "None of us (Sannyâsins) have any longer the right to take back this casket of Sri Ramakrishna, for we have installed him here today. It behoves on you, therefore, to take it on your head back (to Nilambar Babu's garden)." Seeing that the disciple hesitated to touch the casket Swamiji said : "No fear, touch it, you have my order." The disciple gladly obeyed the injunction, lifted the casket on his head, and moved on. He went first, next came Swamiji, and the rest followed. Swamiji said to the disciple on the way : "Sri Ramakrishna has today sat on your head and is blessing you. Take care, never let your mind think of anything transitory, from this day forth." Before crossing a small bridge, Swamiji again said to him, "Beware, now, you must move very cautiously."

Thus all safely reached the Math and rejoiced. Swamiji now entered into a conversation with the disciple, in the course of which he said :

"Through the will of Sri Ramakrishna, his Dharmakshetra—sanctified spot—has been established today. A twelve years' anxiety is off my head. Do you know what I am thinking of at this moment?—This Math will be a centre of learning and spiritual discipline. Householders of a virtuous turn like yourselves will build houses on the surrounding land and live there, and Sannyasins, men of renunciation, will live in the centre, while on that plot of land on the south of the Math, buildings will be erected for English and American disciples to live in. How do you like this idea?"

Disciple:—Sir, it is indeed a wonderful fancy of yours.

Swamiji:—A fancy do you call it? Not at all, everything will come about in time. I am but laying the foundation. There will be lots of further developments in future. Some portion of it I shall live to work out. And I shall infuse into you fellows various ideas, which you will work out in future. It will not do merely to listen to great principles. You must apply them in the practical field, turn them into constant practice. What will be the good of cramming the high-sounding dicta of the scriptures? You have first to grasp the teachings of the Shâstras, and then to work them out in practical life. Do you understand? This is called practical religion.

Thus the talk went on, and gradually drifted to the topic of Shankarâchârya. The disciple was a great adherent of Shankara, almost to the point of fanaticism. He used to look upon Shankara's Advaita philosophy as the crest of all philosophies, and could not bear any criticism of him. Swamiji was aware of this and, as was his wont, wanted to break this onesidedness of the disciple.

Swamiji :—Shankara's intellect was sharp like the razor—he was a good argumentator and a scholar, no doubt of that, but he had no great liberality; his heart too seems to have been like that. Besides, he used to take great pride in his Brâhminism—much like a southern Brahmin of the priest class, you may say. How he has defended in his Commentary on the *Vedanta-Sutras* that the non-Brahmin castes will not attain to a supreme knowledge of Brahman! And how specious arguments! Referring to Vidura* he has said that he became a knower of Brahman by reason of his Brahmin body in the previous incarnation. Well, if nowadays any Shudra attains to a knowledge of Brahman, shall

---

* Uncle of the Pândava brothers, and a most saintly character, considered to be an incarnation of Dharma.

we have to side with your Shankara and maintain that because he had been a Brahmin in his previous birth, therefore he has attained to this knowledge? Goodness! What is the use of dragging in Brahminism with so much ado? The Vedas have entitled anyone belonging to the three upper castes to a study of the Vedas and the realization of Brahman, haven't they? So Shankara had no need whatsoever of displaying this curious bit of pedantry on this subject, contrary to the Vedas. And such was his heart that he burnt to death lots of Buddhist monks— by defeating them in argument! And the Buddhists, too, were foolish enough to burn themselves to death, simply because they were worsted in argument! What can you call such an action on Shankara's part except fanaticism? But look at Buddha's heart!—Ever ready to give his own life to save the life of even a kid— what to speak of बहुजनहिताय बहुजनसुखाय —"for the welfare of the many, for the happiness of the many"! See, what a large-heartedness—what a compassion!

Disciple:—Can't we call that attitude of Buddha, too, as another kind of fanaticism, sir! He went to the length of sacrificing his own body for the sake of a beast!

Swamiji:—But consider how much good to

the world and its beings came out of that "fanaticism" of his—how many monasteries and schools and colleges, how many public hospitals, and veterinary refuges were established, how developed architecture became—think of that. What was there in this country before Buddha's advent ? Only a number of religious principles recorded on bundles of palm leaves—and those too known only to a few. It was Lord Buddha who brought them down to the practical field, and showed how to apply them in the everyday life of the people. In a sense, *he* was the living embodiment of true Vedanta.

Disciple : —But, sir, it was he who by breaking down the Varnâshrama Dharma (duty according to caste and order of life) brought about a revolution within the fold of Hinduism in India, and there seems to be some truth also in the remark that the religion he preached was for this reason banished in course of time from the soil of India.

Swamiji : —It was not through his teachings that Buddhism came to such degradation, it was the fault of his followers. By becoming too philosophic they lost much of their breadth of heart. Then gradually the corruption known as Vâmâchâra (unrestrained mixing with women in the name of religion) crept in and ruined

Buddhism. Such diabolical rites are not to be met with in any modern Tantra! One of the principal centres of Buddhism was Jagannâth or Puri, and you have simply to go there and look at the abominable figures carved on the temple-walls to be convinced of this. Puri has come under the sway of the Vaishnavas since the time of Râmânuja and Sri Chaitanya. Through the influence of great personages like these the place now wears an altogether different aspect.

Disciple :—Sir, the Shastras tell us of various special influences attaching to places of pilgrimage. How far is this claim true?

Swamiji :—When the whole world is the Form Universal of the Eternal Atman, the Ishvara, what is there to wonder at in special influences attaching to particular places? There are places where He manifests Himself specially, either spontaneously or through the earnest longing of pure souls, and the ordinary man, if he visits those places with eagerness, attains his end quite easily. Therefore it may lead to the development of the Self in time to have recourse to holy places. But know it for certain that there is no greater Tirtha (holy spot) than the body of man. Nowhere else is the Atman so manifest as here. That car of Jagannatha that you see is but a concrete symbol of this corporeal car. You have to behold the Atman in this car of the body. Haven't you read— आत्मानं रथिनं विद्धि—"Know the Atman to be seated on the chariot" etc., मध्ये वामनमासीनं विश्वे देवा उपासते —"All the gods worship the Vâmana (the Supreme Being in a diminutive form) seated in the interior of the body"? The sight of the Atman is the real vision of Jagannatha. And the statement— रथे च वामनं दृष्ट्वा पुनर्जन्म न विद्यते —"Seeing the Vamana on the car one is no more subject to rebirth," means, that if you can visualise the Atman which is within you, and disregarding which you are always identifying yourself with this curious mass of matter, this body of yours—if you can see that, then there is no more rebirth for you. If the sight of the Lord's image on a wooden framework confer liberation on people, then crores of them would be liberated every year—specially with such facility of communication by rail nowadays. But I do not mean to say that the notion which devotees in general entertain towards Sri Jagannatha is either nothing or erroneous. There is a class of people who gradually rise to higher and higher truths with the help of that Image. So it is an undoubted fact that in and through that Image there is a special manifestation of the Lord.

Disciple :—Sir, are there different religions then for the ignorant and the wise?

Swamiji :—Quite So. Otherwise why do your scriptures go to such lengths over the specification of the qualifications of an aspirant? All is truth no doubt, but relative truth, different in degrees. Whatever man knows to be truth is of a like nature, some are lesser truths, other higher ones in comparison to them, while the Absolute Truth is God alone. This Atman is altogether dormant in matter; in man, designated as a living being, It is partially conscious; while in personages like Sri Krishna, Buddha, and Shankara the same Atman has reached the super-conscious stage. There is a state even beyond that, which cannot be expressed in terms of thought or language—अवाङ्मनस गोचरम् ।

Disciple :—Sir, there are certain Bhakti sects who hold that we must practise devotion by placing ourselves in a particular attitude or relation with God. They do not understand anything about the glory of the Atman and so forth, and exclusively recommend this constant devotional attitude.

Swamiji :—What they say is true to their own case. By continued practice along this line they too shall feel an awakening of Brahman within them. And what we (Sannyâsins) are doing is another kind of practice. We have renounced the world. So how will it suit us to practise by putting ourselves in some worldly relation—such as that of mother, or father, or wife, or son and so forth—with God? To us all these ideals appear to be narrow. Of course it is very difficult to qualify for the worship of God in His Absolute, unconditioned aspect. But must we go in for poison because we get no nectar? Always talk and hear and reason about this Atman. By continuing to practise in this way, you will find in time that the Lion (Brahman) will wake up in you too. Go beyond all those relative attitudes—mere sports of the mind. Listen to what Yama says in the *Katha Upanishad* उत्तिष्ठत जाग्रत प्राप्यवरान्निबोधत । —Arise! Awake! and stop not till the goal is reached!

Here the subject was brought to a close. The bell for taking Prasâda rang and Swamiji went to partake of it, followed by the disciple.

XV

IN A REMINISCENT MOOD—HIS PSYCHIC POWERS
—AMERICAN MEN AND WOMEN—OPPOSITION FROM
THE BIGOTED CHRISTIANS—SELF-SURRENDER AND
INERTIA—NAG MAHASHAYA.

[Place : *The rented Math premises at Belur.*
Time : *February, 1898.*]

Swamiji has removed the Math from Alambazar to Nilambar Babu's garden at Belur. He is very glad to have come to these new premises. He said to the disciple when the latter came : "See how the Ganga flows by and what a nice building ! I like this place. This is the ideal kind of place for a Math." It was then afternoon.

In the evening the disciple found Swamiji alone in the upper storey, and the talk went on, on various topics, in the course of which he wanted to know about Swamiji's boyhood days. Swamiji began to say : "From my very boyhood I was a daredevil sort of fellow. Otherwise, do you think I could make a tour round the world without a single copper in my pocket ?"

In boyhood Swamiji had a great predilection for hearing the chanting of the Râmâyana by professional singers. Wherever such chanting would take place in the neighbourhood, he would attend it leaving sport and all. Swamiji related how, while listening to the Râmâyana, on some days, he would be so deeply engrossed in it as to forget all about home, and would have no idea that it was late at night and that he must return home, and so forth. One day during the chant he heard that the monkey-god Hanumân lived in banana orchards. Forthwith he was so much convinced that when the chant was over he did not go home straight that night, but loitered in a banana orchard close to his house, with the hope of catching sight of Hanuman, till it was very late in the night.

In his student life he used to pass the daytime only in playing and gamboling with his mates, and study at night, bolting the doors. And none could know when he prepared his lessons.

The disciple asked, "Did you see any visions, sir, during your school-days?"

Swamiji:—While at school one night I was meditating within closed doors and had a fairly deep concentration of mind. How long I meditated in that way, I cannot say. It was over, and I still kept my seat, when from the southern wall of that room a luminous figure stepped out and stood in my front. There was a wonderful radiance on its visage, yet there seemed to be no play of emotion on it. It was the figure of a Sannyâsin absolutely calm, shaven-headed, and staff and Kamandalu (a Sannyâsin's wooden water-bowl) in hand. He gazed at me for some time, and seemed as if he would address me. I too gazed at him in speechless wonder. Then a kind of fright seized me, I opened the door and hurried out of the room. Then it struck me that it was foolish of me to run away like that, that perhaps he might say something to me. But I have never met that figure since. Many a time and often have I thought that if again I saw him, I would no more be afraid but would speak to him. But I met him no more.

Disciple :—Did you ever think on the matter afterwards?

Swamiji :—Yes, but I could find no clue to its solution. I now think it was the Lord Buddha whom I saw.

After a short pause Swamiji said : "When the mind is purified, when one is free from the attachment for lust and gold, one sees lots of visions, most wonderful ones! But one should not pay heed to them. The aspirant cannot advance further if he sets his mind constantly on them. Haven't you heard that Sri Ramakrishna used to say, 'Countless jewels lie uncared for in the outer courts of my beloved

TALKS WITH SWAMI VIVEKANANDA 143

Lord's sanctum'? We must come face to face with the Atman, what is the use of setting one's mind on vagaries like those?"

After saying these words Swamiji sat silent for a while, lost in thought over something. He then resumed:

"Well, while I was in America I had certain wonderful powers developed in me. By looking into people's eyes I could fathom in a trice the contents of their minds. The workings of everybody's mind would be patent to me, like a fruit on the palm of one's hand. To some I used to give out these things, and of those to whom I communicated these, many would become my disciples; whereas those who came to mix with me with some ulterior motive, would not, on coming across this power of mine, even venture into my presence any more.

"When I began lecturing in Chicago and other cities, I had to deliver every week some twelve or fifteen or even more lectures at times. This excessive strain on the body and mind would exhaust me to a degree. I seemed to run short of subjects for lectures, and was anxious where to find new topics for the morrow's lecture. New thoughts seemed altogether scarce. One day after the lecture I lay thinking of what means to adopt next. The thought induced a sort of slumber and in that state I heard as if somebody stood by me and was lecturing—many new ideas and new veins of thought, which I had scarcely heard or thought of in my life. On awaking I remembered them and reproduced them in my lecture. I cannot enumerate how often this phenomenon took place. Many, many days did I hear such lectures while lying in bed. Sometimes the lecture would be delivered in such a loud voice that the inmates of adjacent rooms would hear the sound and ask me the next day, 'With whom, Swamiji, were you talking so loudly last night?' I used to avoid the question somehow. Ah, it was a wonderful phenomenon."

The disciple was wonder-struck at Swamiji's words and after thinking deeply on the matter said, "Sir, then you yourself must have lectured like that in your subtle body, and sometimes it would be echoed by the gross body also."

Swamiji listened and replied, "Well, may be."

The topic of his American experiences came up. Swamiji said: "In that country the women are more learned than men. They are all well versed in science and philosophy and that is why they would appreciate and honour me so much. The men are grinding all day at their work and have very little leisure, whereas the women, by studying and teaching in the schools and colleges, have become highly learned. Whichever side you turn your eyes in America, you see the power and influence of women."

Disciple :—Well, sir, did not the bigoted Christians oppose you ?

Swamiji :—Yes, they did. When people began to honour me, then the Pâdris were after me. They spread many slanders about me by publishing them in the newspapers. Many asked me to contradict these slanders. But I never took the slightest notice of them. It is my firm conviction that no great work is accomplished in this world by low cunning ; so without paying any heed to these vile slanders, I used to work steadily at my mission. The upshot I used to find was that often my slanderers, feeling repentant afterwards, would surrender to me and offer apologies, by contradicting the slanders in the papers, themselves. Sometimes it so happened that learning that I had been invited to a certain house, somebody would communicate those slanders to my host, who hearing them would leave home locking his door. When I went there to attend the invitation, I found it was deserted and nobody was there. Again a few days afterwards, they themselves learning the truth, would feel sorry for their previous conduct, and come to offer themselves as disciples. The fact is, my son, this whole world is full of mean ways of worldliness. But men of real moral courage and discrimination are never deceived by these. Let the world say what it chooses, I shall tread the path of duty—know this to be the line of action for a hero. Otherwise, if one has to attend day and night to what this man says or that man writes, no great work is achieved in this world. Do you know this Sanskrit Shloka: "Let those who are versed in the ethical codes praise or blame, let Lakshmi, the goddess of Fortune, come or go wherever she wisheth, let death overtake him today or after a century, the wise man never swerves from the path of rectitude."* Let people praise you or blame you, let fortune smile or frown upon you, let your body fall today or after a Yuga, see that you do not deviate from the path of Truth. How much of tempests and waves one has to weather, before one reaches the heaven of Peace! The greater a man has become, the fiercer ordeal he has had to pass through. Their lives have been tested true by the touchstone of practical life and only then have they been acknowledged great by the

* Bhartrihari's *Nitishataka*.

world. Those who are faint-hearted and cowardly sink their barks near the shore, frightened by the raging of waves on the sea. He who is a Hero never casts a glance at these. Come what may, I must attain my ideal first—this is Purushakâra, manly endeavour; without such manly endeavour no amount of Divine help will be of any avail to banish your inertia.

Disciple :—Is, then, reliance on Divine help a sign of weakness ?

Swamiji :—In the Shâstras real self-surrender and reliance on God has been indicated as the culmination of human achievement. But in your country nowadays the way people speak of Daiva or reliance on Divine dispensation is a sign of death, the outcome of great cowardliness; conjuring up some monstrous idea of Godhead and trying to saddle that with all your faults and shortcomings. Haven't you heard Sri Ramakrishna's story about "the sin of killing a cow"?* In the end the owner of the garden

---

* A man had laid out a beautiful garden into which a cow strayed one day and did much injury. The man in rage gave some blows to the cow which killed her. Then to avoid the terrible sin he bethought himself of a trick : knowing that Indra was the presiding deity of the hand, he tried to lay the blame on him. Indra perceiving his sophistry appeared on the scene in the guise of a Brâhmin and by a number of questions drew from him the answer that each and every item in

had to suffer for the sin of killing the cow. Nowadays everybody says : "I am acting as I am being directed by the Lord" and thus throws the burden of both his sins and virtues on the Lord. As if he is himself like the lotus-leaf in the water (untouched by it). If everybody can truly live always in this mood, then he is a Free Soul. But what really happens is that for the "good" I have the credit, but for the "bad" Thou God art responsible—praise be to such reliance on God! Without the attainment of the fullness of Knowledge or Divine Love, such a state of absolute reliance on the Lord does not come. He who is truly and sincerely reliant on the Lord goes beyond all idea of the duality of good and bad. The brightest example of the attainment of this state among us, at the present time, is Nâg Mahâshaya.

Then the conversation drifted to the subject of Nâg Mahâshaya. Swamiji said, "One does not find a second devoted Bhakta like him—oh, when shall I see him again!"

Disciple :—He will soon come to Calcutta to meet you, so mother (Nâg Mahâshaya's wife)

---

connection with that garden was the man's own handiwork; whereupon Indra exposed his cunning with the cutting remark, "Well, everything here has been done by you, and Indra alone is responsible for the killing of the cow, eh!"

has written to me.

Swamiji :—Sri Ramakrishna used to compare him to King Janaka. A man with such control over all the senses one does not hear of even, much less come across. You must associate with him as much as you can. He is one of Sri Ramakrishna's nearest disciples.

Disciple :—Many in our part of the country call him a madcap. But I have known him to be a great soul since the very first day of my meeting him. He loves me much and I have his fervent blessings.

Swamiji :—Since you have attained the company of such a Mahâpurusha, what more have you to fear about? As an effect of many lives of Tapasyâ (austerities) one is blessed with the company of such a great soul. How does he live at home?

Disciple :—Sir, he has got no business or anything of the kind. He is always busy in serving the guests who come to his house. Beyond the small sum the Pâl Babus give him, he has no other means of subsistence; his expenses, however, are like those in a rich family. But he does not spend a pice for his own enjoyment, all that expense is for the service of others. Service—service of others—this seems to be the great mission of his life. It sometimes strikes me that realizing the Atman in all creatures he is engrossed in serving the whole world as a part and parcel of himself. In the service of others he works incessantly and is not conscious even of his body. I suppose, he always lives on the plane which you, sir, call the superconscious state of the mind.

Swamiji :—Why should not that be? How greatly was he beloved of Sri Ramakrishna! In your East Bengal, one of Sri Ramakrishna's divine companions has been born in the person of Nâg Mahâshaya. By his radiance Eastern Bengal has become effulgent.

XVI

SWAMI VIVEKANANDA'S EXPERIENCES AT AMARNATH AND KSHIR BHAVANI—HEARING A DIVINE VOICE—EXISTENCE OF GHOSTS AND SPIRITS—SWAMI VIVEKANANDA'S EXPERIENCE OF A DISEMBODIED SPIRIT.

[Place : *The rented Math premises at Belur.*
Year : *1898, November.*]

It is two or three days since Swamiji has returned from Kashmir. His health is indifferent. When the disciple came to the Math, Swami Brahmananda said, "Since returning from Kashmir Swamiji does not speak to anybody, he sits in one place rapt in thought; you go to him and by conversations try to draw his mind a little towards worldly objects."

The disciple coming to Swamiji's room in the upper storey found him sitting as if immersed in deep meditation. There was no smile on his face, his brilliant eyes had no outward look, as if intent on seeing something within. Seeing the disciple he only said, "You have come, my son? Please take your seat," and lapsed into silence. The disciple seeing the inside of his left eye reddened asked, "How is it that your eye is red?" "That is nothing," said Swamiji and was again silent. When even after a long time Swamiji did not speak, the disciple was a little troubled at heart and touching his feet said, "Won't you relate to me what things you have seen at Amarnath?" By the disciple's touching his feet, the tensity of his mood was broken a little; as if his attention was diverted a little outwards. He said, "Since visiting Amarnath I feel as if Shiva is sitting on my head for twenty-four hours and would not come down." The disciple heard it with speechless wonder.

Swamiji :—I underwent great religious austerities at Amarnath and then in the temple of Kshir Bhavâni. Go and prepare me some tobacco, I will relate everything to you.

The disciple joyfully obeyed the order. Swamiji slowly smoking began to say: "On the way to Amarnath, I made a very steep ascent on the mountain. Pilgrims do not generally travel by that path. But the determination came upon me that I must go by that path, and so I did. The labour of the strenuous ascent has told on my body. The cold there is so biting that you feel it like pin-pricks.

Disciple :—I have heard that it is the custom to visit the Image of Amarnath naked, is it so?

Swamiji :—Yes, I entered the cave with only my Kaupin on and my body smeared with the holy ashes; I did not then feel any cold or heat. But when I came out of the temple, I was benumbed by the cold.

Disciple :—Did you see the holy pigeons? I have heard, in that cold no living creatures are found to live, but a flight of pigeons from some unknown place frequents the place occasionally.

Swamiji :—Yes, I saw three or four white pigeons; whether they live in the cave or the neighbouring hills, I could not ascertain.

Disciple :—Sir, I have heard people say that the sight of pigeons on coming out of the temple indicates that one has really been blessed with the vision of Shiva.

Swamiji :—I have heard, the sight of the pigeons brings to fruition whatever desires you may have.

Then Swamiji said, on the way back he returned to Srinagar by the common route by which the pilgrims return. A few days after returning to Srinagar he went to visit Kshir Bhavâni Devi and staying there for seven days worshipped the Devi and made Homa to her with offerings of *kshir* (condensed milk). Every day he used to worship the Devi with a maund of *kshir* as offering. One day, while worshipping, the thought arose in Swamiji's mind : "Mother Bhavâni has been manifesting Her Presence here for untold years. The Mohammedans came and destroyed Her temple, yet the people of the place did nothing to protect Her. Alas, if I were then living, I could never have borne it silently." When, thinking in this strain, his mind was much oppressed with sorrow and anguish, he distinctly heard the voice of the Mother saying : "It was according to My desire that the Mohammedans destroyed this temple. It is My desire that I should live in a dilapidated temple, otherwise, can I not immediately erect a seven-storied temple of gold here if I like ? What can you do ? Shall I protect you or shall you protect me !" Swamiji said: "Since hearing that Divine Voice, I cherish no more plans. The idea of building Maths etc., I have given up; as Mother wills, so it will be." The disciple speechless with wonder began to think, "Did he not one day tell me that whatever I saw and heard was but the echo of the Atman within me, that there was nothing outside?"—and fearlessly spoke it out also—"Sir, you used to say that Divine Voices are the echo of our inward thoughts and feelings." Swamiji gravely said: "Whether it be internal or external, if you actually hear with your ears such a disembodied voice, as I have done, can you deny it and call it false? Divine Voices are actually heard, just as you and I are talking."

The disciple without controverting accepted Swamiji's words, for his words always carried conviction.

He then brought up the subject of departed spirits, and said, "Sir, these ghosts and departed spirits we hear about, which the Shâstras also amply corroborate—are all these true or not?"

Swamiji:—Certainly they are true. Whatever you don't see, are they all false for that? Beyond your sight, millions of universes are revolving at great distances. Because you do not see them, are they non-existent for that? But then, do not put your mind on these subjects of ghosts and spirits. Your mental attitude towards them should be one of indifference. Your duty is to realize the Atman within this body. When you realize the Atman, ghosts and spirits will all be your slaves.

Disciple:—But, sir, I think that, if one sees them, it strengthens one's belief in the hereafter, and dispels all doubts about it.

Swamiji:—You are heroes; do you mean to say that even you shall have to strengthen your belief in the hereafter by seeing ghosts and spirits! You have read so many sciences and scriptures—have mastered so many secrets of this infinite universe—even with such knowledge, you have to acquire the knowledge of the Atman by seeing ghosts and spirits! What a shame!

Disciple:—Well, sir, have you ever seen ghosts and spirits?

Swamiji narrated that a certain deceased relative of his used to come to him as a disembodied spirit. Sometimes it used to bring him information about distant events. But on verification, some of its information were not found to be correct. Afterwards at a certain place of pilgrimage Swamiji prayed for it mentally wishing it might be released—since then he did not see it again.

The disciple then questioned Swamiji if Shrâddha or other obsequial ceremonies appeased the departed spirits in any way. Swamiji replied, "That is not impossible." On the disciple's asking for the grounds of that belief Swamiji said : "I will explain the subject to you at length some day. There are irrefutable arguments to prove that the Shrâddha ceremony appeases the departed beings. Today I don't feel well. I shall explain it to you another day." But the disciple did not get another opportunity to ask that question of Swamiji.

XVII

COMPOSING A SANSKRIT HYMN—ABOUT BENGALI LANGUAGE AND ITS STYLE—"BE FEARLESS"—NEED FOR THE STUDY OF SCRIPTURES—RESULT OF SELF-REALIZATION.

[Place : *The rented Math premises at Belur.* Year : *1898, November.*]

The Math is still situated in Nilambar Babu's garden-house at Belur. It is the month of November. Swamiji is now much engaged in the study and discussion of Sanskrit scriptures. The couplets beginning with "*âchandâlâ-pratihatarayah,*" he composed about this time.

Today Swamiji composed the hymn *"Om hrim ritam"* etc., and making it over to the disciple said, "See if there is any metrical defect in these stanzas." The disciple made a copy of the poem for this purpose.

On this day it seemed as if the goddess of learning has manifested herself on his tongue. With the disciple he fluently talked for about two hours at a stretch in exceedingly melodious Sanskrit.

After the disciple had copied the hymn, Swamiji said, "You see, as I write immersed in thought, grammatical slips sometimes occur; therefore I ask you all to look over them."

Disciple :—Sir, those are not slips, but the licence of genius.

Swamiji :—You may say so; but why will other people assent to that ? The other day I wrote an essay on "What is Hinduism," and some amongst you even are complaining that it is written in very stiff Bengali. I think, like all other things language and thought also become lifeless and monotonous in course of time. Such a state seems to have happened now in this country. On the advent of Sri Ramakrishna, however, a new current has set in, in thought and language. Everything has now to be recast in new moulds. Everything has to be propagated with the stamp of new genius. Look, for example, how the old modes of Sannyâsins are breaking, yielding place to a new mould by degrees. Society is protesting much against it—but is it of any avail? Neither are we frightened by that. The Sannyasins of the present day have to go to distant countries for preaching, and if they go in an ash-besmeared, half-nude body like the Sâdhus of old, in the first place they won't be taken on board the ships; and even if they anyhow reach foreign countries in that dress they will have to stay in jail. Everything requires to be changed a little according to place, time and civilization. Henceforth I am thinking of writing essays in Bengali. Litterateurs will perhaps rail at them. Never mind—I shall try to cast the Bengali language in a new mould. Nowadays, Bengali writers use too many verbs in their writings; this takes away the force of the language. If one can express the ideas of verbs with adjectives, it adds to the force of the language— henceforth try to write in that style. Try to write articles in that style in the *Udbodhan*. Do you know the meaning of the use of verbs in language? It gives a pause to the thought; hence the use of too many verbs in language

TALKS WITH SWAMI VIVEKANANDA 159

is a sign of weakness, like quick breathing, and indicates that there is not much vitality in the language; that is why one cannot lecture well in the Bengali language. He who has control over his language, does not make frequent breaks in his thoughts. As your physique has been rendered languid by living on a dietary of boiled rice and *dâl*, similar is the case with your language. In food, in modes of life, in thought and in language, energy has to be infused. With the infusion of vitality all round and the circulation of blood in all arteries and veins, one should feel the throbbing of new life in everything— then only will the people of this land be able to survive the present terrible struggle for existence; otherwise, the country and the race will vanish in the enveloping shadows of death at no distant date.

Disciple :—Sir, the constitution of the people of this country has been moulded in a peculiar way through long ages. Is it possible to change that within a short time?

Swamiji :—If you have known the old ways to be wrong, then why don't you, as I say, learn to live in a better way? By your example ten other people will follow suit, and by theirs another fifty people will learn. By this process in course of time the new idea will awaken in the hearts of the whole race. But even if after understanding, you do not act accordingly, I shall know that you are wise in words only—but practically you are fools.

Disciple :—Your words, sir, infuse great courage, enthusiasm, energy and strength into the heart.

Swamiji :—By degrees the heart has to be strengthened. If one man is made, it equals the result of a hundred thousand lectures. Making the mind and the lips at one, the ideas have to be practised in life. This is what Sri Ramakrishna meant by "allowing no theft in the chamber of thought." You have to be practical in all spheres of work. The whole country has been ruined by masses of theories. He who is the true son of Sri Ramakrishna, will manifest the practical side of religious ideas and will set to work with one-pointed devotion without paying heed to the prattling of men or of society. Haven't you heard of the couplet of Tulsidâs : "The elephant walks the market-place and a thousand curs bark at him, so the Sadhus have no ill-feeling if worldly people slander them." You have to walk in this way. No count should be taken of the words of people. If one has to pay heed to their praise or blame, no great work can be accomplished in this life.

नायमात्माबलहीनेनलभ्य: —"The Atman is not to be gained by the weak." If there is no strength in body and mind, the Atman cannot be realized. First you have to build the body by good nutritious food—then only will the mind be strong. The mind is but the subtle part of the body. You must retain great strength in your mind and words. "I am low," "I am low," repeating these ideas in the mind man belittles and degrades himself. Therefore the Shâstras say,—

मुक्ताभिमानी मुक्तो हि बद्धो बद्धाभिमान्यपि ।
किंवदन्तीति सत्येयं या मतिः सा गतिर्भवेत् ॥

—"He who thinks himself free, free he becomes; he who thinks himself bound, bound he remains —this popular saying is true; as one thinks, so one becomes." He alone who is always awake to the idea of freedom, becomes free; he who thinks he is bound, endures life after life in the state of bondage. It is a fact. This truth holds good both in spiritual and temporal matters. Those who are always down-hearted and dispirited in this life, can do no work; from life to life they come and go wailing and moaning. "The earth is enjoyed by heroes"—this is the unfailing truth. Be a hero, always say, "I have no fear." Tell this to everybody—"Have no fear." Fear is death, fear is sin, fear is hell, fear is unrighteousness, fear is wrong life. All the negative thoughts and ideas that are in this world have proceeded from this evil spirit of fear. This fear alone has kept the Sun, Air, and Death, in their respective places and functions, allowing none to escape from its bounds. Therefore the Shruti says—

भयादस्याग्निस्तपति भयात्तपति सूर्यः ।
भयादिन्द्रश्च वायुश्च मृत्युर्धावति पञ्चमः ॥

—"Through fear of this fire burns, the sun heats, through fear Indra and Vâyu are carrying on their functions, and Death stalks upon this earth." When the gods Indra, Chandra, Vayu, Varuna will attain to fearlessness, then will they be one with the Brahman, and all this phantasm of the world will vanish. Therefore I say, "Be fearless," "Be fearless."

Swamiji, in saying these words, appeared in the eyes of the disciple like the very embodiment of "fearlessness," and he thought, "How in his presence even the fear of death leaves one and vanishes into nothingness!"

Swamiji continued : In this embodied existence, you will be tossed again and again on the waves of happiness and misery, prosperity and adversity—but know them all to be of momentary duration. Never care for them. "I am the birthless, the deathless Atman, whose nature is Intelligence"—implanting this idea firmly in your heart, you should pass the days of your life. "I have no birth, no death, I am the Atman untouched by anything"—lose yourself completely in this idea. If you can once become one with this idea, then in the hour of sorrow and tribulation, it will rise of itself in your mind, and you will not have to strive with difficulty to bring it up. The other day, I was a guest of Babu Priyanath Mukherjee at Baidyanath. There I had such a spell of asthma that I felt like dying. But from within, with every breath arose the deep-toned sound, "I am He," "I am He." Resting on the pillow, I was waiting for the vital breath to depart, and observing all the time that from within was being heard the sound of "I am He," "I am He!" I could hear all along,— एकमेवाद्वयं ब्रह्म नेह नानास्ति किञ्चन—"The Brahman, the One without a second, alone exists, nothing manifold exists in the world."

The disciple struck with amazement said, "Sir, talking with you and listening to your realizations, I feel no necessity for the study of scriptures."

Swamiji :—No! Scriptures have to be

studied also. For the attainment of Jnâna, study of scriptures is essential. I shall soon open classes in the Math for them. The Vedas, Upanishads, the Gita and Bhâgavata should be studied in the classes and I shall teach the Pânini Ashtâdhyâyi.

Disciple :—Have you studied the Ashtadhyayi of Panini?

Swamiji :—When I was in Jaipur, I met a great grammarian and felt a desire to study Sanskrit grammar with him. Although he was a great scholar in that branch, he had not much aptitude for teaching. He explained to me the commentary on the first aphorism for three days continuously, still I could not grasp a bit of it. On the fourth day the teacher got annoyed and said, "Swamiji, I could not make you understand the meaning of the first aphorism even in three days; I fear, you will not be much benefited by my teaching." Hearing these words a great self-reproach came over me. Putting food and sleep aside I set myself to study the commentary on the first aphorism independently. Within three hours the sense of the commentary stood explained before me as clearly as anything; then going to my teacher I gave him the sense of the whole commentary. My teacher hearing me, said, "How could you gather the sense so excellently within three hours, which I failed to explain to you in three days?" After that, every day I began to read chapter after chapter, with the greatest ease. Through concentration of mind everything can be accomplished—even mountains can be crushed to atoms.

Disciple:—Sir, everything is wonderful about you.

Swamiji:—There is nothing wonderful in this universe. Ignorance constitutes the only darkness, which covers all things and makes them look mysterious. When everything is lighted by Knowledge, the sense of mystery vanishes from the face of things. Even such an inscrutable thing as Mâyâ, which brings the most impossible things to pass, disappears. Know Him, think of Him by knowing whom everything else is known. And when that Atman is realized, the purport of all scriptures will be perceived as clearly as a fruit on the palm of one's hand. The Rishis of old attained realization, and must we fail? We are also men. What has happened once in the life of one individual must, through proper endeavour, be realized in the life of others. History repeats itself. This Atman is the same in all, there is only a difference of manifestation in different individuals. Try to manifest this Atman and you will see your intellect penetrating into all subjects. The intellect of one who has not realized the Atman is one-sided, whereas the genius of the knower of Atman is all-embracing. With the manifestation of the Atman you will find that science, philosophy and everything will be easily mastered. Proclaim the glory of the Atman with the roar of a lion, and impart fearlessness unto all beings by saying, "Arise, awake and stop not till the goal is reached."

XVIII

SWAMI VIVEKANANDA'S EXPERIENCE OF NIRVI-KALPA SAMADHI—EXTRAORDINARY POWER OF AVATARAS.

[Place : *The rented Math premises at Belur*. Year : *1898*.]

The disciple is staying with Swamiji at the garden-house of Nilambar Babu at Belur for the last two days.

Today, Swamiji has given permission to the disciple to stay in his room at night. When the disciple was serving Swamiji and massaging his feet, he spoke to him : "What folly! Leaving such a place as this, you want to go back to Calcutta! See what an atmosphere of holiness is here—the pure air of the Ganges—what an assemblage of Sâdhus, will you find anywhere a place like this!"

Disciple :—Sir, as the fruition of great austerities in past lives, I have been blessed with your company. Now bless me that I may not be overcome by ignorance and delusion any more. Now my mind sometimes is seized with a great longing for some direct spiritual realization.

Swamiji :—I also felt like that many times. One day in the Cossipore garden, I had expressed my prayer to Sri Ramakrishna with great earnestness. Then in the evening, at the hour of meditation, I lost the consciousness of the body, and felt that it was absolutely non-existent. I felt that the sun, moon, space, time, ether and all had been reduced to a homogeneous mass and then melted far away into the unknown; the body-consciousness had almost vanished, and I had nearly merged in the Supreme. But I had just a trace of the feeling of Ego, so I could again return to the world of relativity from the Samâdhi. In this state of Samâdhi all the difference between "I", and the "Brahman" goes away, everything is reduced into unity, like the waters of the Infinite Ocean —water everywhere, nothing else exists—

language and thought, all fail there. Then only is the state "beyond mind and speech" realized in its actuality. Otherwise, so long as the religious aspirant thinks or says, "I am the Brahman,"—"I" and "the Brahman," these two entities persist—there is the involved semblance of duality. After that experience, even after trying repeatedly I failed to bring back the state of Samâdhi. On informing Sri Ramakrishna about it, he said, "If you remain day and night in that state, the work of the Divine Mother will not be accomplished; therefore you won't be able to induce that state again; when your work is finished, it will come again."

Disciple :—On the attainment of the absolute and transcendent Nirvikalpa Samâdhi, can none return to the world of duality through the consciousness of Egoism?

Swamiji :—Sri Ramakrishna used to say that the Avatâras alone can descend to the ordinary plane from that state of Samâdhi, for the good of the world. Ordinary Jivas do not; immersed in that state, they remain alive for a period of twenty-one days; after that their body drops like a sere leaf from the tree of Samsâra.

Disciple :—When in Samâdhi the mind is merged, and there remain no waves on the surface of consciousness, where then is the possibility of mental activity and returning to the world through the consciousness of Ego ? When there is no mind, then who will descend from Samâdhi to the relative plane, and by what means ?

Swamiji :—The conclusion of the Vedanta is that when there is absolute Samâdhi and cessation of all modifications, there is no return from that state; as the Vedanta Aphorism says : अनावृत्तिः शब्दात्—"There is non-return, from scriptural texts." But the Avataras cherish a few desires for the good of the world. By taking hold of that thread they come down from the superconscious to the conscious state.

Disciple :—But, sir, if one or two desires remain, how can that state be called the absolute, transcendent Samâdhi ? For the scriptures say that in that state all the modifications of the mind and all desires are stamped out.

Swamiji :—How then can there be projection of the universe after Mahâpralaya (final dissolution) ? At Mahâpralaya everything is merged in the Brahman. But even after that one hears and reads of creation in the scriptures, that projection and contraction (of the universe) go on in wave forms. Like the fresh creation and dissolution of the universe after Mahâpralaya, the superconscious and conscious states of Avataras also stand to reason.

Disciple :—If I argue that at the time of dissolution the seeds of further creation remain almost merged in Brahman and that it is not absolute dissolution or Nirvikalpa Samâdhi?

Swamiji :—Then I shall ask you to answer how the projection of the universe is possible from Brahman in which there is no shadow of any qualification—which is unaffected and unqualified?

Disciple :—Why, this is but a seeming projection. The reply to the question is given in the scriptures in this way, that the manifestation of creation from the Brahman is only an appearance like the mirage in the desert, but really there has been no creation or anything of the kind. This illusion is produced by Mâyâ, which is the negation of the eternally existing Brahman, and hence unreal.

Swamiji :—If the creation is false then you can also regard the Nirvikalpa Samâdhi of Jiva and his return therefrom as seeming appearances. Jiva is Brahman by his nature. How can he have any experience of bondage? Your desire to realize the truth that you are the Brahman is also an hallucination in that case—for the scripture says, "You are already that." Therefore, अयमेव हि ते बन्धः समाधिमनुतिष्ठसि —"This is verily your bondage that you are practising the attainment of Samâdhi."

Disciple :—This is a great dilemma. If I am the Brahman, why don't I always realize it?

Swamiji :—In order to attain to that realization in the conscious plane some instrumentality is required. The mind is that instrument in us. But it is a non-intelligent substance. It only appears to be intelligent through the light of the Atman behind. Therefore the author of the Panchadasi* says : चिच्छायावेशतः शक्तिश्चेतनेव विभाति सा —"The Shakti appears—to be intelligent by the reflection of the intelligence of the Atman." Hence the mind also appears to us like an intelligent substance. Therefore it is certain that you won't be able to know the Atman, the Essence of Intelligence, through the mind. You have to go beyond the mind. As there is no instrument beyond the mind—for only the Atman exists there—there the object of of knowledge becomes the same as the instrument of knowledge. The knower, knowledge and the instrument of knowledge become one and the same. It is therefore that the Shruti says—विज्ञातारमरे केन विजानीयात्—"Through what are you to know the Eternal Subject ?" The real fact is, that there is a state beyond the conscious

* III. 40.

plane, where there is no duality of the knower, knowledge, and the instrument of knowledge, etc. When the mind is merged, that state is perceived. I say it is "perceived," because there is no other word to express that state. Language cannot express that state. Shankarâchârya has styled it "transcendent perception" (Aparokshânubhuti). Even after that transcendent perception Avataras descend to the relative plane and give glimpses of that—therefore it is said that the Vedas and other scriptures have originated from the perception of Seers. The case of ordinary Jivas is like that of the salt-doll which attempting to sound the depths of the ocean melted into it. Do you see? The sum and substance of it is—you have only got to know that you are the Eternal Brahman.

You are already that, only the intervention of a non-intelligent mind (which is called Mâyâ in the scriptures) is hiding that knowledge. When the mind composed of subtle matter is quelled, the Atman is effulgent by its own radiance. One proof of the fact that Mâyâ or mind is an illusion is, that the mind by itself is non-intelligent and of the nature of darkness; and it is the light of Atman behind that makes it appear as intelligent: When you will understand this, the mind will merge in the unbroken Ocean of Intelligence; then you will realize : अयमात्मा ब्रह्म —"This Atman is the Brahman."

Then Swamiji addressing the disciple said, "You feel sleepy, then go to sleep."

⁂

In the night the disciple had a wonderful dream, as a result of which he earnestly begged Swamiji's permission to worship him. Swamiji had to acquiesce and after the ceremony was over he said to the disciple, "Well, your worship is finished, but Premananda will be in a rage at your sacrilegious act of worshipping my feet in the flower-tray meant for Sri Ramakrishna's worship." Before his words were finished, Swami Premananda came there and Swamiji said to him, "See, what a sacrilege he has committed! With the requisites of Sri Ramakrishna's worship, he has worshipped me!" Swami Premananda, smiling said, "Well done! Are you and Sri Ramakrishna different?"— hearing which the disciple felt at ease.

The disciple is an orthodox Hindu. Not to speak of prohibited food, he does not even take food touched by another. Therefore Swamiji sometimes used to call him by the name of "priest." Swamiji, while he was eating biscuits with his breakfast, said to Swami Sadananda,

"Bring the priest in here." When the disciple came to Swamiji, he gave some portion of his food to him to eat. Finding the disciple accepting them without any demur Swamiji said, "Do you know what you have eaten now, they are made from eggs." In reply, the disciple said, "Whatever may be in it, I have no need to know; taking this sacramental food from you, I have become immortal." Thereupon Swamiji said, "I bless you, that from this day all your egoism of caste, colour, high birth, religious merit and demerit, and all may vanish for ever!"

XIX

NEED FOR FAITH IN ONESELF—SERVICE AND BUSINESS—SO-CALLED EDUCATED PEOPLE—MASSES —THEIR FUTURE.

[Place : *The rented Math premises at Belur*. Year : *1898.*]

The disciple has come to the Math this morning. As soon as he stood after touching the feet of Swamiji, Swamiji said : "What's the use of your continuing in service any more ? Why not go in for some business ?" The disciple was then employed as a private tutor in some family. Asked about the profession of teaching, Swamiji said : "If one does the work of teaching boys for a long time, he gets blunt in intellect; his intelligence is not manifested. If one stays among a crowd of boys day and night, gradually he gets obtuse. So give up the work of teaching boys."

Disciple :—What shall I do then ?

Swamiji :—Why ? If you want to live the life of a worldly man and have a desire for earning money, then go over to America. I shall give you directions for business. You will find that in five years you will get together a lot of money.

Disciple :—What business shall I go in for ? And where am I to get the money ?

Swamiji :—What nonsense are you talking ? Within you lies indomitable power. Only thinking, "I am nothing, I am nothing," you have become powerless. Why you alone! The whole race has become so. Go round the world once and you will find how vigorously the life-current of other nations is flowing. And What are you doing! Even after learning so much, you go about the doors of others, crying, "Give me employment." Trampled under others' feet, doing slavery for others, are you men any more ? You are not worth a pin's head!

In this fertile country with abundant water-supply, where Nature produces wealth and harvest a thousand times more than in others, you have no food for your stomach, no clothes to cover your body! In this country of abundance, the produce of which has been the cause of the spread of civilization in other countries, you are reduced to such straits! Your condition is even worse than that of a dog! And you glory in your Vedas and Vedanta! A nation that cannot provide for its simple food and clothing, which always depends on others for its subsistence—what is there for it to vaunt about? Throw your religious observances overboard for the present and be first prepared for the struggle for existence. People of foreign countries are turning out such golden results from the raw naterials produced in your country, and you, like asses of burden, are only carrying their load. The people of foreign countries import Indian raw goods, manufacture various commodities by bringing their intelligence to bear upon them, and become great; whereas you have locked up your intelligence, thrown away your inherited wealth to others, and roam about crying piteously for food!

Disciple :—In what way, sir, can the means of subsistence be procured?

Swamiji:—Why, the means are in your hands. You blindfold your eyes and say, "I am blind and can see nothing." Tear off the folds from your eyes and you will see the whole world lighted by the rays of the midday sun. If you cannot procure money, go to foreign countries, working your passage as a *lascar*. Take Indian cloth, towel, bamboo-work and other indigenous products and peddle in the streets of Europe and America; you will find how greatly Indian products are appreciated in foreign markets even now. In America I found some Mohammedans of the Hooghly district had grown rich by peddling Indian commodities in this way. Have you even less intelligence than they? Take, for example, such excellent fabric as the Benares-made *sâris* of India, the like of which are not produced anywhere else in the world. Go to America with this cloth. Have gowns made out of this fabric and sell them, and you will see how much you earn.

Disciple:—Sir, why will they wear gowns made of the *sâris* of Benares? I have heard that clothes painted diversely are not to the taste of the ladies in those countries.

Swamiji:—Whether they will receive them or not, I shall look to that. It is for you to exert yourself and go over there. I have many friends in that country, to whom I shall introduce you. At first I shall request them to take this cloth up among themselves. Then you will find many will follow suit and at last you won't be able to keep the supply up to the enormous demand.

Disciple :—Where shall I get the capital for the business?

Swamiji :—I shall anyhow give you a start; for the rest you must depend on your own exertions. "If you fail, you get to heaven, and if you win, you enjoy the earth." (Gitâ). Even if you die in this attempt, well and good, many will take up the work, following your example. And if you succeed, you will live a life of great opulence.

Disciple :—Yes, sir, so it is. But I cannot muster sufficient courage.

Swamiji :—That is what I say, my son, you have no Shraddhâ—no faith in yourselves. What will you achieve? You will have neither material nor spiritual advancement. Either put forth your energy in the way I have suggested and be successful in life, or give up all and take to the path we have chosen. Serve the people of all countries through spiritual instructions— then only will you get your dole of food like us. If there is no mutual exchange, do you think anybody cares for any other? You observe in our case, that because we give the householders some spiritual instructions they in return give us some morsels of food. If you do nothing why will they give you food? You observe so much misery in mere service and slavery of others, still you are not waking up; and so your misery also is never at an end.—This is certainly the delusive power of Mâyâ! In the West I found that those who are in the employment of others have their seats fixed in the back rows in the Parliament; while the front seats are reserved for those who have made themselves famous by self-exertion, or education, or intelligence. In Western countries there is no botheration of caste. Those on whom Fortune smiles for their industry and exertion, are alone regarded as leaders of the country and the controllers of its destiny. Whereas in your country, you are simply vaunting of your superiority in caste, till at last you cannot even get a morsel of food! You have not the capacity to manufacture a needle and you dare to criticize the English—fools! Sit at their feet and learn from them the arts, industries and the practicality necessary for the struggle for existence. You will be esteemed once more when you will become fit. Then they too will pay heed to your words. Without the necessary preparation, what will mere shouting in the Congress avail?

Disciple:—But, sir, all the educated men of the country have joined it.

Swamiji:—Well, you consider a man as educated if only he can pass some examinations and deliver good lectures. The education which does not help the common mass of people to equip themselves for the struggle for life, which does not bring out strength of character, a spirit of philanthropy, and the courage of a lion— is it worth the name? Real education is that which enables one to stand on his own legs. The education that you are receiving now in schools and colleges is only making you a race of dyspeptics. You are working like machines merely, and living a jellyfish existence.

The peasant, the shoemaker, the sweeper, and such other lower classes of India have much greater capacity for work and self-reliance than you. They have been silently working through long ages, and producing the entire wealth of the land, without a word of complaint. Very soon they will get above you in position. Gradually capital is drifting into their hands and they are not so much troubled with wants as you are. Modern education has changed your fashion, but new avenues of wealth lie yet undiscovered for want of the inventive genius. You have so long oppressed these forbearing masses; now is the time for their retribution. And you will become extinct in your vain search for employment, making it the be-all and end-all of your life!

Disciple:—Sir, although our power of originality is less than that of other countries, still the lower classes of India are being guided by our intelligence. So where will they get the power and culture to overcome the higher classes in the struggle for existence?

Swamiji:—Never mind if they have not read a few books like you—if they have not acquired your tailor-made civilization. What do these matter? But they are the backbone of the nation in all countries. If these lower classes stop work, where will you get your food and clothing from? If the sweepers of Calcutta stop work for a day, it creates a panic; and if they strike for three days, the whole town will be depopulated by the outbreak of epidemics. If the labourers stop work, your supply of food and clothes also stops. And you regard them as low-class people and vaunt about your own culture!

Engrossed in the struggle for existence they had not the opportunity for the awakening of knowledge. They have worked so long uniformly like machines guided by human intelligence, and the clever educated section have taken the substantial part of the fruits of their labour. In every country this has been the case. But times have changed. The lower classes are gradually awakening to this fact and making a united front against this, determined to exact their legitimate dues. The masses of Europe and America have been the first to awaken and have already begun the fight. Signs of this awakening have shown themselves in India too, as is evident from the number of strikes among the lower classes nowadays. The upper classes will no longer be able to repress the lower, try they ever so much. The well-being of the higher classes now lies in helping the lower to get their legitimate rights.

Therefore I say, set yourselves to the task of spreading education among the masses. Tell them and make them understand, "You are our brothers—a part and parcel of our bodies, and we love you and never hate you." If they receive this sympathy from you, their enthusiasm for work will be increased a hundred-fold. Kindle their knowledge with the help of modern science. Teach them history, geography, science, literature, and along with these the profound truths of religion. In exchange for that teaching, the poverty of the teachers will also disappear. By mutual exchange both parties will become friendly to each other.

Disciple :—But, Sir, with the spread of learning among them, they too will in course of time have fertile brains but become idle and inactive like us and live on the fruits of the labour of the next lower classes.

Swamiji :—Why shall it be so ? Even with the awakening of knowledge, the potter will remain a potter—the fisherman a fisherman—the peasant a peasant. Why should they leave their hereditary calling ?—सहजं कर्म कौन्तेय सदोषमपि न त्यजेत्—"Don't give up the work to which you are born, even if it be attended with defects." If they are taught in this way, why should they give up their respective callings ? Rather they will apply their knowledge to the better performance of the work to which they have been born. A number of geniuses are sure to arise from among them in course of time. You (the higher classes) will take these into your own fold. The Brâhmanas had acknowledged valiant king Vishwâmitra as a Brâhmana, and think how grateful the whole Kshatriya race became to the Brâhmanas for this act ! By such sympathy and co-operation even birds and beasts become one's own—not to speak of men!

Disciple :—Sir, what you say is true, but there yet seems to be a wide gulf between the higher and lower classes. To bring the higher classes to sympathise with the lower, seems to be a difficult affair in India.

Swamiji :—But without that there is no well-being for you upper classes. You will be destroyed by internecine quarrels and fights—which you have been doing so long. When the masses will wake up they will come to understand your oppression on them and by a puff of their mouth you will be entirely blown off! It is they who have introduced civilization amongst you; and it is they who will then pull it down. Think how at the hands of the Gauls the mighty ancient Roman civilization crumbled into dust! Therefore I say, try to rouse these lower classes from slumber by imparting learning and culture to them. When they will awaken—and awaken one day they must—they also will not forget your good services to them and will remain grateful to you.

After such conversation Swamiji addressing the disciple said : Let these subjects drop now —come, tell me what you have decided. Do something, whatever it be. Either go in for some business, or like us come to the path of real Sannyâsa, आत्मनो मोक्षार्थं जगद्धिताय च —"For your own liberation and for the good of the world." The latter path is of course the best way there is. What good will it do to be a worthless householder? You have understood that everything in life is transitory. नलिनीदलगतजलमतितरलम् तद्वज्जीवनमतिशयचपलम् —"Life is as unstable as the water on the lotus leaf." Therefore if you have the enthusiasm for acquiring this knowledge of the Atman, do not wait any more but come forward immediately. यदहरेव विरजेत् तदहरेव प्रव्रजेत् —"The very day that you feel dispassion for the world, that very day renounce and take to Sannyâsa."* Sacrifice your life for the good of others and go round the doors of people, carrying this message of fearlessness— उत्तिष्ठत जाग्रत प्राप्य वरान् निबोधत —"Arise! Awake! and stop not till the goal is reached."

XX

AT THE ZOOLOGICAL GARDEN AT ALIPUR—DARWIN, THEORY OF EVOLUTION AND PATANJALI—NEED FOR PHYSICAL STRENGTH.

[Place: *Calcutta.* Year: 1898.]

Swamiji accompanied by Sister Nivedita,

* Jâbâlopanishat, 4.

Swami Yogananda and others has come to visit the Zoological Garden at Alipur in the afternoon. Rai Rambrahma Sanyal Bahadur, Superintendent of the Garden, cordially received them and took them round the garden. Swamiji, as he went on seeing the various species of animals, casually referred to the Darwinian theory of the gradual evolution of animals. The disciple remembers how, entering the room for snakes, he pointed to a huge python with circular rings on its body, with the remark : "From this the tortoise has evolved in course of time. That very snake, by remaining stationary at one spot for a long time, has gradually turned hard-backed." Saying this he said in fun to the disciple : "You eat tortoises, don't you ? Darwin holds that it is this snake that has evolved into the tortoise in the process of time—then you eat snakes too!" The disciple protested, saying,—

"Sir, when a thing is metamorphosed into another thing through evolution, it has no more its former shape and habits; then how can you say that eating tortoises means eating snakes also ?"

This answer created a laughter among the party. After seeing some other things Swamiji went to Rambrahma Babu's quarters in the garden, where he took tea, and others also did the same. Finding that the disciple hesitated to sit at the same table and partake of the sweets and tea which Sister Nivedita had touched, Swamiji repeatedly urged him to take them, which he was induced to do, and drinking water himself, he gave the rest of it to the disciple to drink. After this there was a short conversation on Darwin's evolution theory.

Rambrahma Babu :—What is your opinion on the evolution theory of Darwin and the causes he has put forward for it?

Swamiji :—Taking for granted that Darwin is right, I cannot yet admit that it is the final conclusion about the causes of evolution.

Rambrahma Babu :—Did the ancient scholars of our country discuss this subject?

Swamiji :—The subject has been nicely discussed in the Sankhya Philosophy. I am of opinion that the conclusion of the ancient Indian philosophers is the last word on the causes of evolution.

Rambrahma Babu :—I shall be glad to hear of it, if it can be explained in a few words.

Swamiji :—You are certainly aware of the laws of struggle for existence, survival of the fittest, natural selection and so forth, which have been held by the Western scholars to be the causes of elevating a lower species to a higher.

But none of these has been advocated as the cause of that in the system of Patanjali. Patanjali holds that the transformation of one speices into another is effected by the "infilling of nature" (प्रकृत्यापूरात्) It is not that this is done by the constant struggle against obstacles. In my opinion, struggle and competition sometimes stand in the way of a being attaining its perfection. If the evolution of an animal is effected by the destruction of a thousand others, then one must confess that this evolution is doing very little good to the world. Taking it for granted that it conduces to physical well-being, we cannot help admitting that it is a serious obstacle to spiritual development. According to the philosophers of our country, every being is a perfect Soul, and the diversity of evolution and manifestation of Nature is simply due to the difference in the degree of manifestation of this Soul. The moment the obstacles to the evolution and manifestation of Nature are completely removed, the Soul manifests Itself perfectly. Whatever may happen in the lower strata of Nature's evolution, in the higher strata at any rate, it is not true that it is only by constantly struggling against obstacles that one has to go beyond them. Rather it is observed that there the obstacles give way and a greater manifestation of the Soul takes place through education and culture, through concentration and meditation and above all through sacrifice. Therefore, to designate the obstacles not as the effects but as the causes of the Soul-manifestation, and describe them as aiding this wonderful diversity of Nature, is not consonant with reason. The attempt to remove evil from the world by killing a thousand evil-doers, only adds to the evil in the world. But if the people can be made to desist from evil-doing by means of spiritual instruction, there is no more evil in the world. Now see, how horrible the Western struggle theory becomes!

Rambrahma Babu was astonished to hear Swamiji's words and at length said: "India badly needs at the present moment men well-versed in the Eastern and Western philosophies like you. Such men alone are able to point out the mistakes of the educated people who see only one side of the shield. I am extremely delighted to hear your original explanation of the evolution theory."

Shortly after Swamiji with party left for Baghbazar, and reached Balaram Bose's house at about 8 P.M.

After a short rest he came to the drawing room, where there was a small gathering, all eager to hear of the conversation at the Zoological Garden in detail. When Swamiji came to the meeting, the disciple, as the spokesman of the meeting raised that very topic.

Disciple :—Sir, I have not been able to follow all your remarks about the evolution theory at the Zoo Garden. Will you kindly recapitulate them in simple words ?

Swamiji :—Why, which points did you fail to grasp ?

Disciple :—You have often told us that it is the power to struggle with the external forces which constitutes the sign of life and the first step towards improvement. Today you seem to have spoken just the opposite thing.

Swamiji :—Why should I speak differently ? It was you who could not follow me. In the animal kingdom we really see such laws as struggle for existence, survival of the fittest, etc., evidently at work. Therefore Darwin's theory seems true to a certain extent. But in the human kingdom, where there is the manifestation of rationality, we find just the reverse of those laws. For instance, in those whom we consider really great men or ideal characters, we scarcely observe any external struggle. In the animal kingdom instinct prevails ; but the more a man advances, the more he manifests rationality. For this reason, progress in the rational human kingdom cannot be achieved, like that in the animal kingdom, by the destruction of others! The highest evolution of man is effected through sacrifice alone. A man is great among his fellows in proportion as he can sacrifice for the sake of others. While in the lower strata of the animal kingdom, that animal is the strongest which can kill the greatest number of animals. Hence the struggle theory is not equally applicable to both kingdoms. Man's struggle is in the mental sphere. A man is greater in proportion as he can control his mind. When the mind's activities are perfectly at rest, the Atman manifests Itself. The struggle which we observe in the animal kingdom for the preservation of the gross body, obtains in the human plane of existence for gaining mastery over the mind or for attaining the state of balance. Like a living tree and its reflection in the water of a tank, we find opposite kinds of struggle in the animal and human kingdoms!

Disciple :—Why then do you advocate so much the improvement of our physique?

Swamiji :—Well, do you consider yourselves as men? You have got only a bit of rationality—that's all. How will you struggle with the mind unless the physique be strong? Do you deserve to be called men any longer—the highest evolution in the world? What have you got besides eating, sleeping and satisfying the creature-comforts? Thank your stars that you have not developed into quadrupeds yet! Sri Ramakrishna used to say, "He is the man who is conscious of his dignity." You are but standing witnesses to the lowest class of insect-like existence of which the scripture speaks that they simply undergo the round of births and deaths, without being allowed to go to any of the higher spheres! You are simply living a life of jealousy among yourselves and are objects of hatred in the eyes of the foreigner! You are animals, therefore I recommend you to struggle. Leave aside theories and all that. Just reflect calmly on your own every-day acts and dealings, and find out whether you are not a species of beings intermediate between the animal and human planes of existence! First build up your physique. Then only you can get control over the mind—नायमात्मा बल्हीनेन लभ्यः —"This Self is not to be attained by the weak."

Disciple :—But, sir, the commentator (Shankara) has interpreted the word "weak" to mean "devoid of Brahmacharya or continence."

Swamiji :—Let him. I say—"The physically weak are unfit for the realization of the Self."

Disciple :—But many dull-headed persons also have strong bodies.

Swamiji :—If you can take the pains to give them good ideas once, they will be able to work them out sooner than physically unfit people. Don't you find, in a weak physique it is difficult to control the sex-appetite or anger? Lean people are quickly incensed and are quickly overcome by the sex-instinct.

Disciple :—But we find exceptions to the rule also.

Swamiji :—Who denies it? Once a person gets control over the mind, it matters little whether the body remains strong or becomes emaciated. The gist of the thing is that unless one has a good physique one can never aspire to Self-realization. Sri Ramakrishna used to say, "One fails to attain Realization if there be but a slight defect in the body."

Finding that Swamiji had grown excited, the disciple did not dare to push on the topic further, but remained quiet accepting Swamiji's view. Shortly after, Swamiji addressing those present, said, "By the bye, have you heard that this 'priest' has today taken food which was touched by Nivedita? That he took the sweets touched by her did not matter so much, but"— here he addressed the disciple—"how did you drink the water she had touched?"

Disciple:—But it was you, sir, who ordered me to do so. Under the Guru's orders I can do anything. I was unwilling to drink the water, though. But you drank it and I had to take it as Prasâda.

Swamiji:—Well, your caste is gone for ever. Now nobody will respect you as a Brâhmana of the priest class.

Disciple:—I don't care if they do not. I can take the rice from the house of a pariah if you order me to.

These words set Swamiji and all those present in a roar of laughter.

The conversation lasted till it was past midnight, when the disciple came back to his lodging, only to find it bolted. So he had to pass the night out of doors.

The wheel of Time has rolled on in its unrelenting course, and Swamiji, the Swami Yogananda and Sister Nivedita are now no more on earth. Only the sacred memory of their lives remains—and the disciple considers himself blessed to be able to record, in ever so meagre a way, these reminiscences.

XXI

SWAMI VIVEKANANDA'S FUTURE PLAN ABOUT BELUR MATH—WORK AND MEDITATION—NESCIENCE —BRAHMAN AND THE WORLD OF MATTER.

[Place : *The rented Math premises at Belur.*
Year : *1898.*]

The disciple has come to the Math today. It has now been removed to Nilambar Babu's graden-house, and the site of the present Math has recently been purchased. Swamiji is out visiting the new Math-grounds at about four o'clock, taking the disciple with him. The site was then full of jungles, and on the north side of it there was a one-storeyed brick-built house. Swamiji began to walk over the site and to discuss, in the course of conversation, the plan of work of the future Math and its rules and regulations.

Reaching by degrees the verandah on the east side of the one-storied house, Swamiji said : "Here would be the place for the Sâdhus to live in. It is my wish to convert this Math into a chief centre of spiritual practices and the culture of knowledge. The power that will have its rise from here will flood the whole world, and turn the course of men's lives into different channels; from this place will spring forth ideals which will be the harmony of Knowledge, Devotion, Yoga and Work; at a nod from the men of this Math a life-giving impetus will in time be given to the remotest corners of the globe; while all true seekers after spirituality will in course of time assemble here—a thousand thoughts like these are arising in my mind.

"Yonder plot of land on the south side of the Math will be the centre of learning, where Grammar, Philosophy, Science, Literature, Rhetoric, the Shrutis, Bhakti scriptures and English will be taught; this Temple of Learning will be fashioned after the *Tols* of old days. Boys who are Brahmachârins from their childhood will live there and study the scriptures. Their food and clothing and all will be supplied from the Math. After a course of five years' training these Brahmachârins may, if they like, go back to their homes and lead householders' lives; or they may embrace the monastic life with the sanction of the venerable Superiors of the Math. The authorities of the Math will have the power to turn out at once any of these Brahmachârins who will be found refractory or of a bad character. Teaching will be imparted here irrespective of caste or creed, and those who will have objection to this will not be admitted. But those who would like to observe their particular caste-rites, should make separate arrangements for their food etc. They will attend the classes only, along with the rest. The Math authorities shall keep a vigilant watch over the character of these also. None but those that are trained here shall be eligible for Sannyâsa. Won't it be nice when by degrees this Math will begin to work like this?"

Disciple :—Then you want to reintroduce into the country the ancient institution of living a Brahmachârin's life in the house of the Guru?

Swamiji :—Exactly. The modern system of education gives no facility for the development of the knowledge of Brahman. We must found Brahmacharya Homes as in times of old. But now we must lay their foundations on a broad basis, that is to say, we must introduce a good deal of change into it to suit the requirements of the times. Of this I shall speak to you later on.

"That piece of land to the south of the Math," Swamiji resumed, "we must also purchase in time. There we shall start an Annasatra— a Feeding Home. There arrangements will be made for serving really indigent people in the spirit of God. The Feeding Home will be named after Sri Ramakrishna. Its scope will at first be determined by the amount of funds. For the matter of that, we may start it with two or three inmates. We must train energetic Brahmachârins to conduct this Home. They will have to collect the funds for its maintenance,—aye, even by begging. The Math will not be allowed to give any pecuniary help in this matter. The Brahmachârins themselves shall have to raise funds for it. Only after completing their five years' training in this Home of Service, will they be allowed to join the Temple of Learning branch. After a training of ten years—five in the Feeding Home and five in the Temple of Learning—they will be allowed to enter the life of Sannyâsa, having initiation from the Math authorities—provided of course they have a mind to become Sannyâsins and the Math authorities consider them fit for Sannyâsa and are willing to admit them into it. But the Head of the Math will be free to confer Sannyâsa on any exceptionally meritorious Brahmachârin, at any time, in defiance of this rule. The ordinary Brahmachârins, however, will have to qualify themselves for Sannyâsa by degrees, as I have just said. I have all these ideas in my brain."

Disciple :—Sir, what will be the object of starting three such sections in the Math?

Swamiji :—Didn't you understand me? First

of all comes the gift of food; next is the gift of learning, and the highest of all is the gift of knowledge. We must harmonise these three ideals in this Math. By continuously practising the gift of food, the Brahmachârins will have the idea of practical work for the sake of others and that of serving all beings in the spirit of the Lord firmly impressed on their minds. This will gradually purify their minds and lead to the manifestation of Sâttvika (pure and unselfish) ideas. And having this the Brahmachârins will in time acquire the fitness for attaining the knowledge of Brahman, and become eligible for Sannyâsa.

Disciple :—Sir, if, as you say, the gift of knowledge is the highest, why then start sections for the gift of food and the gift of learning ?

Swamiji :—Can't you understand this point even now ? Listen—if in these days of food scarcity you can, for the disinterested service of others, get together a few morsels of food by begging or any other means, and give them to the poor and suffering, that will not only be doing good to yourself and the world, but you will at the same time get everybody's sympathy for this noble work. The worldly-minded people, tied down to lust and wealth, will have faith in you for this labour of love and come forward to help you. You will attract a thousand times as many men by this unasked-for gift of food, as you will by the gift of learning or of knowledge. In no other work will you get so much public sympathy as you will in this. In a truly noble work, not to speak of men, even God Himself befriends the doer. When people have thus been attracted, you will be able to stimulate the desire for learning and knowledge in them. Therefore the gift of food comes first.

Disciple :—Sir, to start Feeding Homes we want a site first, then bulidings, and then the funds to work them. Where will so much money come from ?

Swamiji :—The southern portion of the Math premises I am leaving at your disposal immediately, and I am getting a thatched house erected under that Bael tree. You just find out one or two blind or infirm people and apply yourself to their service. Go and beg food for them yourself; cook with your own hands and feed them. If you continue this for some days, you will find that lots of people will be coming forward to assist you, with plenty of money. नहि कल्याणकृत्कश्चिद्दुर्गतिं तात गच्छति "Never, my Son, does a doer of good come to grief." (Gitâ).

Disciple :—Yes, it is true. But may not

that kind of continuous work become a source of bondage in the long run?

Swamiji:—If you have no eye to the fruits of work, and if you have a passionate longing to go beyond all selfish desires, then those good works will help to break your bonds, I tell you. How thoughtless of you to say that such work will lead to bondage! Such disinterested work is the only means of rooting out the bondage due to selfish work. नान्यः पन्था विद्यतेऽयनाय—"There is no other way out."

Disciple:—Your words encourage me to hear in detail about your ideas of the Feeding Homes and Home of Service.

Swamiji:—We must bulid small well-ventilated rooms for the poor. Only two or three of them will live in each room. They must be given good bedding, clean clothes and so on. There will be a doctor for them, who will inspect them once or twice a week according to his convenience. The Sevâshrama will be as a ward attached to the Annasatra, where the sick will be nursed. Then gradually, as funds will accumulate, we shall build a big kitchen. The Annasatra must be astir with constant shouts of food demanded and immediately supplied. The rice-gruel must run into the Ganga and whiten its water! When I see such a Feeding

Home started, it will bring solace to my heart.

Disciple :—When you have this kind of desire, most likely it will materialise into action in course of time.

Hearing the disciple's words Swamiji remained motionless for a while, gazing on the Ganga. Then with a beaming countenance he addressed the disciple saying : "Who knows which of you will have the lion roused up in him, and when ? If in a single one amongst you Mother rouses the fire, there will be hundreds of Feeding Homes like that. The thing is, that Knowledge, and Power, and Devotion—everything exists in the fullest measure in all beings. We only notice the varying degrees of their manifestation, and call one great and another little. In the minds of all creatures a screen intervenes, as it were, and hides the perfect manifestation from view. The moment that is removed, everything is settled; whatever you will want, whatever you will desire, will come to pass."

Swamiji continued : "If the Lord wills, we shall make this Math a great centre of harmony. Our Lord is the visible embodiment of the harmony of all ideals. He will be established on earth if we keep alive that spirit of harmony here. We must see to it that people of all creeds and sects, from the Brâhmana down to the

Chandâla, may come here and find their respective ideals manifested. The other day when I installed Sri Ramakrishna on the Math grounds, I felt as if his ideas shot forth from this place and flooded the whole universe, sentient and insentient. I, for one, am doing my best, and shall continue to do so—all of you too explain to people the liberal ideas of Sri Ramakrishna; what is the use of merely reading the Vedanta? We must prove the truth of pure Advaitism in practical life. Shankara left this Advaita philosophy in the hills and forests; while I have come to bring it out of those places and scatter it broadcast before the work-a-day world and society. The lion-roar of Advaita must resound in every hearth and home, in meadows and groves, over hills and plains. Come all of you to my assistance, and set yourselves to work."

Disciple:—Sir, it appeals to me rather to realize that state through meditation than to manifest it in action.

Swamiji:—That is but a state of stupefaction, as under liquors. What will be the use of merely remaining like that? Through the urge of Advaitic realization, you should sometimes dance wildely and sometimes remain lost to outward sense. Does one feel happy to taste of a good thing all by himself? One should share it with others. Granted that you attain personal liberation by means of the realization of the Advaita, but what matters it to the world? You must liberate the whole universe before you leave this body. Then only you will be established in the eternal Truth. Has that bliss any match, my boy? You will be established in the bliss of the Infinite, which is limitless like the skies. You will be struck dumb to find your presence everywhere in the world of soul and matter! You will feel the whole sentient and insentient world as your own self. Then you can't help treating all with the same kindness as you show towards yourself. This is indeed practical Vedanta. Do you understand me? Brahman is one, but is at the same time appearing to us as many, on the relative plane. Name and form are at the root of this relativity. For instance, what do you find when you abstract name and form from a jar? Only earth, which is its essence. Similarly, through delusion you are thinking of and seeing a jar, a cloth, a monastery and so on. The phenomenal world depends on this Nescience which obstructs knowledge and which has no real existence. One sees variety such as wife, children, body, mind —only in the world created by Nescience by means of name and form. As soon as this

Nescience is removed, the realization of Brahman which eternally exists, is the result.

Disciple :—Where has this Nescience come from?

Swamiji :—Where it has come from, I shall tell you later on. When you began to run, mistaking the rope for the snake, did the rope actually turn into a snake? Or, was it not your ignorance which put you to flight in that way?

Disciple :—I did it from sheer ignorance.

Swamiji :—Well, then, consider whether, when you will again come to know the rope as rope, you will not laugh at your previous ignorance. Will not name and form appear to be a delusion then?

Disciple :—They will.

Swamiji :—If that be so, the name and form turn out to be unreal. Thus Brahman, the Eternal Existence, proves to be the only reality. Only through this twilight of Nescience you think this is your wife, that is your child, this is your own, that is not your own, and so on, and fail to realize the existence of the Atman, the illuminator of everything. When through the Guru's instructions and your own conviction you will see, not this world of name and form, but the essence which lies as its substratum, then only you will realize your identity with the whole universe from the Creator down to a clump of grass—then only you will get the state— भिद्यते हृदयग्रन्थिः छिद्यन्ते सर्वसंशयाः —"in which the knots of the heart are cut asunder and all doubts are dispelled."

Disciple :—Sir, one wishes to know of the origin and cessation of this Nescience.

Swamiji :—You have understood, I presume, that a thing that ceases to exist afterwards, is a phenomenon merely? He who has truly realized the Brahman will say—where is Nescience, in faith? He sees the rope as rope only, and never as the snake. And he laughs at the alarm of those who see it as the snake. For this reason, Nescience has no absolute reality. You can call Nescience neither real nor unreal. सन्नाप्यसन्नाप्युभयात्मिका नो—"Neither real, nor unreal, nor a mixture of both." About a thing that is thus proved to be false, neither question nor answer is of any significance. Moreover, any question on such a thing is unreasonable. I shall explain how. Are not this question and answer made from the standpoint of name and form, of time and space? And can you explain Brahman which transcends time and space, by means of questions and answers? Hence the Shâstras and Mantras and such other things are only relatively and not absolutely true. Nescience has verily no essence to call its own, how then can you understand it? When Brahman will manifest Itself, there will be no more room for such questions. Have you not heard that story of Sri Ramakrishna about "the shoemaker coolie"?* The moment one recognises Nescience, it vanishes.

Disciple:—But, sir, whence has this Nescience come?

Swamiji:—How can that come which has no existence at all? It must exist first, to admit the possibility of coming.

Disciple:—How then did this world of souls and matter originate?

Swamiji:—There is only one Existence, viz,

---

* Once a Brâhmana, desirous of going to a disciple's house, was in need of a coolie to carry his load. Not finding anyone belonging to a good caste, he at last asked a shoemaker to perform the function. The man at first refused on the ground that he was a man belonging to an untouchable caste. But the Brâhmana insisted on engaging him, telling him that he would escape detection by keeping perfectly silent. The man was at last persuaded to go, and when the party reached their destination, someone asked the shoemaker-servant to remove a pair of shoes. The servant who thought it best to keep silent, as instructed, paid no attention to the order, which was repeated, whereupon the man getting annoyed shouted out, "Why dost thou not hear me, sirrah? Art thou a shoemaker?" "O Master," cried the bewildered shoemaker, "I am discovered. I cannot stay any longer." Saying this he immediately took to his heels.

Brahman. You are but seeing That under different forms and names, through the veil of name and form which are unreal.

Disciple :—But why this unreal name and form ? Whence have they come ?

Swamiji :—The Shâstras have described this ingrained notion or ignorance as almost endless as a series. But it has a termination. While Brahman ever remains as It is, without suffering the least change, like the rope which causes the delusion of the snake. Therefore the conclusion of the Vedanta is that the whole universe has been superimposed on the Brahman—appearing like a juggler's magic. It has not caused the least aberration of Brahman from Its real nature. Do you understand me ?

Disciple :—One thing I cannot yet understand.

Swamiji :—What is that ?

Disciple :—You have just said that creation, maintenance and dissolution, etc., are superimposed on the Brahman, and have no absolute existence. But how can that be ? One can never have the delusion of something that he has not already experienced. Just as one who has never seen a snake cannot mistake a rope for a snake, so how can one who has not experienced this creation, come to mistake Brahman for the creation ? Therefore creation must have been or is, to have given rise to the delusion of creation. But this brings in a dualistic position.

Swamiji :—The man of realization will in the first place refute your objection by stating that to his vision creation and things of that sort do not at all appear. He sees Brahman and Brahman alone. He sees the rope and not the snake. If you argue that you at any rate are seeing this creation, or snake—then he will try to bring home to you the real nature of the rope, with a view to curing your defective vision. When through his instructions and your reasoning you will be able to realize the truth of the rope, or Brahman, then this delusive idea of the snake, or creation, will vanish. At that time, what else can you call this delusive idea of creation, maintenance and dissolution, but a superimposition on the Brahman ? If this appearance of creation etc., has continued as a beginningless series, let it do so ; no advantage will be gained by settling this question. Until Brahman is realized as vividly as a fruit on the palm of one's hand, this question cannot be adequately settled, and then neither such a question crops up, nor is there need for a solution. The tasting of the reality of Brahman is then like a dumb man tasting something nice, but without the power to express his feelings.

Disciple :—What then will be the use of reasoning about it so much?

Swamiji :—Reasoning is necessary to understand the point intellectually. But the Reality transcends reasoning—नैषा तर्केण मतिरापनेया—"This conviction cannot be reached through reasoning."

In the course of such conversation Swamiji reached the Math, accompanied by the disciple. Swamiji then explained to the Sannyâsins and Brahmachârins of the Math the gist of the above discussion on Brahman. While going upstairs he remarked to the disciple, नायमात्मा बल्हीनेन लभ्यः —"This Atman cannot be attained by the weak."

XXII

THE BENGALI MONTHLY 'UDBODHAN'—ITS FUTURE POLICY.

[Place : *The rented Math premises at Belur*. Year : *1899.*]

The Bengali fortnightly magazine, *Udbodhan*, was just started by Swami Trigunâtita under the directions of Swamiji for spreading the religious views of Sri Ramakrishna among the general public. After the first number had been out, the disciple came to the Math at Nilambar Babu's garden one day. Swamiji opened the following conversation with him about the *Udbodhan*—

Swamiji :—(Humorously caricaturing the name of the magazine) Have you seen the *Udbandhan**?

Disciple :—Yes, sir, it is a good number.

Swamiji :—We must mould the ideas, language, and everything of this magazine in a new fashion.

Disciple :—How ?

Swamiji :—Not only must we give out Sri Ramakrishna's ideas to all, but we must also introduce a new vigour into the Bengali language. For instance, the frequent use of verbs diminishes the force of a language. We must restrict the use of verbs by the use of adjectives. Begin to write articles in that way, and show them to me before you give them to print in the *Udbodhan*.

Disciple :—Sir, the way Swami Trigunatita is labouring for this magazine, it is impossible for any other man to do.

Swamiji :—Do you think these Sannyâsin children of Sri Ramakrishna are born simply to sit under trees lighting *dhuni*-fires ? Whenever

---

* The word means 'suicide by hanging'.

any of them will take up some work, people will be astonished to see their energy. Learn from them how to work. Here, for instance, Trigunatita has given up his spiritual practices, his meditation and everything, to carry out my orders, and has set himself to work. Is this a matter of small sacrifice?—What an amount of love for me is at the back of this spirit of work, do you see? He will not stop short of success! Have you householders such determination?

Disciple:—But, sir, it looks rather odd in our eyes that Sannyâsins in ochre robe should go about from door to door as the Swami is doing.

Swamiji:—Why? The circulation of the magazine is only for the good of householders. By the spread of new ideas within the country the public at large will be benefited. Do you think this unselfish work is any way inferior to devotional practices? Our object is to do good to humanity. We have no idea of making money from the income of this paper. We have renounced everything, and have no wives or children to provide for after our death. If the paper be a success, the whole of its income will be spent in the service of humanity. Its surplus money will be profitably spent in the opening of monasteries and homes of service in different places, and all sorts of work of public utility. We are not certainly working like householders with the plan of filling our own pockets. Know for certain that all our movements are for the good of others.

Disciple :—Even then, all will not be able to appreciate this spirit.

Swamiji :—What if they cannot ? It neither adds nor takes away anything from us. We do not take up any work with an eye to criticism.

Disciple :—Sir, this magazine will be a fortnightly. We would like it to be a weekly.

Swamiji :—Yes, but where are the funds ? If through the grace of Sri Ramakrishna funds are raised, it can be made into a daily even, in future. A hundred thousand copies may be struck off daily and distributed free in every street and lane of Calcutta.

Disciple :—This idea of yours is a capital one.

Swamiji :—I have a mind to make the paper self-supporting first, and then set you up as its editor. You have not yet got the capacity to make any enterprise stand on its legs. That is reserved only for these all-renouncing Sannyâsins to do. They will work themselves to death, but never yield. Whereas a little resistance, or just a trifle of criticism is bewildering to you.

Disciple :—Sir, the other day I saw Swami Trigunatita worshipped the photo of Sri Ramakrishna in the Press before opening the work and asked for your blessings for the success of the work.

Swamiji :—Well, Sri Ramakrishna is our centre. Each one of us is a ray of that light-centre. So, Trigunatita worshipped Sri Ramakrishna before opening the work, did he? It was excellently done. But he told me nothing of it.

Disciple :—Sir, he fears you and yesterday he told me to come to you and ask your opinion of the first issue of the magazine, after which, he said, he would see you.

Swamiji :—Tell him when you go that I am exceedingly delighted with his work. Give him my loving blessings. And all of you help him as far as you can. You will be doing Sri Ramakrishna's work by that.

Immediately after saying these words Swamiji called Swami Brahmananda to him and directed him to give Swami Trigunatita more money for the *Udbodhan*, if it was needed.

The same evening, after supper, Swamiji again referred to the topic of *Udbodhan* in the following words :—

"In the *Udbodhan* we must give the public only positive ideals. Negative thoughts weaken men. Do you not find that where parents are constantly taxing their sons to read and write, telling them they will never learn anything, and calling them fools and so forth, the latter do actually turn out to be so in many cases. If you speak kind words to boys and encourage them, they are bound to improve in time. What holds good of children, also holds good of children in the region of higher thoughts. If you can give them positive ideas, people will grow up to be men and learn to stand on their own legs. In language and literature, in poetry and the arts, in everything we must point out not the mistakes that people are making in their thoughts and actions, but the way in which they will gradually be able to do these things better. Pointing out mistakes wounds man's feelings. We have seen how Sri Ramakrishna would encourage even those whom we considered as worthless, and change the very course of their lives thereby! His very method of teaching was a unique phenomenon!"

After a short pause, Swamiji continued : "Never take the preaching of religion to mean the turning up of one's nose at everything and at everybody. In matters physical, mental and spiritual—in everything we must give men positive ideas—and never hate anybody. It is your hatred of one another that has brought about your degradation. Now we shall have to raise men by scattering broadcast only positive thoughts. First we must raise the whole Hindu race in this way, and then the whole world. That is why Sri Ramakrishna was incarnated. He never destoryed a single man's special inclinations. He gave words of hope and encouragement even to the most degraded of persons and lifted them up. We too must follow in his footsteps and lift all up, and rouse them. Do you understand?

"Your history, literature, mythology and all other Shâstras are simply frightening people. They are only telling them, 'You will go to hell, you are doomed!' Therefore has this lethargy crept into the very vitals of India. Hence we must explain to men in simple words the highest ideas of the Vedas and the Vedanta. Through the imparting of moral principles, good behaviour and education we must make the Chandâla come up to the level of the Brâhmana. Come, write out all these things in the *Udbodhan* and awaken everyone, young and old, man and woman. Then only shall I know that your study of the Vedas and Vedanta has been a success.

What do you say? Will you be able to do this?"

Disciple :—Through your blessings and command I think I shall succeed in everything.

Swamiji :—Another thing. You must learn to make the physique very strong, and teach the same to others. Don't you find me exercising everyday with dumbbells even now? Walk on mornings and evenings, and do physical labour. Body and mind must run parallel. It won't do to depend on others in everything. When the necessity of strengthening the physique is brought home to people, they will of themselves exert in that. It is to make them feel this need that education is necessary at the present moment.

XXIII

INDIA WANTS NOT LECTURING BUT WORK—THE CRYING PROBLEM IN INDIA IS POVERTY—YOUNG SANNYASINS TO BE TRAINED BOTH AS SECULAR AND SPIRITUAL TEACHERS AND WORKERS FOR THE MASSES—EXHORTATIONS TO YOUNG MEN TO WORK FOR OTHERS.

[Place : *The Belur Math while under construction.* Year : *1898.*]

Disciple :—How is it, Swamiji, that you do

not lecture in this country? You have stirred Europe and America with your lectures, but coming back here you have kept silence.

Swamiji:—In this country, the ground should be prepared first; and then if the seed is sown, the plant will come out best. The ground in the West, in Europe and America, is very fertile and fit for sowing seeds. There, they have reached the climax of Bhoga (enjoyment). Being satiated with Bhoga to the full, their minds are not getting peace now even in those enjoyments, and they feel as if they wanted something else. In this country you have not either Bhoga or Yoga (renunciation). When one is satiated with Bhoga, then it is that one will listen to and understand the teachings on Yoga. What good will lectures do in a country like India which has become the birthplace of disease, sorrow and affliction, and where men are emaciated through starvation, and weak in mind?

Disciple:—How is that? Do you not say that ours is the land of religion and that here the people understand religion as they do nowhere else? Why then will not this country be animated by your inspiring eloquence and yield to the full the fruits thereof?

Swamiji:—Now understand what religion

means. The first thing required is the worship of the Kurma (tortoise) Incarnation, and the belly-god is this Kurma, as it were. Until you pacify this, no one will welcome your words about religion. India is restless with the thought of how to face this spectre of hunger. The drainage of the best resources of the country by the foreigners, the unrestricted exports of merchandise, and, above all, the abominable jealousy natural to slaves, are eating into the very bones and marrow of India. First of all, you must remove this evil of hunger and starvation, this constant thought for bare existence, from those to whom you want to preach religion; otherwise, lectures and such things will be of no benefit.

Disciple:—What should we do then to remove that evil?

Swamiji:—First, some young men full of the spirit of renunciation are needed—those who will be ready to sacrifice their lives for others, instead of devoting themselves to their own happiness. With this object in view I shall establish a Math to train young Sannyâsins, who will go from door to door and make the people realize their pitiable condition by means of facts and reasoning, and instruct them in the ways and means for their welfare, and at the same time will explain to them as clearly as possible, in very simple and easy language, the higher truths of religion. The mass of people in our country is like the sleeping Leviathan. The education imparted by the present university system reaches to one or two per cent of the masses only. And even those who get that do not succeed in their endeavours of doing any good to their country. But it is not their fault, poor fellows! As soon as they come out of their college, they find themselves fathers of several children! Somehow or other they manage to secure the position of a clerk, or at the most, a deputy magistrate. This is the finale of education! With the burden of a family on their backs, they find no time to do anything great or think anything high. They do not find means enough to fulfil their personal wants and interest—so what can be expected of them in the way of doing anything for others?

Disciple :—Is there then no way out for us?

Swamiji :—Certainly there is. This is the land of Religion Eternal. The country has fallen, no doubt, but will as surely rise again, and that upheaval will astound the world. The lower the hollows the billows make, the higher and with equal force will they rise again.

Disciple :—How would India rise again?

Swamiji :—Do you not see? The dawn has

already appeared in the eastern sky, and there is little delay in the sun's rising. You all set your shoulders to the wheel! What is there in making the world the all in all, and thinking of "My Samsâra, my Samsâra"? Your duty at present is to go from one part of the country to another, from village to village, and make the people understand that mere sitting about idly won't do any more. Make them understand their real condition and say, "O ye brothers, all arise! Awake! How much longer would you remain asleep!" Go and advise them how to improve their own condition, and make them comprehend the sublime truths of the Shâstras, by presenting them in a lucid and popular way. So long the Brâhmanas have monopolized religion; but since they cannot hold their ground against the strong tide of time, go and take steps so that one and all in the land may get that religion. Impress upon their minds that they have the same right to religion as the Brâhmanas. Initiate all, even down to the Chandâlas, in these fiery Mantras. Also instruct them, in simple words, about the necessities of life, and in trade, commerce, agriculture, etc. If you cannot do this, then fie upon your education and culture, and fie upon your studying the Vedas and Vedanta!

Disciple :—But where is that strength in us ? I should have felt myself blessed if I had had a hundredth part of your powers, Swamiji.

Swamiji :—How foolish! Power and things like that will come by themselves. Put yourself to work, and you will find such tremendous power coming to you that you will feel it hard to bear. Even the least work done for others awakens the power within; even thinking the least good of others gradually instils into the heart the strength of a lion. I love you all ever so much, but I would wish you all to die working for others—I should be rather glad to see you do that!

Disciple :—What will become of those, then, who depend on me?

Swamiji :—If you are ready to sacrifice your life for others, God will certainly provide some means for them. Have you not read in the Gitâ the words of Sri Krishna ? न हि कल्याणकृत्कश्चित् दुर्गतिं तात गच्छति —"Never does a doer of good, O my beloved, come to grief."

Disciple :—I see, sir.

Swamiji :—The essential thing is renunciation—without renunciation none can pour out his whole heart in working for others. The man of renunciation sees all with an equal eye and devotes himself to the service of all. Does not our Vedanta also teach us to see all with an equal eye—why then do you cherish the idea that wife and children are your own, more than others? At your very threshold, Nârâyana Himself in the form of a poor beggar is dying of starvation! Instead of giving him anything, would you only satisfy the appetites of your wife and children with delicacies? Why, that is beastly!

Disciple:—To work for others requires a good deal of money at times, and where shall I get that?

Swamiji:—Why not do as much as lies within your power? Even if you cannot give to others for want of money, surely you can at least breathe into their ears some good words or impart some good instruction, can't you? Or does that also require money?

Disciple:—Yes, sir, that I can do.

Swamiji:—But saying, "I can," won't do. Show me through action what you can do, and then only shall I know that your coming to me is turned to some good account. Get up, and set your shoulder to the wheel—how long is this life for? As you have come into this world, leave some mark behind. Otherwise, where is the difference between you and the trees and stones? They, too, come into existence, decay and die. If you like to be born and to die like them, you are at liberty to do so. Show me by your actions that your reading the Vedanta has been fruitful of the highest good. Go and tell all, "In every one of you lies that Eternal Power," and try to wake It up. What will you do with individual salvation? That is sheer selfishness. Throw aside your meditation, throw away your salvation and such things! Put your whole heart and soul in the work to which I have consecrated myself.

With bated breath the disciple heard these inspiring words and Swamiji went on with his usual fire and eloquence.

Swamiji:—First of all, make the soil ready, and thousands of Vivekanandas will in time be born into this world to deliver lectures on religion. You needn't worry yourself about that! Don't you see why I am starting orphanages, famine-relief works, etc.? Don't you see how Sister Nivedita, an English lady, has learnt to serve Indians so well, by doing even menial work for them? And can't you, being Indians, similarly serve your own fellow-countrymen? Go, all of you, wherever there is an outbreak of plague or famine, or wherever the people are in distress, and mitigate their sufferings. At the most you may die in the attempt—what of that? How many like you are taking birth and dying like worms every day? What difference does that make to the world at large? Die you must, but have a great ideal to die for and it is better to die with a great ideal in life. Preach this ideal from door to door, and you will yourselves be benefited by it at the same time that you are doing good to your country. On you lie the future hopes of our country. I feel extreme pain to see you leading a life of inaction. Set yourselves to work—to work! Do not tarry—the time of death is approaching day by day! Do not sit idle, thinking that everything will be done in time, later on! Mind—nothing will be done that way!

XXIV

RECONCILIATION OF JNANA AND BHAKTI—SATCHIT-ANANDA—HOW SECTARIANISM ORIGINATES—BRING IN SHRADDHA AND THE WORSHIP OF SHAKTI AND AVATARAS—THE IDEAL OF THE HERO WE WANT NOW, NOT THE MADHURA-BHAVA—SRI RAMAKRISHNA—AVATARAS.

[Place: *The Belur Math while under construction.* Year: *1896.*]

Disciple:—Pray, Swamiji, how can Jnâna and Bhakti be reconciled? We see the followers of the path of devotion (Bhaktas) close their ears at the name of Shankara, and again, the followers of the path of knowledge (Jnânis) call the Bhaktas fanatics, seeing them weep in torrents, or sing and dance in ecstasy, in the name of the Lord.

Swamiji :—The thing is, all this conflict is in the preliminary (preparatory) stages of Jnâna and Bhakti. Have you not heard Sri Ramakrishna's story about Shiva's demons and Râma's monkeys ?†

Disciple :—Yes, sir, I have.

Swamiji :—But there is no difference between the supreme Bhakti and the supreme Jnâna. The supreme Bhakti is to realize God as the form of Prema (Love) itself. If you see the loving form of God manifested everywhere and in everything, how can you hate or injure others ? That realization of Love can never come so long as there is the least desire in the heart, or what Sri Ramakrishna used to say attachment for Kâma-Kânchana (sense-pleasure and wealth). In the perfect realization of Love,

---

† There was once a fight between Shiva and Râma. Shiva was the Guru of Râma, and Râma was the Guru of Shiva. They fought but became friendly again. But there was no end to the quarrels and wranglings between the demons of Shiva and the monkeys of Râma!

even the consciousness of one's own body does not exist. Also, the supreme Jnâna is to realize the oneness everywhere, to see one's own self as the self in everything. That too cannot come so long as there is the least consciousness of the ego (Aham).

Disciple :—Then what you call Love is the same as supreme Knowledge?

Swamiji :—Exactly so. Realization of Love comes to none unless one becomes a perfect Jnâni. Does not the Vedanta say that Brahman is Sat-Chit-Ananda—the Absolute Existence-Knowledge-Bliss?

Disciple :—Yes, sir.

Swamiji :—The word Sat-Chit-Ananda means—Sat, i.e., Existence, Chit, i.e., Consciousness, or Knowledge, and Ananda, i.e., Bliss, which is the same as Love. There is no controversy between the Bhakta and the Jnâni regarding the Sat aspect of Brahman. Only, the Jnânis lay greater stress on His aspect of Chit, or Knowledge, while the Bhaktas keep the aspect of Ananda, or Love, more in view. But no sooner is the essence of Chit realized, than the essence of Ananda is also realized. Because what is Chit is verily the same as Ananda.

Disciple :—Why then is so much sectarianism prevalent in India? And why is there so much controversy between the scriptures on Bhakti and Jnâna?

Swamiji:—The thing is, all this waging of war and controversy is concerning the preliminary ideals, i.e., those ideals which men take up to attain the real Jnâna or real Bhakti. But which do you think is the higher—the end or the means? Surely, the means can never be higher than the end. Because the means to realize the same end must be numerous, as they vary according to the temperament or mental capacities of individual followers. The counting of beads, meditation, worship, offering oblations in the sacred fire—all these and such other things are the limbs of religion; they are but the means; and to attain to supreme devotion (Parâ-Bhakti) or to the highest realization of Brahman is the pre-eminent end. If you look a little deeper you will understand what they are fighting about. One says, "If you pray to God facing the East, then you will reach Him." "No," says another, "you will have to sit facing the West, and then only you will see Him." Perhaps someone realized God in meditation, ages ago, by sitting with his face to the East and his disciples at once began to preach this attitude, asserting that none can ever see God unless he assumes this position. Another party comes forward and inquires—"How is that? Such and such a person realized God while facing the West, and we have seen this ourselves." In this way all these sects have originated. Someone might have attained supreme devotion by repeating the name of the Lord as Hari, and at once it entered into the composition of the Shâstra as :—

हरेर्नाम हरेर्नाम हरेर्नामैव केवलम् ।
कलौ नास्त्येव नास्त्येव नास्त्येव गतिरन्यथा ॥

"The name of the Lord Hari, the name of the Lord Hari, the name of the Lord Hari alone. Verily, there is no other, no other, no other path than this, in the age of Kali."

Someone, again, let us suppose, might have attained perfection with the name of Allah, and immediately another creed originated by him began to spread, and so on. But we have to see what is the end to which all these forms of worship and other religious practices are intended to lead. The end is the Shraddhâ. We have not any synonym in our Bengali language to express the Sanskrit word Shraddhâ. The Upanishad says that Shraddhâ entered into the heart of Nachiketâ. Even with the word Ekâgratâ (one-pointedness) we cannot express the whole significance of the word Shraddhâ. The word Ekâgranishthâ (one-pointed devotion) conveys, to a certain extent, the meaning of the word Shraddhâ. If you meditate on any truth with steadfast devotion and concentration, you will see that the mind is more and more tending onwards to Oneness, i.e., taking you towards the realization of the Absolute Existence-Knowledge-Bliss. The scriptures on Bhakti or Jnâna give special advice to men to take up in life the one or the other of such a Nishthâ and make it their own. With the lapse of ages, these great truths become distorted and gradually transform themselves into Deshâchâras, or the prevailing customs of a country. It has happened, not only in India, but in every nation and every society in the world. And the common people, lacking in discrimination, make these the bone of contention and fight among themselves. They have lost sight of the end, and hence sectarianism, quarrels and fights continue.

Disciple :—What then is the saving means, Swamiji ?

Swamiji :—That true Shraddhâ, as of old, has to be brought back again. The weeds have to be taken up by the roots. In every faith and in every path, there are, no doubt, truths which transcend time and space, but a good deal of rubbish has accumulated over them. This has to be cleared away, and the true eternal principles have to be held before the people ; and then only, our religion and our country will be really benefited.

Disciple :—How will that be effected ?

Swamiji :—Why, first of all, we have to introduce the worship of the great saints. Those great-souled ones who have realized the eternal truths are to be presented before the people as the ideals to be followed ; as in the case of India —Sri Râmachandra, Sri Krishna, Mahâvira and Sri Ramakrishna, among others. Can you bring in the worship of Sri Râmachandra and Mahâvira in this country ? Keep aside for the present the Vrindâvan aspect of Sri Krishna, and spread far and wide the worship of Sri Krishna roaring the Gitâ out, with the voice of a lion. And bring into daily use the worship of Shakti—the Divine Mother, the source of all power.

Disciple :—Is the divine play of Sri Krishna with the Gopis of Vrindâvan not good, then ?

Swamiji :—Under the present circumstances, that worship is of no good to you. Playing on the flute and so on will not regenerate the country. We now mostly need the ideal of a hero with the tremendous spirit of Rajas thrilling through his veins from head to foot—the hero who will dare and die to know the Truth—

the hero whose armour is renunciation, whose sword is wisdom. We want now the spirit of the brave warrior in the battle-field of life, and not of the wooing lover who looks upon life a pleasure-garden!

Disciple :—Is then the path of Love, as depicted in the ideal of the Gopis, false?

Swamiji :—Who says so? Not I! That is a very superior form of worship (Sâdhanâ). In this age of tremendous attachment to sense-pleasure and wealth, very few are able even to comprehend those higher ideals.

Disciple :—Then are not those who are worshipping God as husband or lover (मधुर) following the proper path?

Swamiji :—I daresay not. There may be a few honourable exceptions among them, but know, that the greater part of them are possessed of dark Tâmasika nature. Most of them are full of morbidity and affected with exceptional weakness! The country must be raised. The worship of Mahâvira must be introduced; the Shakti-pujâ must form a part of our daily practice; Sri Râmachandra must be worshipped in every home. Therein lies your welfare, therein lies the good of the country—there is no other way.

Disciple :—But I have heard that Bhagavân

Sri Ramakrishna used to sing the name of God very much?

Swamiji :—Quite so, but his was a different case. What comparison can there be between him and ordinary men? He practised in his life all the different ideals of religion to show that each of them leads but to the One Truth. Shall you or I ever be able to do all that he has done? None of us has understood him fully. So, I do not venture to speak about him anywhere and everywhere. He only knows what he himself really was; his frame was a human one only, but everything else about him was entirely different from others.

Disciple :—Do you, may I ask, believe him to be an Avatâra (Incarnation of God)?

Swamiji :—Tell me first—what do you mean by an Avatâra?

Disciple :—Why, I mean one like Sri Râmachandra, Sri Krishna, Sri Gauranga, Buddha or Jesus, etc.

Swamiji :—I know Bhagavân Sri Ramakrishna to be even greater than those you have just named. What to speak of believing, which is a petty thing—I *know*! Let us, however, drop the subject now; more of it another time.

After a pause Swamiji continued :—To reestablish the Dharma there come Mahâpurushas (great teachers of humanity), suited to the needs of the times and society. Call them what you will, either Mahapurushas, or Avataras, it matters little. They reveal, each in his life, the Ideal. Then, by degrees, shapes are moulded in their matrices—MEN are made! Gradually, sects arise and spread. As time goes on, these sects degenerate, and similar reformers come again—this has been the law flowing in uninterrupted succession, like a current, down the ages.

Disciple :—Why do you not preach Sri Ramakrishna as an Avatara? You have, indeed, power, eloquence and everything else needed to do it.

Swamiji :—Truly, I tell you, I have understood him very little. He appears to me to have been so great that, whenever I have to speak anything of him, I am afraid lest I ignore or explain away the truth, lest my little power does not suffice, lest in trying to extol him I present his picture by painting him according to my lights and belittle him thereby!

Disciple :—But many are now preaching him as an Avatara.

Swamiji :—Let them do so if they like. They are doing it in the light in which they have understood him. You too can go and do the same, if you have understood him.

Disciple :—I cannot even grasp you, what to say of Sri Ramakrishna! I should consider myself blessed in this life if I get a little of your grace.

XXV

BRAHMAN AND DIFFERENTIATION—PERSONAL REALIZATION OF ONENESS—SUPREME BLISS IS THE GOAL OF ALL—THINK ALWAYS, I AM BRAHMAN—DISCRIMINATION AND RENUNCIATION ARE THE MEANS—BE FEARLESS.

[Place : *The Belur Math while under construction.* Year : *1898.*]

Disciple :—Pray, Swamiji, if the One Brahman is the only Reality, why then exists all this differentiation in the world ?

Swamiji :—Are you not considering this question from the point of view of phenomenal existence ? Looking from the phenomenal side of existence, one can, through reasoning and discrimination, gradually arrive at the very root of Unity. But if you were firmly established in that Unity, how from that standpoint, tell me, could you see this differentiation ?

Disciple :—True, if I had existed in the Unity, how should I be able to raise this question of "why"? As I put this question, it is already taken for granted that I do so by seeing this diversity.

Swamiji :—Very well. To enquire about the root of Oneness through the diversity of phenomenal existence, is named by the Shâstras as Vyatireki reasoning, or the process of arguing by the indirect method, that is, first taking for granted something that is non-existent or unreal as existing or real, and then showing through the course of reasoning that that is not a substance existing or real. You are talking of the process of arriving at the truth through assuming that which is not-true as true—are you not?

Disciple :—To my mind, the state of the existing or the seen seems to be self-evident, and hence true, and that which is opposite to it seems, on the other hand, to be unreal.

Swamiji :—But the Vedas say, "One only without a second." And if in reality there is the One only that exists—the Brahman—then, your differentiation is false. You believe in the Vedas, I suppose?

Disciple :—Oh, yes, for myself I hold the Vedas as the highest authority; but if, in argument, one does not accept them to be so, one must, in that case, have to be refuted by other means.

Swamiji :—That also can be done. Look here, a time comes when what you call differentiation vanishes, and we cannot perceive it at all. I have experienced that state in my own life.

Disciple :—When have you done so?

Swamiji :—One day in the temple-garden at Dakshineswar Sri Ramakrishna touched me over the heart, and first of all I began to see that the houses—rooms, doors, windows, verandahs—the trees, the sun, the moon—all were flying off, shattering to pieces as it were—reduced to atoms and molecules—and ultimately became merged in the Akâsha. Gradually again, the Akâsha also vanished, and after that, my consciousness of the ego with it; what happened next I do not recollect. I was at first frightened. Coming back from that state, again I began to see the houses, doors, windows, verandahs and other things. On another occasion, I had exactly the same realization by the side of a lake in America.

Disciple :—Might not this state as well be brought about by a derangement of the brain? And I do not understand what happiness there can be in realizing such a state.

Swamiji :—A derangement of the brain! How can you call it so, when it comes neither as the result of delirium from any disease, nor of intoxication from drinking, nor as an illusion produced by various sorts of queer breathing exercises—but when it comes to a normal man in full possession of his health and wits ? Then again, this experience is in perfect harmony with the Vedas. It also coincides with the words of realization of the inspired Rishis and Achâryas of old. Do you take me, at last, to be a crack-brained man ? (smiling).

Disciple :—Oh, no, I did not mean that of course. When there are to be found hundreds of illustrations about such realization of Oneness, in the Shâstras, and when you say that it can be as directly realized as a fruit in the palm of one's hand, and when it has been your own personal experience in life, perfectly coinciding with the words of the Vedas and other Shâstras —how dare I say that it is false ? Sri Shankarâchârya also realizing that state has said, "Where is the universe vanished ?" and so on.

Swamiji :—Know—this knowledge of Oneness is what the Shâstras speak of as realization of the Brahman, by knowing which, one gets rid of fear, and the shackles of birth and death break for ever. Having once realized that Supreme Bliss, one is no more overwhelmed by pleasure and pain of this world. Men being fettered by base lust-and-wealth cannot enjoy that Bliss of Brahman.

Disciple :—If it is so, and if we are really of the essence of the Supreme Brahman, then why do we not exert ourselves to gain that Bliss ? Why do we again and again run into the jaws of death, being decoyed by this worthless snare of lust-and-wealth ?

Swamiji :—You speak as if man does not desire to have that Bliss! Ponder over it, and you will see that whatever anyone is doing, he is doing in the hope of gaining that Supreme Bliss. Only, not everyone is conscious of it and so cannot understand it. That Supreme Bliss fully exists in all, from Brahmâ down to the blade of grass. You are also that undivided Brahman. This very moment you can realize, if you think yourself truly and absolutely to be so. It is all mere want of direct perception. That you have taken service and work so hard for the sake of your wife also shows that the aim is ultimately to attain to that Supreme Bliss of Brahman. Being again and again entangled in the intricate maze of delusion and hard hit by sorrows and afflictions, the eye will turn of itself to one's own real nature, the Inner Self. It is owing to the presence of this desire for bliss in the heart, that man, getting hard shocks, one after another, turns his eye inwards—to his own Self. A time is sure to come to everyone, without exception, when he will do so—to one it may be in this life, to another after thousands of incarnations.

Disciple :—It all depends upon the blessings of the Guru and the grace of the Lord!

Swamiji :—The wind of grace of the Lord is blowing on, for ever and ever. Do you spread your sail? Whenever you do anything, do it with your whole heart concentrated on it. Think day and night—"I am of the essence of that Supreme Existence-Knowledge-Bliss—what fear and anxiety have I? This body, mind and intellect are all transient, and That which is beyond these is myself."

Disciple :—Thoughts like these come only for a while now and then, but quickly vanish, and I think all sorts of trash and nonsense.

Swamiji :—It happens like that in the initial stage, but gradually it is overcome. But from the beginning, intensity of desire in the mind is needed. Think always—"I am ever-pure, ever-knowing and ever-free; how can I do anything evil? Can I ever be befooled like ordinary men with the insignificant charms of lust and wealth?" Strengthen the mind with such thoughts. This will surely bring real good.

Disciple :—Once in a while Strength of mind comes. But then again I think that if I would appear at the Deputy Magistrateship examination—wealth and name and fame would come and I should live well and happy.

Swamiji :—Whenever such thoughts come in the mind, discriminate within yourself between the real and the unreal. Have you not read the Vedanta ? Even when you sleep, keep the sword of discrimination at the head of your bed, so that covetousness cannot approach you even in dream. Practising such strength, renunciation will gradually come, and then you will see—the portals of heaven are wide open to you.

Disciple :—If it is so, Swamiji, how is it then that the texts on Bhakti say that too much of renunciation kills the feelings that make for tenderness ?

Swamiji :—Throw away, I say, texts which teach things like that! Without renunciation, without burning dispassion for sense-objects, without turning away from wealth and lust as from filthy abominations— न सिध्यति ब्रह्मशतान्तरेऽपि— "Never can one attain salvation even in hundreds of Brahmâ's cycles." Repeating the names of the Lord, meditation, worship, offering libations in sacred fire, penance—all these are for bringing forth renunciation. One who has not gained renunciation, know his efforts to be like unto those of the man who is pulling at the oars all the while that the boat is at anchor. न प्रजया न धनेन त्यागेनैके अमृतत्वमानशुः —"Neither by progeny nor by wealth, but by renunciation alone some attained immortality."

Disciple :—Will mere renouncing of wealth and lust accomplish everything ?

Swamiji :—There are other hindrances on the path even after renouncing those two; then, for example, comes name and fame. Very few men, unless of exceptional strength, can keep their balance under that. People shower honours upon them, and various enjoyments creep in by degrees. It is owing to this that three-fourths of the Tyâgis are debarred from further progress! For establishing this Math and other things, who knows but that I may have to come back again!

Disciple :—If you say things like that, then we are undone!

Swamiji :—What fear ? अभीरभीरभीः —"Be fearless, be fearless, be fearless!" You have seen Nâg Mahâshaya—how even while living the life of a householder, he is more than a Sannyâsin! This is very uncommon; I have rarely seen one like him. If anyone wants to be a householder, let him be like Nâg Mahâshaya. He shines like a brilliant luminary in the spiritual firmament of East Bengal. Ask the people of that part of the country to visit him often; that will do much good to them.

Disciple:—Nâg Mahâshaya, it seems, is the living personification of humility in the play of Sri Ramakrishna's divine drama on earth.

Swamiji:—Decidedly so, without a shadow of doubt! I have a wish to go and see him once. Will you go with me? I love to see fields flooded over with water in the rains. Will you write to him?

Disciple:—Certainly I will. He is always mad with joy when he hears about you, and says that East Bengal will be sanctified into a place of pilgrimage by the dust of your feet.

Swamiji:—Do you know, Sri Ramakrishna used to speak of Nâg Mahâshaya as a "flaming fire"?

Disciple:—Yes, so I have heard.

At the request of Swamiji, the disciple partook of some Prasâda, and left for Calcutta late in the evening; he was deeply thinking over the message of fearlessness that he had heard from the lips of the inspired teacher—"I am free!" "I am free!"

XXVI

RENUNCIATION OF KAMA-KANCHANA—GOD'S MERCY FALLS ON THOSE WHO STRUGGLE FOR REALIZATION—UNCONDITIONAL MERCY AND BRAHMAN ARE ONE.

[Place : *The Belur Math (under construction).* Year : *1898.*]

Disciple :—Sri Ramakrishna used to say, Swamiji, that a man cannot progress far towards religious realization unless he first relinquishes Kâma-Kânchana (lust and wealth). If so, what will become of householders? For their whole minds are set on these two things.

Swamiji :—It is true that the mind can never turn to God until the desire for lust and wealth has gone from it, be a man householder or Sannyâsin. Know this for a fact, that as long as the mind is caught in these, so long true devotion, firmness and Shraddhâ (faith) can never come.

Disciple :—Where will the householders be, then? What way are they to follow?

Swamiji :—To satisfy our smaller desires and have done with them for ever, and to relinquish the greater ones by discrimination—that is the way. Without renunciation God can never be realized—यदि ब्रह्मा स्वयं वदेत्—"Even if Brahmâ himself enjoined otherwise!"

Disciple :—But does renunciation of everything come as soon as one becomes a monk?

Swamiji :—Sannyâsins are at least struggling to make themselves ready for renunciation, whereas householders are in this matter like boatmen who work at their oars while the boat lies at anchor. Is the desire for enjoyment ever appeased? भूय एवाभिवर्धते—"It increases ever and ever."

Disciple :—Why? May not world-weariness come, after enjoying the objects of the senses over and over for a long time?

Swamiji :—To how many does that come? The mind becomes tarnished by constant contact with the objects of the senses and receives a permanent moulding and impress from them. Renunciation, and renunciation alone, is the real secret, the Mulamantra, of all Realization.

Disciple :—But there are such injunctions of the seers in the scriptures as these :— गृहेषु पञ्चेन्द्रियनिग्रहस्तपः—"To restrain the five senses while living with one's wife and children is Tapas." निवृत्तरागस्य गृहं तपोवनं—"For him whose desires are under control, living in the midst of his family is the same as retiring into a forest for Tapasyâ."

Swamiji :—Blessed indeed are those who can renounce Kâma-Kânchana, living in their homes with their family! But how many can do that?

Disciple :—But then, what about the Sannyâsins? Are they all able to relinquish lust and love for riches fully?

Swamiji :—As I said just now, Sannyâsins are on the path of renunciation, they have taken the field, at least, to fight for the goal; but householders, on the other hand, having no knowledge as yet of the danger that comes through lust and gold, do not even attempt to realize the Self; that they must struggle to get rid of these is an idea that has not yet entered their minds.

Disciple :—But many of them are struggling for it.

Swamiji :—Oh, yes, and those who are doing so will surely renounce by degrees; their inordinate attachment for Kâma-Kânchana will diminish gradually. But for those who procrastinate, saying, "Oh, not so soon! I shall do it when the time comes," Self-realization is very far off. "Let me realize the Truth this moment! In this very life!"—these are the words of a hero. Such heroes are ever ready to renounce the very next moment, and to such the scripture says— यदहरेव विरजेत् तदहरेव प्रव्रजेत् —"The moment you feel disgust for the vanities of the world, leave it all and take to the life of a monk."

Disciple :—But was not Sri Ramakrishna wont to say, "All these attachments vanish through the grace of God when one prays to Him ?"

Swamiji :—Yes, it is so, no doubt, through His mercy, but one needs to be pure first before one can receive this mercy—pure in thought, word and deed; then it is that His grace descends on one.

Disciple :—But of what necessity is grace to him who can control himself in thought, word and deed ? For then he would be able to develop himself in the path of spirituality by means of his own exertions!

Swamiji :—The Lord is very merciful to him whom He sees struggling heart and soul for Realization. But remain idle, without any struggle, and you will see that His grace will never come.

Disciple :—Everyone longs to be good, and yet the mind, for some inscrutable reasons, turns to evil! Does not everyone wish to be good— to be perfect—to realize God ?

Swamiji :—Know them to be already struggling who desire this. God bestows His mercy when this struggle is maintained.

Disciple :—In the history of the Incarnations, we find many persons who, we should say, had led very dissipated lives and yet were able to realize God without much trouble and without performing any Sâdhanâ or devotion. How is this accounted for?

Swamiji :—Yes, but a great restlessness must already have come upon them; long enjoyment of the objects of the senses must already have created in these deep disgust. Want of peace must have been consuming their very hearts. So deeply they had already felt this void in their hearts that life even for a moment had seemed unbearable to them unless they could gain that peace which follows in the train of the Lord's mercy. So God was kind to them. This development took place in them direct from Tamas to Sattva.

Disciple :—Then, whatever was the path, they may be said to have realized God truly in that way?

Swamiji :—Yes, why not? But is it not better to enter into a mansion by the main entrance than by its doorway of dishonour?

Disciple :—No doubt that is true. Yet, the point is established that through mercy alone one can realize God.

Swamiji :—Oh, yes, that one can, but few

indeed are there who do so!

Disciple :—It appears to me that those who seek to realize God by restraining their senses and renouncing lust and wealth hold to the (free-will) theory of self-exertion and self-help; and that those who take the name of the Lord and depend on Him are made free by the Lord Himself of all worldly attachments, and led by Him to the supreme stage of Realization.

Swamiji :—True, those are the two different standpoints, the former held by the Jnânis, and the latter by the Bhaktas. But the ideal of renunciation is the keynote of both.

Disciple :—No doubt about that! But Srijut Girish Chandra Ghosh[*] once said to me that there could be no condition in God's mercy; there could be no law for it! If there were, then it could no longer be termed mercy. The realm of grace or mercy must transcend all law.

Swamiji :—But there must be some higher law at work in the sphere alluded to by G. C. of which we are ignorant. Those are words, indeed, for the last stage of development, which alone is beyond time, space and causation. But, when we get there, who will be merciful, and to whom, where there is no law of causation?

[*] The great Bengalee actor-dramatist, a staunch devotee of Sri Ramakrishna.

There the worshipper and the worshipped, the meditator and the object of meditation, the knower and the known, all become one—call that Grace, or Brahman, if you will. It is all one uniform homogeneous entity!

Disciple:—Hearing these words from you, Swamiji, I have come to understand the essence of all philosophy and religion (Vedas and Vedanta); it seems as if I had hitherto been living in the midst of high-sounding words without any meaning.

XXVII

THE DOCTRINE OF AHIMSA AND MEAT-EATING—THE SATTVA, RAJAS AND TAMAS IN MAN—DISCRIMINATION OF FOOD AND SPIRITUALITY—'AHARA'—THE THREE DEFECTS IN FOOD—DON'T-TOUCHISM AND CASTE-PREJUDICES—PLAN OF RESTORING THE OLD CHATURVARNA AND THE LAWS OF THE RISHIS.

[Place: *The Belur Math (under construction)*. Year: *1898*.]

Disciple:—Pray, Swamiji, do tell me if there is any relation between the discrimination of food taken and the development of spirituality in man.

Swamiji:—Yes, there is, more or less.

Disciple:—Is it proper or necessary to take fish and meat?

Swamiji:—Aye, take them, my boy! And if there be any harm in doing so, I will take care of that. Look at the masses of our country! What a look of sadness on their faces and want of courage and enthusiasm in their hearts, with large stomachs and no strength in their hands and feet—a set of cowards frightened at every trifle!

Disciple:—Does the taking of fish and meat give strength? Why do Buddhism and Vaishnavism preach अहिंसा परमो धर्मः —"Non-killing is the highest virtue"?

Swamiji:—Buddhism and Vaishnavism are not two different things. During the decline of Buddhism in India, Hinduism took from her a few cardinal tenets of conduct and made them her own, and these have now come to be known as Vaishnavism. The Buddhist tenet, "Non-killing is supreme virtue," is very good, but in trying to enforce it upon all by legislation without paying any heed to the capacities of the people at large, Buddhism has brought ruin upon India. I have come across many a "religious heron"*

---

* Meaning, religious hypocrite. The heron, so the story goes, gave it out to the fishes that he had forsaken his old habit of catching fish and turned highly religious. So he took his stand by the brink of the water and feigned to be meditating, while in reality he was always watching his opportunity to catch the unwary fish.

in India, who fed ants with sugar, and at the same time would not hesitate to bring ruin on his own brother for the sake of "filthy lucre"!

Disciple :—But in the Vedas as well as in the laws of Manu, there are injunctions to take fish and meat.

Swamiji :—Aye, and injunctions to abstain from killing as well. For the Vedas enjoin मा हिंस्यात् सर्वभूतानि —"Cause no injury to any being," and Manu also has said निवृत्तिस्तु महाफल —"Cessation of desire brings great results." Killing and non-killing have both been enjoined, according to the individual capacity, or fitness and adaptability, of those who will observe the one practice or the other.

Disciple :—It is the fashion here nowadays to give up fish and meat as soon as one takes to religion, and to many it is more sinful not to do so than to commit such great sins as adultery. How, do you think, such notions came into existence ?

Swamiji :—What's the use of your knowing how they came, when you see clearly, do you not, that such notions are working ruin to our country and our society ? Just see—the people of East Bengal eat much fish, meat and turtle, and they are much healthier than those of this part of Bengal. Even the rich men of East

Bengal have not yet taken to *loochis* or *châpâtis* at night, and they do not suffer from acidity and dyspepsia like us. I have heard that in the villages of East Bengal the people have not the slightest idea of what dyspepsia means!

Disciple :—Quite so, Swamiji. We never complain of dyspepsia in our part of the country. I first heard of it after coming to these parts. We take fish with rice, mornings and evenings.

Swamiji :—Yes, take as much of that as you can, without fearing criticism. The country has been flooded with dyspeptic *bâbâjis* living on vegetables only. That is no sign of Sattva but of deep Tamas—the shadow of death. Brightness in the face, undaunted enthusiasm in the heart, and tremendous activity—these result from Sattva; whereas idleness, lethargy, inordinate attachment and sleep are the signs of Tamas.

Disciple :—But do not fish and meat increase Rajas in man?

Swamiji :—That is what I want you to have. Rajas is badly needed just now! More than ninety per cent. of those whom you now take to be men with the Sattva quality are only steeped in the deepest Tamas. Enough if you find one-sixteenth of them to be really Sâttvika! What we want now is an immense awakening of Râjasika energy, for the whole country is wrapped in the shroud of Tamas. The people of this land must be fed and clothed—must be awakened—must be made more fully active. Otherwise they will become inert, as inert as trees and stones. So, I say, eat large quantities of fish and meat, my boy!

Disciple:—Does a liking for fish and meat remain when one has fully developed the Sattva quality?

Swamiji:—No, it does not. All liking for fish and meat disappears when pure Sattva is highly developed, and these are the signs of its manifestation in a soul:—sacrifice of everything for others, perfect non-attachment to lust and wealth, want of pride and egoism. The desire for animal food goes when these things are seen in a man. And where such indications are absent, and yet you find men siding with the non-killing party, know it for a certainty that here there is either hypocrisy or a show of religion. When you yourself come to that stage of pure Sattva, give up fish and meat, by all means.

Disciple:—But in the Chhândogya Upanishad there is this passage— आहारशुद्धौ सत्वशुद्धिः— "Through pure food the Sattva quality in a man becomes pure."

TALKS WITH SWAMI VIVEKANANDA

Swamiji:—Yes, I know. Shankarâchârya has said that the word Âhâra there means "objects of the senses," whereas Sri Râmânuja has taken the meaning of Âhâra to be "food". In my opinion we should take that meaning of the word which reconciles both these points of view. Are we to pass our lives discussing all the time about the purity and impurity of food only, or are we to practise the restraining of our senses? Surely, the restraining of the senses is the main object; and the discrimination of good and bad, pure and impure foods, only helps one, to a certain extent, in gaining that end. There are, according to our scriptures, three things which make food impure : (1) Jâti-dosha, or natural defects of a certain class of food, like onions, garlic, etc.; (2) Nimitta-dosha, or defects arising from the presence of external impurities in it, such as dead insects, dust, etc., that attach to sweetmeats bought in shops; (3) Âshraya-dosha, or defects that arise by the food coming from evil sources, as when it has been touched and handled by wicked persons. Special care should be taken to avoid the first and second classes of defects. But in this country men pay no regard to these very two, and go on fighting for the third alone, the very one that none but a Yogi could really discriminate! The country from end to end is being bored to extinction by the cries, "Don't touch," "Don't touch," of the non-touchism party. In that exclusive circle of theirs, too, there is no discrimination of good and bad men, for their food may be taken from the hands of anyone who wears a thread round his neck and calls himself a Brâhmana! Sri Ramakrishna was quite unable to take food in this indiscriminate way from the hands of any and all. It happened many a time that he would not accept food touched by a certain person or persons, and on rigorous investigation it would turn out that these had some particular stain to hide. Your religion seems nowadays to be confined to the cooking-pot alone. You put on one side the sublime truths of religion and fight, as they say, for the skin of the fruit and not for the fruit itself!

Disciple :—Do you mean, then, that we should eat the food handled by anyone and everyone?

Swamiji :—Why so? Now, look here. You being a Brâhmana of a certain class, say, of the Bhattâchârya class, why should you not eat rice cooked by Brâhmanas of all classes? Why should you, who belong to the Rârhi section, object to take rice cooked by a Brâhmana of the Bârendra section, or why should a Barendra object to taking your rice? Again, why should not the other subcastes in the west and south of India, e.g., the Mahratti, Telingi, Kanouji, do the same? Do you not see that hundreds of Brahmanas and Kâyasthas in Bengal now go secretly to eat dainties in public restaurants, and when they come out of those places pose as leaders of society and frame rules to support don't-touchism! Must our society really be guided by laws dictated by such hypocrites? No, I say. On the contrary we must turn them out. The laws laid down by the great Rishis of old must be brought back and be made to rule supreme once more. Then alone can national well-being be ours.

Disciple:—Then, do not the laws laid down by the Rishis rule and guide our present society?

Swamiji:—Vain delusion! Where indeed is that the case nowadays? Nowhere have I found the laws of the Rishis current in India, even when during my travels I searched carefully and thoroughly. The blind and not unoften meaningless customs sanctioned by the people, local prejudices and ideas, and the usages and ceremonials prevalent amongst women, are what really govern society everywhere! How many care to read the Shâstras or to lead society according to their ordinances after careful study?

Disciple:—What are we to do, then?

Swamiji:—We must revive the old laws of the Rishis. We must initiate the whole people into the codes of our old Manu and Yâjnavalkya, with a few modifications here and there to adjust them to the changed circumstances of the time. Do you not see that nowhere in India now are the original four castes (Châturvarnya) to be found? We have to redivide the whole Hindu population, grouping it under the four main castes of Brahmanas, Kshatriyas, Vaishyas and Shudras, as of old. The numberless modern sub-divisions of the Brahmanas that split them up into so many castes, as it were, have to be abolished and a single Brahmana caste to be made by uniting them all. Each of the three remaining castes also will have to be brought similarly into single groups, as was the case in Vedic times. Without this will the Motherland be really benefited by your simply crying, as you do nowadays, "We won't touch you!"; "We won't take him back into our caste!" Never, my boy!

XXVIII

CAUSE OF INDIA'S DEGRADATION—ANCIENT VEDIC CUSTOMS MUST BE REMODELLED ACCORDING TO THE NEED OF THE SOCIETY AND THE TIMES—NEW SMRITI TO BE COMPILED.

[Place : *The Belur Math (under construction).* Year : *1899.*]

Disciple :—Why is it, Swamiji, that our society and country have come to such degradation ?

Swamiji :—It is you who are responsible for it.

Disciple :—How, sir ? You surprise me.

Swamiji :—You have been despising the lower classes of the country for a very long time and as a result, you have now become the objects of contempt in the eyes of the world.

Disciple :—When did you find us despising them ?

Swamiji :—Why, you priest-class never let the non-Brahmin classes read the Vedas and Vedanta and all such weighty Shâstras—never touch them even. You have only kept them down. It is you who have always done like that through selfishness. It was the Brâhmanas who made a monopoly of the religious books and kept the question of sanction and prohibition in their own hands. And repeatedly calling the other races of India low and vile, they put this belief into their heads that they were really such. If you tell a man, "You are low, you are vile," in season and out of season, then he is bound to believe in course of time that he is really such. This is called hypnotism. The non-Brahmin classes are now slowly rousing themselves. Their faith in Brahminical Scriptures and Mantras is getting shaken. Through the spread of Western education all the tricks of the Brâhmanas are giving way, like the banks of the Padmâ in the rainy season do you not see that?

Disciple :—Yes, sir, the stricture of orthodoxy is gradually lessening nowadays.

Swamiji :—It is as it should be. The Brâhmanas, in fact, gradually took to a course of gross immorality and oppression. Through selfishness they introduced a large number of strange, non-Vedic, immoral and unreasonable doctrines—simply to keep intact their own prestige. And the fruits of that they are reaping forthwith.

Disciple :—What may these fruits be, sir?

Swamiji :—Don't you perceive them? It is simply due to your having despised the masses of India that you have now been living a life of slavery for the last thousand years; it is therefore that you are objects of hatred in the eyes of foreigners and are looked upon with indifference by your countrymen.

Disciple:—But, sir, even now it is the Brâhmanas who direct all ceremonials, and people are observing them according to the opinions of the Brâhmanas. Why then do you speak like that?

Swamiji:—I don't find it. Where do the tenfold Samskâra, or purifying ceremonies, enjoined by the Shâstras, obtain still? Well, I have travelled the whole of India, and everywhere I have found society to be guided by local usages which are condemned by the Shrutis and Smritis. Popular customs, local usages, and observances prevalent among women only—have not these taken the place of the Smritis everywhere? Who obeys, and whom? If you can but spend enough money, the priest-class is ready to write out whatever sanctions or prohibitions you want! How many of them read the Vedic Kalpa (Ritual), Grihya and Shrauta Sutra? Then look here, in Bengal the code of Raghunandana is obeyed: a little further on you will find the *Mitâksharâ* in vogue; while in another part the code of Manu holds sway! You seem to think that the same laws hold good everywhere! What I want therefore is to introduce the study of the Vedas by stimulating a greater regard for them in the minds of the people, and to pass everywhere the injunctions of the Vedas.

Disciple :—Sir, is it possible nowadays to set them going?

Swamiji :—It is true that all the ancieut Vedic laws will not have a go, but if we introduce additions and alterations in them to suit the needs of the times, codify them, and hold them up as a new model to society, why will they not pass current?

Disciple :—Sir, I was under the impression that at least the injunctions of Manu were being obeyed all over India even now.

Swamiji :—Nothing of the kind. Just look to your own province and see how the Vâmâchâra (immoral practices) of the Tantras has entered into your very marrow. Even modern Vaishnavism, which is the skeleton of the defunct Buddhism, is saturated with Vâmâchâra! We must stem the tide of this Vâmâchâra, which is contrary to the spirit of the Vedas.

Disciple :—Sir, is it possible now to cleanse this Augean stable?

Swamiji :—What nonsense do you say, you coward! You have well-nigh thrown the country into ruin by crying. "It is impossible, It is impossible." What cannot human effort achieve ?

Disciple :—But, sir, such a state of things seems impossible unless sages like Manu and Yâjnavalkya are again born in the country.

Swamiji :—Goodness gracious! Was it not purity and unselfish labour that made them Manu and Yâjnavalkya, or was it something else ? Well, we ourselves can be far greater than even Manu and Yâjnavalkya if we try to; why will not our views prevail then ?

Disciple :—Sir, it is you who said just now that we must revive the ancient usages and observances within the country. How then can we think lightly of sages like Manu and the rest?

Swamiji :—What an absurd deduction! You altogether miss my point. I have only said that the ancient Vedic customs must be remodelled according to the need of the society and the times, and passed under a new form in the land. Have I not ?

Disciple :—Yes, sir.

Swamiji :—What then were you talking ? You have read the Shâstras, and my hope and faith rest in men like you. Understand my words in their true spirit and apply yourselves to work in their light.

Disciple :—But, sir, who will listen to us? Why should our countrymen accept them?

Swamiji :—If you can truly convince them and practise what you preach, they must. If, on the contrary, like a coward you simply utter Shlokas as a parrot, be a mere talker and quote authority only, without showing them in action —then who will care to listen to you?

Disciple :—Please give me some advice in brief about social reform.

Swamiji :—Why, I have given you advice enough; now put at least one in practice. Let the world see that your reading of the scriptures and listening to me has been a success. The codes of Manu and lots of other books that you have read—what is their basis and underlying purpose? Keeping that basis intact, compile in the manner of the ancient Rishis the essential truths of them and supplement them with thoughts that are suited to the times; only take care that all races and all sects throughout India be really benefited by following these rules. Just write out a Smriti like that; I shall revise it.

Disciple :—Sir, it is not an easy task; and even if such a Smriti be written, will it be accepted?

Swamiji :—Why not? Just write it out.

कालो ह्ययं निरवधिविपुला च पृथ्वी —"Time is infinite, and the world is vast." If you write it in the proper way, there must come a day when it will be accepted. Have faith in yourself. You people were once the Vedic Rishis. Only, you have come in different forms, that's all. I see it clear as daylight that you all have infinite power in you! Rouse that up; arise, arise— apply yourselves heart and soul, gird up your loins. What will you do with wealth and fame that are so transitory? Do you know what I think? I don't care for Mukti and all that. My mission is to arouse within you all such ideas; I am ready to undergo a hundred thousand rebirths to train up a single man.

Disciple :—But, sir, what will be the use of undertaking such works? Is not death stalking behind?

Swamiji :—Fie upon you! If you die, you will die but once. Why will you die every minute of your life by constantly harping on death like a coward?

Disciple :—All right, sir, I may not think of death, but what good will come of any kind of work in this evanescent world?

Swamiji :—My boy, when death is inevitable, is it not better to die like heroes than as stocks and stones? And what is the use of living a day or two more in this transitory world? It is better to wear out than to rust out—specially for the sake of doing the least good to others.

Disciple:—It is true, sir. I beg your pardon for troubling you so much.

Swamiji:—I don't feel tired even if I talk for two whole nights to an earnest enquirer; I can give up food and sleep and talk and talk. Well, if I have a mind, I can sit up in Samâdhi in a Himalayan cave. And you see that nowadays through the Mother's grace I have not to think about food, it comes anyhow. Why then don't I do so? And why am I here? Only the sight of the country's misery and the thought of its future do not let me remain quiet any more!—Even Samâdhi and all that appear as futile—even the sphere of Brahmâ with its enjoyments becomes insipid! My vow of life is to think of your welfare. The day that vow will be fulfilled, I shall leave this body and make a straight run up!

Hearing Swamiji's words the disciple sat speechless for a while, gazing at him, wondering in his heart. Then with a view to taking his leave, he saluted Swamiji reverently and asked his permission to go.

Swamiji:—Why do you want to go? Why

not live in the Math ? Your mind will again be polluted if you go back to the worldly-minded. See here, how fresh is the air, there is the Ganga, and the Sâdhus are practising meditation, and holding lofty talks! While the moment you will go to Calcutta, you will be thinking of nasty stuff.

The disciple joyfully replied, "All right, sir, I shall stay today at the Math."

Swamiji :—Why today ?—Can't you live here for good ? What is the use of going back to the world ?

The disciple bent down his head, hearing Swamiji's words. Various thoughts crowded into his brain and kept him speechless.

XXIX

AUSPICIOUSNESS OF TIME AND PLACE—WORK AND SELF-REALIZATION—KARMA-YOGA—INDIA WANTS MANIFESTATION OF RAJAS—BRIGHT FUTURE FOR THE COUNTRY.

[Place : *The Belur Math (under construction).* Year : *Beginning of 1899.*]

Today Swamiji is walking round the new Math grounds in the afternoon in company with the disciple. Standing at a little distance off the Bael tree Swamiji took to singing slowly a

Bengalee song :* "O Himalaya, Ganesh is auspicious to me," etc., ending with the line—"And many Dandis (Sannyâsins) and Yogis with matted hair will also come." While singing the song Swamiji repeated this line to the disciple and said : "Do you understand ? In course of time many Sâdhus and Sannyâsins will come here." Saying this he sat under the tree and remarked : "The ground under the Bilva tree is very holy. Meditating here quickly brings about an awakening of the religious instinct. Sri Ramakrishna used to say so."

Disciple :—Sir, those who are devoted to the discrimination between the Self and not-Self—have they any need to consider the auspiciousness of place, time, and so forth ?

Swamiji :—Those who are established in the knowledge of the Atman, have no need for such discrimination, but that state is not attained offhand. It comes as the result of long practice. Therefore in the beginning one has to take the help of external aids and learn to stand on one's own legs. Later on, when one is established in the knowledge of the Atman, there is no more need for any external aid.

The various methods of spiritual practice

* This is one of the songs sung in the homes of Bengal on the eve of Durgâpujâ.

that have been laid down in the scriptures are all for the attainment of the knowledge of Atman. Of course these practices vary according to the qualifications of different aspirants. But they also are a kind of work, and so long as there is work, the Atman is not discovered. The obstacles to the manifestation of the Atman are overcome by practices as laid down in the scriptures, but work has no power of directly manifesting the Atman ; it is only effective in removing some veils that cover knowledge. Then the Atman manifests by Its own effulgence. Do you see ? Therefore does your commentator (Shankara) say—"In the knowledge of Brahman, there can not be the least touch of work."

Disciple :—But, sir, Since the obstacles to Self-manifestation are not overcome without the performance of work in some form or other, therefore indirectly work stands as a means to knowledge.

Swamiji :—From the standpoint of the causal chain, it so appears *prima facie*. Taking up this view it is stated in the Purva-Mimâmsâ that work for a definite end infallibly produces a definite result. But the vision of the Atman which is Absolute, is not to be compassed by means of work. For, the rule with regard to a seeker of the Atman is that he should undergo spiritual practice, but have no eye to its results. It follows thence that these practices are simply the cause of the purification of the aspirant's mind. For if the Atman could be directly realized as a result of these practices, then scriptures would not have enjoined on the aspirant to give up the results of work. So it is with a view to combating the Purva-Mimâmsâ doctrine of work with motive producing results, that the philosophy of work without motive has been set forth in the Gitâ. Do you see?

Disciple :—But, sir, if one has to renounce the fruits of work, why should one be induced to undertake work which is always troublesome?

Swamiji :—In this human life, one cannot help doing some kind of work always. When man has perforce to do some work, Karma-Yoga enjoins on him to do it in such a way as will bring freedom through the realization of the Atman. As to your objection that none will be induced to work—the answer is, that whatever work you do has some motive behind it; but when by the long performance of work, one notices that one work merely leads to another, through a round of births and rebirths, then the awakened discrimination of man naturally begins to question itself—where is the end to this interminable chain of work? It is then that he appreciates the full import of the words of the Lord in the Gitâ—"Inscrutable is the course of work." Therefore, when the aspirant finds that work with motive brings no happiness, then he renounces action. But man is so constituted that to him the performance of work is a necessity. so what work should he take up ? He takes up some unselfish work, but gives up all desire for its fruits. For he has known then that in those fruits of work lie countless seeds of future births and deaths. Therefore the knower of Brahman renounces all actions—although to outward appearances he engages himself in some work, he has no attachment for it. Such men have been described in the scriptures as Karma-Yogins.

Disciple :—Is then the work without motive of the unselfish knower of Brahman like the activities of a lunatic ?

Swamiji :—Why so ? Giving up the fruits of work means not to perform work for the good of one's own body or mind. The knower of Brahman never seeks his own happiness. But what is there to prevent him from doing work for the welfare of others ? Whatever work he does without attachment for its fruits brings only good to the world—it is all "for the good of the many, for the happiness of the many." Sri

Ramakrishna used to say, "They never take a false step."—Haven't you read in the *Uttara-Râma-Charita* ?— ऋषीणाम् पुनराद्यानां वाचमर्थोऽनुधावति —"The words of the ancient Rishis have always some meaning, they are never false." When the mind is merged in the Atman by the suppression of all modifications, it produces "a dispassion for the enjoyment of fruits of work here or hereafter," i.e. there remains no desire in the mind for any enjoyment here, or, after death, in any heavenly sphere. There is no action and interaction of desires in the mind. But when the mind descends from the superconscious state into the world of "I and mine," then by the momentum of previous work or habit, or Samskâras (impressions) the functions of the body go on as before. The mind then is generally in the superconscious state, eating and other functions of the body are done from mere necessity, and the body consciousness is very much attenuated. Whatever work is done after reaching this transcendental state is done rightly ; it conduces to the real well-being of men and the world ; for then the mind of the doer is not contaminated by selfishness or calculation of personal gain or loss. The Lord has created this wonderful universe, remaining always in the realm of superconsciousness ; therefore there is nothing imperfect in this world. So I was saying that the actions which the knower of the Atman does without attachment for fruits, are never imperfect, but they conduce to the real well-being of man and the world.

Disciple :—Sir, you said just now that knowledge and work are contradictory, that in the supreme knowledge there is no room at all for work, or in other words, that by means of work the realization of Brahman cannot be attained. Why then do you now and then speak words calculated to awaken great Rajas (activity)? You were telling me the other day, "Work, work, work—there is no other way besides it."

Swamiji :—Going round the whole world, I find that people of this country are immersed in great Tamas (inactivity), compared with people of other countries. On the outside, there is a simulation of the Sâttvika (calm and balanced) state, but inside, downright inertness like that of stocks and stones— what work will be done in the world by such people? How long can such an inactive, lazy, and sensual people live in the world? First travel in Western countries, then contradict my words. How much of enterprise and devotion to work, how much enthusiasm and manifestation of Rajas are there in the lives of the Western people! While in your country it is as if the blood has become congealed in the heart, so that it cannot circulate in the veins—as if paralysis has overtaken the body and it has become languid. So my idea is first to make the people active by developing their Rajas, and thus make them fit for the struggle for existence. With no strength in the body, no enthusiasm at heart, and no originality in the brain, what will they do—these lumps of dead matter! By stimulating them I want to bring life into them—to this I have dedicated my life. I will rouse them through the infallible power of Vedic Mantras. I am born to proclaim to them that fearless message—"Arise, Awake!" Be you my helpers in this work. Go over from village to village, from one portion of the country to another, and preach this message of fearlessness to all, from the Brâhmana to the Chandâla. Tell each and all that infinite power resides within them, that they are sharers of immortal Bliss. Thus rouse up the Rajas within them—make them fit for the struggle for existence, and then speak to them about salvation. First make the people of the country stand on their legs by rousing their inner power, first let them learn to have good food and clothes and plenty of enjoyment—then tell them how to be free from this bondage of enjoyment. Laziness, meanness and hypocrisy have covered the whole length and breadth of the country. Can an intelligent man look on all this and remain quiet? Does it not bring tears to the eyes? Madras, Bombay, Punjab, Bengal—whichever way I look, I see no signs of life. You are thinking yourselves highly educated. What nonsense have you learnt? Getting by heart the thoughts of others in a foreign language, and stuffing your brain with them and taking some university degrees, you consider yourselves educated! Fie upon you! Is this education? What is the goal of your education? Either a clerkship, or being a rougish lawyer, or at the most a Deputy Magistracy, which is another form of clerkship —isn't that all? What good will it do you or the country at large? Open your eyes and see what a piteous cry for food is rising in the land of Bhârata, proverbial for its wealth! Will your education fulfil this want? Never. With the help of Western science set yourselves to dig the earth and produce foodstuffs—not by means of mean servitude of others—but by discovering new avenues to production by your own exertions aided by Western science. Therefore I teach the people of this country to be full of activities, so as to be able to produce food and clothing for themselves. For want of food and clothing and plunged in anxiety for it, the country has come to ruin—what are you doing to remedy this? Throw aside your scriptures in the Ganga and teach the people first the means of procuring their food and clothing, and then you will find time to read to them the scriptures. If their material wants are not removed by the rousing of intense activity, none will listen to words of spirituality. Therefore I say, first rouse the inherent power of the Atman within you, then rousing the faith of the general people in that power as much as you can, teach them first of all to make provision for food, and then teach them religion. There is no time to sit idle—who knows when death will overtake one?

While saying these words, a mingled expression of remorse, sorrow, compassion and power shone on his face. Looking at his majestic appearance, the disciple was awed into silence. A little while afterwards Swamiji said again: "That activity and self-reliance must come in the people of the country in time—I see it clearly. There is no escape. The intelligent man can distinctly see the vision of the next three Yugas (ages) ahead. Ever since the advent of Sri Ramakrishna the eastern horizon has been aglow with the dawning rays of the sun which

XXX

LAWS OF BRAHMACHARYA—NEW ORDER OF SANNYASINS—WANTED KARMA-YOGA AS TAUGHT IN THE GITA.

[Place : *The Belur Math (under construction).* Year : *Beginning of 1899.*]

The present Math buildings are almost complete now. Swamiji is not in good health ; therefore doctors have advised him to go out on boat in the mornings and evenings on the Ganga.

Today is Sunday. The disciple is sitting in Swamiji's room and conversing with him. About this time Swamiji framed certain rules for the guidance of the Sannyâsins and Brahmachârins of the Math ; the object of which was to keep them from indiscriminate mixing with worldly people. The conversation turned on this topic.

Swamiji :—Nowadays I feel a peculiar smell of lax self-control in the dress and clothes of worldly people ; therefore I have made it a rule in the Math that householders should not sit or lie on the beds of Sâdhus. Formerly I used to read in the Shâstras that such a smell is felt and therefore Sannyâsins cannot bear the smell of householders. Now I see it is true. By strictly observing the rules that have been framed, the Brahmachârins will in time grow into genuine Sannyâsins. When they are established in the ideal of Sannyâsa, they will be able to mix on an equal footing with worldly men without any harm. But now if they are not kept within the barriers of strict rules, they will all go wrong. In order to attain to ideal Brahmacharya one has in the beginning to observe strict rules regarding chastity. Not only should one keep oneself strictly aloof from the least association with the opposite sex, but also give up the company of married people even.

The disciple who was a householder was awed at these words of Swamiji, felt dejected that he would not be able to associate freely as before with Sadhus of the Math and said : "Sir, I feel more intimacy with the Math and its inmates than with my own family. As if they are known to me from a long long time. The unbounded freedom that I enjoy in the Math, I feel nowhere else in the world."

Swamiji :—All those who are pure in spirit will feel like that here. Those who do not feel so must be taken as not belonging to this Math and its ideals. That is the reason why many people come here out of mere sensation-mongering and then run away. Those who are devoid of continence, and are running after money day and night, will never be able to appreciate the ideals of the Math, nor regard the Math people as their own. The Sannyâsins of this Math are not like those of old, ash-besmeared, with matted hair and iron tongs in their hands, and curing disease by medicinal tit-bits; therefore seeing the contrast, people cannot appreciate them. The ways, movements and ideas of our Master were all cast in a new mould, so we are also of a new type. Sometimes dressed like gentlemen, we are engaged in lecturing, at other times, throwing all aside, with "Hara, Hara, Vyom Vyom" on the lips, ash-clad, we are immersed in meditation and austerities in mountains and forests.

Now it won't do to quote merely the authority of our ancient books. The tidal wave of Western civilization is now rushing over the length and breadth of the country. It won't do now simply to sit in meditation on mountain tops without realizing in the least its usefulness. Now is wanted—as said in the Gitâ by the Lord—intense Karma-Yoga, with unbounded courage and indomitable strength in the heart. Then only will the people of the country be roused, otherwise they will continue to be as much in the dark as you are.

The day is nearly ended. Swamiji came downstairs, dressed for the boating excursion on the Ganga. Swamiji, accompanied by the disciple and two others, boarded the boat, which passed the Dakshineswar temple and reached Pânihaty where it was anchored below the garden-house of Babu Govinda Kumar Chaudhury. It had once been proposed to rent this house for the use of the Math. Swamiji descended from the boat, went round the house and the garden and looking over the place minutely said: "The garden is nice but is at a great distance from Calcutta. The devotees of Sri Ramakrishna would have been put to trouble to walk such a long distance from Calcutta. It is fortunate that the Math has not been established here." The boat then returned to the Math amid the enveloping darkness.

XXXI

MEETING WITH NAG MAHASHAYA.

[Place: *Belur Math*. Year: *Beginning of 1899.*]

The disciple has today come to the Math with Nâg Mahâshaya in company.

Swamiji to Nag Mahashaya (saluting him):

You are all right, I hope?

Nag Mahashaya :—I have come today to visit you. Glory to Shankara! Glory to Shankara! I am blessed today verily with the sight of Shiva!

Saying these words, Nag Mahashaya out of reverence stood with folded hands before him.

Swamiji :—How is your health?

Nag Mahashaya :—Why are you asking about this trifling body—this cage of flesh and bones? Verily I am blessed today to see you.

Saying these words, Nag Mahashaya prostrated before Swamiji.

Swamiji (lifting him up):—Why are you doing that to me?

Nag Mahashaya :—I see with my inner eye that today I am blessed with the vision of Shiva Himself. Glory to Ramakrishna!

Swamiji (addressing the disciple) :—Do you see? How real Bhakti transforms human nature! Nag Mahashaya has lost himself in the Divine, his body-consciousness has vanished altogether. (To Swami Premananda) Get some Prasâda for Nag Mahashaya.

Nag Mahashaya :—Prasada! (To Swamiji with folded hands) Seeing you, all my earthly hunger has vanished today.

The Brahmachârins and Sannyâsins of the

Math were studying the Upanishads. Swamiji said to them, "Today a great devotee of Sri Ramakrishna has come amongst us. Let it be a holiday in honour of Nag Mahashaya's visit to the Math." So all closed their books and sat in a circle round Nag Mahashaya; Swamiji also sat in front of him.

Swamiji (addressing all):—Do you see? Look at Nag Mahashaya; he is a householder, yet he has no knowledge of the mundane existence; he always lives lost in Divine conscousness. (To Nag Mahashaya) Please tell us and these Brahmachârins something about Sri Ramakrishna.

Nag Mahashaya (in reverence):—What do you say, sir? What shall I say? I have come to see you—the hero, the helper in the divine play of Sri Ramakrishna. Now will people appreciate his message and teachings. Glory to Ramakrishna!

Swamiji:—It is you who have really appreciated and understood Sri Ramakrishna. We are only spent in useless wanderings.

Nag Mahashaya:—What do you say, sir? You are the image of Sri Ramakrishna—the obverse and reverse of the same coin. Those who have eyes, let them see.

Swamiji:—Is the starting of these Maths and

Ashramas, etc., a step in the right direction?

Nag Mahashaya:—I am an insignificant being, what do I understand? Whatever you do, I know for a certainty, will conduce to the well-being of the world,—aye, of the world.

Many out of reverence proceeded to take the dust of Nag Mahashaya's feet, which made him much agitated. Swamiji addressing all said, "Don't act so as to cause pain to Nag Mahashaya; he feels uncomfortable." Hearing this everybody desisted.

Swamiji:—Do please come and stay at the Math. You will be an object-lesson to the boys here.

Nag Mahashaya:—I once asked Sri Ramakrishna about that, to which he replied, "Stay as a householder as you are doing." Therefore I am continuing in that life. I see you all occasionally and feel myself blessed.

Swamiji:—I will go to your place once.

Nag Mahashaya, mad with joy, said: "Shall such a day dawn? My place will be made holy by your visit, like Varanasi. Shall I be so fortunate as that!"

Swamiji:—Well, I have the desire. Now it depends on "Mother" to take me there.

Nag Mahashaya:—Who will understand you? Unless the inner vision opens, nobody can understand you. Only Sri Ramakrishna understood you; all else have simply put faith in his words, but none has understood you really.

Swamiji:—Now my one desire is to rouse the country—the sleeping Leviathan that has lost all faith in his power and makes no response. If I can wake it up to a sense of the Eternal Religion, then, I shall know that Sri Ramakrishna's advent and our birth are fruitful. That is the one desire in my heart; Mukti and all else appear of no consequence to me. Please give me your blessings that I may succeed.

Nag Mahashaya:—Sri Ramakrishna will bless! Who can turn the course of your will? Whatever you will, shall come to pass.

Swamiji:—Well, nothing comes to pass—without his will behind it.

Nag Mahashaya:—Your will and his have become one. Whatever is your will is his. Glory to Sri Ramakrishna!

Swamiji:—To work, one requires a strong body; since coming to this country, I am not doing well; in the West I was in very good health.

Nag Mahashaya:—"Whenever one is born in a body," Sri Ramakrishna used to say, "one has to pay the house tax." Disease and sorrow are the tax. But your body is a box of gold *mohurs,* and very great care should be taken of it. But who will do it? Who will understand? Only Sri Ramakrishna understood. Glory to Ramakrishna!

Swamiji :—All at the Math take great care of me.

Nag Mahashaya :—It will be to their good if they do it, whether they know it or not. If proper attention is not paid to your body, then the chances are that it will fall off.

Swamiji :—Nag Mahashaya, I do not fully understand whether what I am doing is right or not. At particular times I feel a great inclination to work in a certain direction, and I work according to that. Whether it is for good or evil, I cannot understand.

Nag Mahashaya :—Well, Sri Ramakrishna said, "The treasure is now locked".—Therefore he does not let you know fully. The moment you know it, your play of human life will be at an end.

Swamiji was pondering something with steadfast gaze. Then Swami Premananda brought some Prasada for Nag Mahashaya who was ecstatic with joy. Shortly after Nag Mahashaya found Swamiji slowly digging the ground with a spade near the pond, and held him by the hand saying, "When we are present, why should you do that?" Swamiji leaving the spade walked about the garden talking the while, and began to narrate to a disciple : "After Sri Ramakrishna's passing away we heard one day that Nag Mahashaya was lying in fast in his humble tiled lodgings in Calcutta. Myself, Swami Turiyananda and another went together and appeared at Nag Mahashaya's cottage. Seeing us he rose from his bed. We said, 'We shall have our Bhikshâ (food) here today.' At once Nag Mahashaya brought rice, cooking pot and fuel, etc., from the bazar and began to cook. We thought that we would eat and make Nag Mahashaya also eat. Cooking over, he gave the food to us; we set apart something for him and then sat down to eat. After this, we requested him to take food; he at once broke the pot of rice and striking his forehead began to say : 'Shall I give food to the body in which God has not been realized?' Seeing this we were struck with amazement. Later on, after much persuasion we induced him to take some food and then returned."

Swamiji :—Will Nag Mahashaya stay in the Math tonight?

Disciple :—No, he has some work; he must return today.

Swamiji :—Then look for a boat. It is getting dark.

When the boat came, the disciple and Nag Mahashaya saluted Swamiji and started for Calcutta.

XXXII

BRAHMAN, ISHVARA, JIVA AND AVIDYA—RENUNCIATION AND SELF-REALIZATION—HOW TO CONTROL THE MIND—ATMAN AS THE OBJECT OF MEDITATION—JNANA, BHAKTI, KARMA AND YOGA—THE DOCTRINE OF INCARNATION OF GOD—EXHORTATION FOR SELF-REALIZATION—WORK OF A JNANI.

[Place : *Belur Math.* Year : *1899.*]

Swamiji is now in very good health. The disciple has come to the Math on a Sunday morning. After visiting Swamiji he has come downstairs and is discussing the Vedantic scriptures with Swami Nirmalananda. At this moment Swamiji himself came downstairs and addressing the disciple said, "What were you discussing with Nirmalananda ?"

Disciple :—Sir, he was saying, "The Brahman of the Vedanta is only known to you and your Swamiji. We on the contrary know— कृष्णस्तु भगवान् स्वयं —that Sri Krishna is the Lord Himself."

Swamiji :—What did you say?

Disciple :—I said that the Atman is the one Truth, and that Krishna was merely a person who had realized this Atman. Swami Nirmalananda is at heart a believer in the Vedanta—but outwardly he takes up the dualistic side of arguments. His first idea seems to be to moot the personal aspect of the Ishvara and then by a gradual process of reasoning to strengthen the foundations of Vedanta. But as soon as he calls me a "Vaishnava" I forget his real intention and begin a heated discussion with him.

Swamiji :—He loves you and so enjoys the fun of teasing you. But why should you be upset by his words? You will also answer, "You, sir, are an atheist, a believer of Nihility."

Disciple :—Sir, is there any such statement in the Upanishads that Ishvara is an all-powerful Personality? But people generally believe in such an Ishvara.

Swamiji :—The highest principle, the Lord of all, cannot be a Person. The Jiva is an individual and the sum total of all Jivas is the Ishvara. In the Jiva, Avidyâ or Nescience, is predominant, but the Ishvara controls Mâyâ composed of Avidyâ and Vidyâ and independently projects this world of movable and immovable things out of Himself. But Brahman transcends both the individual and collective aspects, the Jiva and Ishvara. In Brahman there is no part. It is for the sake of easy comprehension that parts have been imagined in It. That part of Brahman in which there is the superimposition of creation, maintenance and dissolution of the universe, has been spoken of as Ishvara in the scriptures. While the other unchangeable portion, with reference to which there is no thought of duality, is indicated as Brahman. But do not on that account think that Brahman is a distinct and separate substance from the Jivas and the universe. The Qualified Monists hold that it is Brahman that has transformed Itself into Jivas and the universe. The Advaitins on the contrary maintain that on the Brahman, Jivas and the universe have been merely superimposed. But in reality there has been no modification in the Brahman. The Advaitin says that the universe consists only in name and form. It endures only so long as there are name and form. When through meditation and other practices name and form are dissolved, then only the transcendent Brahman remains. Then the separate reality of Jivas and the universe is felt no longer. Then it is realized that I am the Eternal, Pure Essence of Intelligence or Brahman. The real nature of the Jiva is Brahman. When the veil of name and form vanishes through meditation etc., then that idea is simply realized. This is the substance of pure Advaita. The Vedas, the Vedanta and all other scriptures only explain this idea in different ways.

Disciple:—How then is it true that the Ishvara is an almigthy Person?

Swamiji:—Man is man in so far as he is qualified by the limiting adjunct of mind. Through the mind he has to understand and grasp everything, and therefore whatever he thinks must be limited by the mind. Hence it is the natural tendency of man to argue, from the analogy of his own personality, the personality of Ishvara (God). Man can only think of his ideal as a human being. When buffeted by sorrows in this world of disease and death he is driven to desperation and helplessness, then he seeks refuge with someone, relying on whom he may feel safe. But where is that refuge to be found. The omnipresent Atman which depends on nothing else to support It, is the only Refuge. At first man does not find that. When discrimination and dispassion arise in the course of meditation and spiritual practices, he comes to know it. But in whatever way he may progress on the path of spirituality, everyone is unconsciously awakening the Brahman within him. But the means may be different in different cases. Those who have faith in the Personal God, have to undergo spiritual practices holding on to that idea. If there is sincerity, through that will come the awakening of the lion of Brahman within. The knowledge of Brahman is the one goal of all beings but the various ideas are the various paths to it. Although the real nature of the Jiva is the Brahman, still as he has identification with the qualifiying adjunct of mind, he suffers from all sorts of doubts and difficulties, pleasure and pain. But everyone from Brahmâ down to a blade of grass is advancing towards the realization of his real nature. And none can escape the round of births and deaths until he realizes his identity with the Brahman. Getting the human birth, when the desire for freedom becomes very strong, and along with it comes the grace of a person of realization, then man's desire for Self-knowledge becomes intensified. Otherwise the mind of men given to lust and wealth never inclines that way. How should the desire to know Brahman arise in one who has the hankering in his mind for the pleasures of family-life, for wealth and for fame? He who is prepared to renounce all, who amid the strong current of the duality of good and evil, happiness and misery, is calm, steady, balanced, and awake to his Ideal, alone endeavours to attain to Self-knowledge. He alone by the might of his own power tears asunder the net of the world, and breaking the barriers of Maya emerges like a mighty lion—निर्गच्छति जगज्जालात् पिञ्जरादिव केसरी ।

Disciple :—Well then, is it true that without Sannyâsa, there can be no knowledge of Brahman ?

Swamiji :—That is true, a thousand times. One must have both internal and external Sannyâsa—renunciation in spirit as well as formal renunciation. Shankarâchârya in commenting on the Upanishadic text, "Neither by Tapas (spiritual practice) devoid of the necessary accompaniments," has said that by practising Sâdhanâ without the external badge of Sannyâsa (the geruâ-robe, the staff and Kamandalu, etc.), the Brahman, which is difficult to attain, is not realized. Without dispassion for the world, without renunciation, without giving up the desire for enjoyment, absolutely nothing can be accomplisned in the spiritual life. "It is not like a sweetmeat in the hands of a child which you can snatch by a trick."*

Disciple :—But, sir, in the course of spiritual practices, that renunciation may come.

---

* Song of Ramprasâd. a Saint and Poet of Bengal.

Swamiji :—Let those to whom it will come gradually, have it in that way. But why should you sit and wait for that? At once begin to dig the channel which will convey the waters of spirituality to your life. Sri Ramakrishna used to deprecate lukewarmness in spiritual attainments, as for instance, saying that religion would come gradually, and that there was no hurry for it. When one is thirsty, can one sit idle? Does he not run about for water? Because your thirst for spirituality has not come, therefore you are sitting idly. The desire for knowledge has not grown strong, therefore you are satisfied with the little pleasures of family life.

Disciple :—Really I do not understand why I don't get that idea of renouncing everything. Do make some way for that, please.

Swamiji :—The end and the means are all in your hands. I can only stimulate them. You have read so many scriptures and are serving and associating with the Brahmajnâni Sâdhus (Monks who have known Brahman)—if even this does not bring the idea of renunciation, then your life is in vain. But it will not be altogether vain—the effects of this will manifest some way or other in time.

The disciple was much dejected and then again addressing Swamiji said, "Sir, I have come under your refuge, do open the path of Mukti for me—that I may realize the Truth in this body."

Swamiji :—What fear is there ? Always discriminate—your body, your house, these Jivas and the world are all absolutely unreal like a dream. Always think that this body is only an inert instrument. And the self-contained Purusha within is your real nature. The adjunct of mind is His first and subtle covering, then, there is this body which is His gross, outer covering. The indivisible, changeless, self-effulgent Purusha is lying hidden under these delusive veils, therefore your real nature is unknown to you. The direction of the mind which always runs after the senses has to be turned within. The mind has to be killed. The body is but gross—it dies and dissolves in the five elements. But the bundle of mental impressions which is the mind, does not die soon. It remains for some time in seed-form and then sprouts and grows in the form of a tree—it takes on another physical body and goes the round of birth and death—until Self-knowledge arises. Therefore do I say that by meditation and concentration and by the power of philosophical discrimination plunge this mind in the Ocean of Existence-Knowledge-Bliss Absolute. When the mind dies, all limiting adjuncts vanish and you are established in the Brahman.

Disciple :—Sir, it is so difficult to direct this uncontrollable mind towards the Brahman.

Swamiji :—Is there anything difficult for the hero? Only men of faint hearts speak so. वीराणामेव करतलगता मुक्तिः, न पुनः कापुरुषाणाम् —"Mukti is easy of attainment only to the hero—but not to the cowards." Says the Gitâ, अभ्यासेन तु कौन्तेय वैराग्येन च गृह्यते —"By renunciation and by practice is the mind brought under control, O Arjuna." The Chitta or mind-stuff is like a transparent lake, and the waves which rise in it by the impact of sense-impressions constitute Manas or the mind. Therefore the mind consists of a succession of thought-waves. From these mental waves arises desire. Then that desire transforms itself into will and works through its gross instrument, the body. Again as work is endless, so its fruits also are endless. Hence the mind is always being tossed by the countless myriads of waves—the fruits of work. This mind has to be divested of all modifications (Vrittis) and reconverted into the transparent lake, so that there remains not a single wave of modification in it. Then will the Brahman manifest Itself. The scriptures give a glimpse of this state in such passages as, "Then all the knots of the heart are cut asunder," etc. Do you understand?

Disciple:—Yes, sir, but meditation must base itself on some object?

Swamiji:—You yourself will be the object of your meditation. Think and meditate that you are the omnipresent Atman. "I am neither the body, nor the mind, nor the Buddhi (determinative faculty), neither the gross nor the subtle body"—by this process of elimination, immerse your mind in the transcendent knowledge which is your real nature. Kill the mind by thus plunging it repeatedly in this. Then only you will realize the Essence of Intelligence, or be established in your real nature. Knower and known, meditator and object meditated upon, will then become one, and the cessation of all phenomenal superimpositions will follow. This is styled in the Shâstras as the transcendence of the triad of relative knowledge (Triputibheda). There is no relative or conditioned knowledge in this state. When the Atman is the only knower, by what means can you possibly know It? The Atman is Knowledge, the Atman is Intelligence, the Atman is Sacchidânanda. It is through that inscrutable power of Mâyâ which cannot be indicated as either existent or non-existent that the relative consciousness has come upon the Jiva who is none other than Brahman. This is

TALKS WITH SWAMI VIVEKANANDA

generally known as the conscious state. And the state in which this duality of relative existence becomes one in the pure Brahman, is called in the scriptures the superconscious state and described in such words as, स्तिमितसलिलराशिप्रख्यमाख्या विहीनम् —"It is like an ocean perfectly at rest and without a name."

Swamiji spoke these words as if from within the profound depths of the realization of Brahman.

Swamiji :—All philosophy and scriptures have come from the plane of relative knowledge of subject and object. But no thought or language of the human mind can fully express the Reality which lies beyond the plane of relative knowledge! Science and philosophy etc., are only partial truths. So they can never be the adequate channels of expression for the transcendent reality. Hence viewed from the transcendent standpoint, everything appears to be unreal—religious creeds, and works, I and thou, and the universe—everything is unreal! Then only it is perceived that I am the only reality; I am the all-pervading Atman, and I am the proof of my own existence. Where is the room for a separate proof to establish the reality of my existence? I am, as the scriptures say, नित्यमस्मत्प्रसिद्धम्—"always known to myself as the eternal subject." I have actually seen that state, realized it. You also see and realize it and preach this truth of Brahman to all. Then only would you attain to peace.

While speaking these words, Swamiji's face wore a serious expression and he was lost in thought. After some time he continued: "Realize in your own life this knowledge of Brahman which comprehends all theories, and is the *rationale* of all truths, and preach it to the world. This will conduce to your own good and the good of others as well. I have told you today the essence of all truths; there is nothing higher than this."

Disciple :—Sir, now you are speaking of Jnâna; but sometimes you proclaim the superiority of Bhakti, sometimes of Karma, and sometimes of Yoga. This confuses our understanding.

Swamiji :—Well, the truth is this, the knowledge of Brahman is the ultimate goal—the highest destiny of man. But man cannot remain absorbed in Brahman all the time! When he comes out of It he must have something to engage himself. At that time he should do such work as will contribute to the real well-being of people. Therefore do I urge you in the service of Jivas in a spirit of oneness. But my son, such are the intricacies of work, that even great saints are caught in them and become attached. Therefore work has to be done without any desire for results. This is the teaching of the Gitâ. But know that in the knowledge of Brahman there is no touch of any relation with work. Good works, at the most, purify the mind. Therefore has the commentator Shankara so sharply criticized the doctrine of the combination of Jnana and Karma. Some attain to the knowledge of Brahman by means of unselfish work. This is also a means, but the end is the realization of Brahman. Know this thoroughly that the goal of the path of discrimination and of all other modes of practice is the realization of Brahman.

Disciple :—Now, sir, please tell me about the utility of Râja-Yoga and Bhakti-Yoga.

Swamiji :—Striving in these paths also some attain to the realization of Brahman. The path of Bhakti, or devotion to God, is a slow process, but is easy of practice. In the path of Yoga there are many obstacles; perhaps the mind runs after the psychic powers and thus draws you away from attaining your real nature. Only the path of Jnana is of quick fruition and the *rationale* of the other creeds; hence it is equally esteemed in all countries and all ages. But even in the path of discrimination there is the chance of the mind getting stuck in the interminable net of vain argumentation. Therefore along with it meditation should be practised. By means of discrimination and meditation, the goal, or Brahman, has to be reached. One is sure to reach the goal by practising in this way. This, in my opinion, is the easy path ensuring quick success.

Disciple :—Now please tell me something about the doctrine of Incarnation of God.

Swamiji :—You want to master everything in a day, it seems!

Disciple :—Sir, if the doubts and difficulties of the mind be solved in one day, then I shall not have to trouble you time and again.

Swamiji :—By whose grace the knowledge of this Atman which is extolled so much in the scriptures, is attained in a minute, they are the moving Tirthas (seats of holiness)—the Incarnations. From their very birth they are knowers of Brahman, and between Brahman and the knower of Brahman there is not the least difference. ब्रह्म वेद ब्रह्मैव भवति —"He who knows the Brahman becomes the Brahman." The Atman cannot be known by the mind for It is Itself the Knower—this I have already said. Therefore man's relative knowledge reaches up to the

Avatâras—those who are always established in the Atman. The highest ideal of Ishvara which the human mind can grasp is the Avatara. Beyond this there is no relative knowledge. Such knowers of Brahman are rarely born in the world. And very few people can understand them. They alone are the proof of the truths of scriptures—the pillars of light in the ocean of the world. By the company of such Avataras and by their grace, the darkness of the mind disappears in a trice—and realization flashes immediately in the heart. Why or by what process it comes it cannot be ascertained. But it does come. I have seen it happen like that. Sri Krishna spoke the Gitâ, establishing Himself in the Atman. Those passages of the Gitâ where references to the word "I" occur, invariably indicate the Atman : "Take refuge in Me alone"—means, "be established in the Atman." This knowledge of the Atman is the highest aim of the Gitâ. The references to Yoga etc., are but incidental to this realization of the Atman. Those who have not this knowledge of the Atman are "suicides". "They kill themselves by the clinging to the unreal"—they lose their life in the noose of sense-pleasures. You are also men, and can't you ignore this trash of sensual enjoyment that won't last for two days ? Should you also swell the ranks of those who are born and die in utter ignorance ? Accept the "beneficial" and discard the "pleasant". Speak of this Atman to all, even to the lowest. By continued speaking your own intelligence also will clear up. And always repeat the great Mantras— तत्त्वमसि —"Thou art That," सोऽहमस्मि—"I am That," सर्वं खल्विदं ब्रह्म,—"All this is Brahman"—and have the courage of a lion in the heart. What is there to fear ? Fear is death—fear is the greatest sin. The human soul, represented by Arjuna, was touched with fear—therefore Bhagavân Sri Krishna, established in the Atman, spoke to him the teachings of the Gitâ. Still his fear would not leave him. Later, when Arjuna saw the Universal Form of the Lord, and became established in the Atman, then with all bondages of Karma burnt by the fire of knowledge, he fought the battle.

Disciple :—Sir, can a man do work even after realization ?

Swamiji :—After realization, what is ordinarily called work does not persist. It changes its character. The work which the Jnani does only conduces to the well-being of the world. Whatever a man of realization says or does contributes to the welfare of all. We have observed Sri Ramakrishna—he was, as it were, देहस्योऽपि न देहस्थः: —"in the body but not of it!"

TALKS WITH SWAMI VIVEKANANDA

About the motive of the actions of such personages only this can be said—लोकवत्तु लीलाकैवल्यम्—"Everything they do like men is simply by way of sport."

XXXIII

ON ART—DIFFERENCE BETWEEN INDIAN AND WESTERN ARTS—SEAL OF THE RAMAKRISHNA MISSION, ITS SIGNIFICANCE—PLAN OF THE RAMAKRISHNA TEMPLE.

[Place : *Belur Math*. Year : *1901*.]

The disciple has come to the Math today accompanied by Srijut Ranadaprasad Das Gupta, the founder and professor of the Jubilee Art Academy, Calcutta. Ranada Babu is an expert artist, a learned man and an admirer of Swamiji. After the exchange of courtesies, Swamiji began to talk with Ranada Babu on various topics relating to art.

Swamiji :—I had the opportunity of seeing the beauties of art of nearly every civilized country in the world, but I saw nothing like the development of art which took place in our country during the Buddhistic period. During the regime of the Moghul Emperors also, there was a marked development of art—and the Taj and the Jumma Masjid etc., are standing monuments of that culture.

Art has its origin in the expression of some idea in whatever man produces. Where there is no expression of idea, however much there may be a display of colours and so on, it cannot be styled as true art. Even the articles of everyday use, such as water vessels, or cups and saucers, should be fashioned so as to express an idea. In the Paris Exhibition I saw a wonderful figure carved in marble. In explanation of the figure, the following words were inscribed underneath : Art unveiling Nature That is, how Art sees the inner beauty of Nature by drawing away with its own hands the covering veils. The work has been so designed as to indicate that the beauty of Nature has not yet become fully unveiled ; but the artist is fasicanted, as it were, with the beauty of the little that has become manifest. One cannot refrain from praising the sculptor who has tried to express this exquisite idea. You should also try to produce something original like this.

Ranada Babu :—Yes, I also have the desire to do some original modelling at leisure. But I meet with no encouragement in this country ; it is a poor country and there is want of appreciation.

Swamiji :—If you can with your whole heart produce one real thing, if you can rightly express a single idea in art, it must win appreciation in course of time. A real thing never suffers from want of appreciation in this world. It is also heard that some artists have gained appreciation for their works a thousand years after their death!

Ranada Babu :—That is true. But we have become so worthless, that we haven't got the courage to spend a lot of energy to no purpose. Through these five years' struggle I have succeeded to some extent. Bless me that my efforts be not in vain.

Swamiji :—If you set to work in right earnest, then you are sure to be successful. Whoever works at a thing heart and soul, not only achieves success in it, but through his absorption in that he also realizes the supreme Truth—Brahman. Whoever works at a thing with his whole heart, receives help from God.

Ranada Babu :—What difference did you find between the art of the West and that of India ?

Swamiji :—It is nearly the same everywhere. Originality is rarely found. In those countries pictures are painted with the help of models obtained by photographing various objects. But no sooner does one take the help of machinery than all originality vanishes—one cannot give expression to one's ideas. The ancient artists used to evolve original ideas from their brains and try to express them in their paintings. Now the picture being a likeness of photographs, the power of originality and the attempt to develop are getting scarce. But each nation has a Characteristic of its own. In its manners and customs, in its mode of living in painting and sculpture is found the expression of that characteristic idea. For instance, music and dancing in the West are all pointed in their expression. In dance, they look as if jerking the limbs; in instrumental music, the sounds prick the ear like a sword thrust, as it were; so also in vocal music. In this country, on the other hand, the dance has a rolling wave-like movement and there is the same rounded movement in the varieties of pitch in vocal song. So also in instrumental music. Hence with regard to art also, a different expression is found among different people. People who are very materialistic take Nature as their ideal, and try to express in art ideas allied thereto. While the people whose ideal is the transcendent Reality beyond Nature try to express that in art through the powers of Nature. With regard to the former class of people, Nature is the primary basis of art, while with the second class, ideality is the principal motive of artistic development. Thus, though starting with two different deals in art, they have advanced in it each in its own way. Seeing some paintings in the West you will mistake them for real natural objects. With respect to this country also, when in ancient times sculpture attained a high degree of perfection, if you look at a statue of the period it will make you forget the material world and transport you to a new ideal world. As in Western countries paintings like those of the ancient are not produced now, so in our country also, attempts to give expression to original ideas in art are no longer seen. For example, the paintings from your art school have got no expression, as it were. It would be well, if you try to paint the objects of everyday meditation of the Hindus by giving in them the expression of ancient ideals.

Ranada Babu :—I feel much encouraged by your words. I shall try to act up to your suggestions.

Swamiji :—Take, for instance, the figure of Mother Kâli. In it there is the union of the blissful and terrible aspects. But in none of the pictures can be seen the true expression of these two aspects. Far from this, there is no attempt to express adequately even one of these two aspects! I have tried to put down some ideas of the terrible aspect of Mother Kali in my English poem, *"Kali the Mother"*, can you express those ideas in a picture?

Ranada Babu :—Please let me know them.

Swamiji had the poem brought from the library, and began to read it out most impressively to Ranada Babu. Ranada Babu silently listened to the poem, and after a while, as if visualizing the figure with his mind's eye, he turned to Swamiji with frightened looks.

Swamiji :—Well, will you be able to express this idea, in the picture?

Ranada Babu :—Yes, I shall try;* but it turns one's head even to imagine the idea.

Swamiji :—After drawing the picture, please show it to me. Then I will tell you about the points necessary to perfect it.

Then Swamiji had the design which he had sketched for the seal of the Ramakrishna Mission brought, showed it to Ranada Babu and asked his opinion on it. It depicted a lake in which a lotus blossomed, and there was a swan, and

---

* Ranada Babu began to paint this picture the very next day, but it was never finished, nor shown to Swamiji.

the whole was encircled by a serpent. Ranada Babu at first could not catch the significance of it and asked Swamiji to explain. Swamiji said: "The wavy waters in the picture are symbolic of Karma, the lotus, of Bhakti and the rising-sun, of Jnâna. The encircling serpent is indicative of Yoga and the awakened Kundalini Shakti, while the swan in the picture stands for the Paramâtman. Therefore, the idea of the picture is that by the union of Karma, Jnana, Bhakti and Yoga, the vision of the Paramatman is obtained."

Ranada Babu kept silent, gratified to hear the *motif* of the picture. After a while he said, "I wish I could learn about art from you!"

Then Swamiji showed to Ranada Babu a drawing depicting his plan of the future Ramakrishna Temple and Math. Then he began to say: "In the building of this prospective Temple and Math I have the desire to bring together all that is best in Eastern and Western art. I shall try to apply in its construction all the ideas about architecture which I have gathered in my travels all over the world. A big prayer-hall will be built supported on numerous clustered pillars. In its walls, hundreds of lotuses will be in full bloom. It must be big enough to accommodate a thousand person sitting in meditation. The Ramakrishna temple and prayer-hall should be built together in such a way that from a distance it would be taken for a representation of the symbol, 'Om'. Within the temple there would be a figure of Sri Ramakrishna seated on a swan. On the two sides of the door will be represented the figure of a lion and a lamb licking each other's body in love—expressing the idea that great power and gentleness have become united in love. I have these ideas in my mind; and if I live long enough I shall carry them out. Otherwise future generations will try if they can do it by degrees. It is my opinion that Sri Ramakrishna was born to vivify all branches of art and culture in this country. Therefore this Math has to be built up in such a way that Religion, work, learning, Jnana and Bhakti may spread over the world from this centre. Be you my helpers in this work."

Ranada Babu and the assembled Sannyâsins and Brahmachârins listened to Swamiji in mute wonder. After a while Swamiji resumed, "I am discussing the subject at length with you as you are yourself adept in the line. Now please tell me what you have learnt about the highest ideals of art as the result of your long study of it."

Ranada Babu:—What new thing can I tell you? On the contrary, it is you who have opened my eyes on this subject. I have never heard such instructive words on the subject of art in my life. Bless me, sir, that I can work out the ideas I have got from you.

Then Swamiji got up from his seat and paced the lawn, remarking to the disciple. "He is a very spirited young man."

Disciple:—Sir, he is astonished to hear your words.

Swamiji, without answering the disciple, began to hum the lines of a song which Sri Ramakrishna used to sing, "The controlled mind is a great treasure, the philosopher's stone, which can yield you whatever you want."

After walking a while, Swamiji washing his face entered his room with the disciple in company and read the article on Art in the *Encyclopaedia Britannica* for some time. After finishing it, he began to make fun with the disciple caricaturing the words and accents of East Bengal.

XXXIV

A POWER WORKING THROUGH SWAMI VIVEKANANDA—REMINISCENCE OF EAST BENGAL AND THE VISIT TO NAG MAHASHAYA'S HOUSE—RENUNCIATION AND NOT THE OBSERVANCE OF EXTERNAL FORMS IS THE TEST OF SPIRITUAL PROGRESS—FIRM DETERMINATION NEEDED TO REALIZE THE SELF.

[Place : *Belur Math.* Year : *1901.*]

Swamiji has returned from East Bengal and Assam a few days back. He is ill, and his feet have swollen. Coming to the Math, the disciple went upstairs and prostrated himself at Swamiji's feet. In spite of his illhealth, Swamiji wore his usual smiling face and affectionate look.

Disciple :—How are you, Swamiji ?

Swamiji :—What shall I speak of my health, my son ? The body is getting unfit for work day by day. It has been born on the soil of Bengal, and some disease or other is always overtaking it. The physique of this country is not at all good. If you want to do some strenuous work, it cannot bear the strain. But the few days that the body lasts, I will work for you. I shall die in harness.

Disciple :—If you give up work for some time and take rest, then you will be all right.

Your life means good to the world.

Swamiji :—Am I able to sit quiet, my son? Two or three days before Sri Ramakrishna's passing away, She whom he used to call "Kâli" has entered this body. It is She who takes me here and there and makes me work, without letting me remain quiet, or allowing me to look to my personal comforts.

Disciple :—Are you speaking it metaphorically?

Swamiji :—Oh, no; two or three days before his leaving the body, he called me to his side one day, and asking me to sit before him, looked steadfastly at me and fell into Samâdhi. Then I really felt that a subtle force like an electric shock was entering my body! In a little while, I also lost outward consciousness and sat motionless! How long I stayed in that condition I do not remember; when consciousness returned I found Sri Ramakrishna shedding tears. On questioning him, he answered me affectionately: "Today, giving you my all I have become a beggar. With this power you are to do many works for the world's good before you will return." I feel that that power is constantly directing me to this or that work. This body has not been made for remaining idle.

Hearing these words with speechless wonder

the disciple thought—who knows how common people will take these words? Thereupon he changed the topic and said, "Sir, how did you like our East Bengal?"

Swamiji:—I liked it on the whole. The fields, I saw, were rich in crops, the climate also is good, and the scenery on the hill-side is charming. The Brahmaputra Valley is incomparable in its beauty. The people of East Bengal are a little stronger and more active than those of this part. It may be due to their taking plenty of fish and meat. Whatever they do, they do with great persistence. They use a good deal of oil and fat in their food, which is not good, because taking too much of oily and fatty food produces fat in the body.

Disciple:—How did you find their religious consciousness?

Swamiji:—About religious ideas, I noticed the people are very conservative, and many have turned into fanatics in trying to be liberal in religion. One day a young man brought to me in the house of Mohini Babu at Dacca, a photograph and said, "Sir, please tell me who he is. Is he an Avatâra?" I told him gently many times that I know nothing of it. When even on my telling him three or four times the boy did not cease from his persistent questioning,

I was constrained to say at last: "My boy, henceforth take a little nutritious food and then your brain will develop. Without nourishing food, I see your brain has become dried up." At these words the young man may have been much displeased. But what could I do? Unless I spoke like this to the boys, they would turn into madcaps by degrees.

Disciple:—In our East Bengal a great many Avataras have cropped up recently.

Swamiji:—People may call their Guru an Avatara; they may have any idea of him they like. But Incarnations of God are not born anywhere and everywhere and at all seasons. At Dacca itself I heard there were three or four Avataras!

Disciple:—How did you find the women of that side?

Swamiji:—The women are very nearly the same everywhere. I found Vaishnavism strong at Dacca. The wife of H—seemed to be very intelligent. With great care she used to prepare food and send it to me.

Disciple:—I hear you had been to Nâg Mahâshaya's place.

Swamiji:—Yes, going so far, should I not visit the birthplace of such a great soul? His wife fed me with many delicacies prepared by her own hand. The house is charming, like a peace retreat. There I took a swimming bath in a village pond. After that I had such a sound sleep that I woke at half past two in the afternoon. Of the few days I had sound sleep in my life, that in Nâg Mahâshaya's house was one. Rising from sleep I had a plentiful repast. Nâg Mahâshaya's wife presented me a cloth which I tied round my head as a turban and started for Dacca. I found that the photograph of Nâg Mahâshaya was being worshipped there. The place where his remains lie interned ought to be well kept. Even now it is not as it should be.

Disciple :—The people of that part have not been able to appreciate Nâg Mahâshaya.

Swamiji :—How can ordinary people appreciate a great man like him ? Those who had his company are blessed indeed.

Disciple :—What did you see at Kamakhya ?

Swamiji :—The Shillong hills are very beautiful. There I met Sir Henry Cotton, the Chief Commissioner of Assam. He asked me, "Swamiji, after travelling Europe and America, what have you come to see here in these distant hills ?" Such a good and kindhearted man as Sir Henry Cotton is rarely found. Hearing of my illness, he sent the Civil Surgeon and inquired after my health mornings and evenings. I could not do much lecturing there, because my health was very bad. On the way Nitai served and looked after me nicely.

Disciple :—What did you find the religious ideas of that part to be?

Swamiji :—It is the land of the Tantras. I heard of one "Hankar Deva" who is worshipped there as an Avatara. I heard his sect is very wide-spread. I could not ascertain if "Hankar Deva" was but another form of the name of Shankarâchârya. They are monks—perhaps Tântrika Sannyâsins. Or perhaps one of the Shankara sects.

Disciple :—The people of East Bengal have not been able to appreciate you as is the case with Nâg Mahâshaya.

Swamiji :—Whether they appreciate me or not, the people there are more active and energetic than those of these parts. In time it will develop more. What are nowadays known as refined or civilized ways have not yet thoroughly entered those parts. Gradually they will. In all times, etiquette and fashion spread to the country side from the capital. And this is happening in East Bengal also. The land that has produced a great soul like Nâg Mahâshaya is blessed and has a hopeful future. By the light of his personality Eastern Bengal is radiant.

Disciple :—But, sir, ordinary people did not know him as a great soul. He hid himself in great obscurity.

Swamiji :—There they used to make much fuss about my food and say, "Why should you eat that food or eat from the hands of such and such?"—and so on. To which I had to reply, "I am a Sannyâsin and a mendicant friar and what need have I to observe so much outward formality with regard to food etc.?" Do not your scriptures say—चरेन्माधुकरीं वृत्तिमपि म्लेच्छकुलादपि —"One should beg his food from door to door, aye even from the house of an outcast"? But of course external forms are necessary in the beginning, for the inner realization of religion, in order to make the truth of the scriptures practical in one's life. Haven't you heard of Sri Ramakrishna's story of "wringing out the almanac for water"?* Outward forms and observances are only for the manifestation of the great inner powers of man. The object of all scriptures is to awaken those inner powers and make him understand and realize his real nature. The means are of the nature of ordin-

---

* The Bengali almanac makes a forecast of the annual rainfall but not a drop comes out of squeezing the pages of the book! Similarly scriptural truths have to be *realized* in life.

ances and prohibitions. If you lose sight of the ideal and fight over the means only, what will it avail? In every country I have visited, I find this fighting over the means going on and people have no eye on the ideal. Sri Ramakrishna came to show the truth of this.

Realization of the truth is the essential thing. Whether you bathe in the Ganga for a thousand years or live on vegetable food for a like period, unless it helps towards the manifestation of the Self, know that it is all of no use. If on the other hand any one can realize the Atman, without the observance of outward forms, then that very non-observance of forms is the best means. But even after the realization of Atman, one should observe outward forms to a certain extent for setting an example to the people. The thing is you must make the mind steadfast on something. If it is steadfast on one object, it attains to concentration, that is, its other modifications die out and there is a uniform flow in one direction. Many become wholly pre-occupied with the outward forms and observances merely, and fail to direct their mind to thoughts of the Atman! If you remain day and night within the narrow groove of ordinances and prohibitions, how will there be any expression of the soul? The more one has advanced in the realization of the Atman, the less is he dependent on the observances of forms. Shankaracharya also has said, निस्त्रैगुण्ये पथि विचरतं को विधि: को निषेध: —"Where is there any ordinance or prohibition for him whose mind is always above the play of the Gunas?" Therefore the essential truth is Realization. Know that to be the goal. Each distinct creed is but a way to the Truth. The test of progress is the amount of renunciation that one has attained. Where you find the attraction for lust and wealth considerably diminished, to whatever creed he may belong, know that his inner spirit is awakening. The door of Self-realization has surely opened for him. On the contrary if you observe a thousand outward rules, and quote a thousand scriptural texts, still, if it has not brought the spirit of renunciation in you, know that your life is in vain. Be earnest over this realization and set your heart on it. Well, you have read enough of scriptures. But tell me, of what avail has it been? Some perhaps thinking of money have become millionaires, whereas you have become a Pandit by thinking of scriptures. But both are bondages. Attain the supreme knowledge and go beyond Vidyâ and Avidyâ, relative knowledge and ignorance.

Disciple:—Sir, through your grace I understand it all, but my past Karma does not allow me to assimilate these teachings.

Swamiji :—Throw aside your Karma and all such stuff. If it is a truth that by your own past action you have got this body, then nullifying the effects of evil works by good works, why should you not be a Jivanmukta in this very body ? Know that Freedom or Self-knowledge is in your own hands. In real knowledge there is no touch of work. But those who work after being Jivanmuktas do so for the good of others. They do not look to the results of works. No seed of desire finds any room in their mind. And strictly speaking it is almost impossible to work like that for the good of the world from the householder's position. In the whole of Hindu scriptures there is the single instance of King Janaka in this respect. But you nowadays want to pose as Janakas (lit. fathers) in every home by begetting children year after year, while he was without the body-consciousness!

Disciple :—Please bless me that I may attain Self-realization in this very life.

Swamiji :—What fear ? If there is sincerity of spirit, I tell you, for a certainty, you will attain it in this very life. But manly endeavour is wanted. Do you know what it is ? "I shall certainly attain Self-knowledge. Whatever obstacles may come, I shall certainly overcome them"—a firm determination like this is Purushakâra. "Whether my mother, father, friends, brothers, wife and children live or die, whether this body remains or goes, I shall never turn back till I attain to the vision of the Atman"— this resolute endeavour to advance towards one's goal, setting at naught all other considerations, is termed manly endeavour. Otherwise, endeavour for creature comforts even beasts and birds possess. Man has got this body simply to realize Self-knowledge. If you follow the common run of people in the world and float with the general current, where then is your manliness? Well, the common people are going to the jaws of death! But you have come to conquer it! Advance like a hero. Don't be thwarted by anything. How many days will this body last, with its happiness and misery? When you have got the human body, then rouse the Atman within and say—I have reached the state of fearlessness! Say—I am that Atman in which my lower ego has become merged for ever. Be perfect in this idea; and then as long as the body endures, speak unto others this message of fearlessness—"Thou art That," "Arise, awake and stop not till the goal is reached!"

If you can achieve this, then shall I know that you are really a tenacious East Bengal man.

XXXV

PLAN OF THE FUTURE MATH FOR WOMEN—SOUL HAS NO SEX—WOMEN HAVE EQUAL OPPORTUNITY FOR REALIZING THE BRAHMAN—RELIGION TO BE THE CENTRE OF FEMALE EDUCATION—DEFINITION OF GOOD WORK—WORK AND KNOWLEDGE.

[Place : *Belur Math*. Year : *1901*.]

Swamiji is in indifferent health since his return to the Math from the Shillong hills. His feet have swollen. All this has made his brother-disciples very anxious. At the request of Swami Niranjanananda Swamiji has agreed to take Kaviraji medicine. He is to begin this treatment from next Tuesday and entirely give up taking water and salt. Today is Sunday. The disciple asked him, "Sir, it is terribly hot now and you drink water very frequently ; it will be unbearable for you now to stop taking water altogether for this treatment."

Swamiji :—What do you say ? I shall make a firm resolve on the morning of the day I shall begin this treatment, not to take any water. After that no water shall pass down the throat any more. For three weeks not a drop of water shall be able to go down the throat. The body is but an outer covering of the mind and whatever the mind will dictate to it, it will have to carry out. So there is nothing to be afraid of. At the request of Niranjan I have to undergo this treatment. Well, I cannot be indifferent to the request of my brother-disciples.

It is now about ten o'clock. Swamiji cheerfully raised the topic of his future Math for women, saying : "With the Holy Mother as the centre of inspiration a Math is to be established on the eastern bank of the Ganga. As Brahmachârins and Sâdhus will be trained in this Math, so in the other Math also, Brahmachârinis and Sâdhvis will be trained.

Disciple :—Sir, history does not tell us of any Maths for women in India in ancient times. Only during the Buddhistic period one hears of Maths for women; but from it in course of time many corruptions arose. The whole country was overrun by great evil practices.

Swamiji :—It is very difficult to understand why in this country so much difference is made between men and women, whereas the Vedanta declares that one and the same conscious Self is present in all beings. You always criticize the women, but say, what have you done for their uplift ? Writing down Smritis etc., and binding them by hard rules, the men have turned the women into mere manufacturing machines! If you do not raise the women who are the living embodiment of the Divine Mother, don't think that you have any other way to rise.

Disciple :—Women are a bondage and a snare to men. By their Mâyâ they cover the knowledge and dispassion of men. It is for this I suppose that scriptural writers hint that knowledge and devotion are difficult of attainment to them.

Swamiji :—In what scriptures do you find statements that women are not competent for knowledge and devotion ? In the period of degradation, when the priests made the other castes incompetent to the study of the Vedas, they deprived the women also of all their rights. Otherwise you will find that in the Vedic or Upanishadic age Maitreyi, Gârgi and other ladies of revered memory have taken the places of Rishis through their skill in discussing about Brahman. In an assembly of a thousand Brâhmanas who were all erudite in the Vedas, Gargi boldly challenged Yâjnavalkya in a discussion about Brahman. When such ideal women were entitled to spiritual knowledge, then why shall not the women have the same privilege now ? What has happened once can certainly happen again. History repeats itself. All nations have attained greatness, by paying proper respect to the women. That country and that nation which do not respect the women have never become great, nor will ever be in future. The principal reason why your race has so much degenerated is that you had no respect for these living images of Shakti. Manu says, "Where women are respected there the gods delight; and where they are not, there all works and efforts come to naught."* There is no hope of rise for that family or country where there is no estimation of women, where they live in sadness. For this reason, they have to be raised first; and an ideal Math has to be started for them.

Disciple :—Sir, when you first returned from the West, in your lecture at the Star Theatre you sharply criticized the Tantras. Now by your supporting the worship of women as taught in the Tantras, you are contradicting yourself.

Swamiji :—I denounced only the present corrupted form of Vâmâchâra of the Tantras. I did not denounce the Mother-worship of the Tantras, or even the real Vâmâchâra. The purport of the Tantras is to worship women in a spirit of Divinity. During the downfall of

* III—56.

Buddhism, the Vâmâchâra became very much corrupted, and that corrupted form obtains to the present day. Even now the Tantra literature of India is influenced by those ideas. I denounced only these corrupt and horrible practices—which I do even now. I never objected to the worship of women who are the living embodiment of Divine Mother, whose external manifestations appealing to the senses have maddened men, but whose internal manifestations such as knowledge, devotion, discrimination and dispassion make man omniscient, of unfailing purpose, and a knower of Brahman. सैषा प्रसन्ना वरदा नृणां भवति मुक्तये—"She when pleased becomes propitious and the cause of the freedom of man." (*Durga Sapta Sati*, I. 57) Without propitiating the Mother by worship and obeisance not even Brahmâ and Vishnu have the power to elude Her grasp and attain to freedom. Therefore for the worship of these family goddesses, in order to manifest the Brahman within them, I shall establish the women's Math.

Disciple :—It may be a good idea, but where will you get the women inmates ? With the present hard restrictions of society, who will permit the ladies of their household to join your Math ?

Swamiji :—Why so ? Even now there are

lady disciples of Sri Ramakrishna. With their help I shall start this Math. The Holy Mother will be their central figure and the wives and daughters of the devotees of Sri Ramakrishna will be its first inmates. For they will easily appreciate the usefulness of such a Math. After that, following their example, many householders will help in this noble work.

Disciple:—The devotees of Sri Ramakrishna will certainly join this work. But I don't think the general public will help in this work.

Swamiji:—No great work has been done in the world without sacrifice. Who on seeing the tiny sprout of the Banyan can imagine that in course of time it will develop into a gigantic Banyan tree? At present I shall start the Math in this way. Later on you will see that after a generation or two people of the country will appreciate the worth of this Math. The lady-disciples of mine will lay down their lives for it. Casting off fear and cowardice, you also be helpers in this noble mission, and hold this high ideal before all. You will see, it will shed its lustre over the whole country in time.

Disciple:—Sir, please tell me all about your plan of this Math for women.

Swamiji:—On the other side of the Ganga a big plot of land would be acquired, where unmarried girls or Brahmachârini widows will live; devout married ladies will also be allowed to stay now and then. Men will have no concern with this Math. The elderly Sadhus of the Math will manage the affairs of this Math from a distance. There shall be a girls' school attached to this female Math, in which religious scriptures, literature, Sanskrit, grammar and even some amount of English should be taught. Other matters such as sewing, culinary art, rules of domestic work, and upbringing of children will also be taught. While Japa, worship and meditation, etc., shall form an indispensable part of the teaching. Those who will be able to live here permanently, renouncing home and family ties, will be provided with food and clothing from this Math. Those who will not be able to do that will be allowed to study in this Math as day-scholars. With the permission of the head of the Math the latter will be allowed even to stay in the Math occasionally, and during such stay will be maintained by the Math. The elder Brahmachârinis will take charge of the training of the girl stduents in Brahmacharya. After five or six year's training in this Math, the guardians of the girls may give them in marriage. If deemed fit for Yoga and religious life, with the permission of their guardians they will be allowed to stay in this Math, taking the vow of celibacy. These celibate nuns will in time be the teachers and preachers of the Math. In villages and towns they will open centres and strive for the spread of women's education. Through such devout preachers of character there will be the real spread of women's education in the country. So long as the students will remain in association with this Math, they must observe Brahmacharya as the basic idea of this Math.

Spirituality, sacrifice and self-control will be the motto of the pupils of this Math, and service, or Seva-Dharma, the vow of their life. In view of such ideal lives, who will not respect and have faith in them ? If the life of the women of this country be moulded in such fashion, then only will there be the re-appearance of such ideal characters as Sitâ, Sâvitri and Gârgi. To what straits the strictures of local usages have reduced the women of this country, rendering them lifeless and inert, you could only understand if you visited the Western countries. You alone are responsible for this miserable condition of the women, and it rests with you also to raise them again. Therefore I say, set to work. What will it do to memorise a few religious books like the Vedas and so on ?

Disciple :—Sir, if the girl students after

being trained in this Math marry, how will one find ideal characters in them? Will it not be better if the rule is made that those who will be educated in this Math shall not marry?

Swamiji :—Can that be brought about all at once? They must be given education and left to themselves. After that they will act as they think best. Even after marriage and entering the world, the girls educated as above will inspire their husbands with noble ideals and be the mothers of heroic sons. But there must be this rule that the guardians of the students in the women's Math must not even think of giving them in marriage, before they attain the age of fifteen.

Disciple :—Sir, then those girls will not command reputation in society. Nobody would like to marry them.

Swamiji :—Why will not they be wanted in marriage? You have not yet understood the trend of society. These learned and accomplished girls will never be in want of bridegrooms. Society nowadays does not follow the texts recommending child-marriage nor will do it in future. Even now don't you see?

Disciple :—But there is sure to be a violent opposition against this in the beginning.

Swamiji :—Let it be. What is there to be

afraid of in that? Opposition to a righteous work initiated with moral courage will only awaken the moral power of the initiators the more. That which meets with no obstruction, no opposition, only takes men to the path of moral death. Struggle is the sign of life.

Disciple:—Yes, sir.

Swamiji:—In the highest truth of the Parabrahman, there is no distinction of sex. We only notice this in the relative plane. And the more the mind becomes introspective, the more that idea of difference vanishes. Ultimately when the mind is wholly merged in the homogenous and undifferentiated Brahman, then such ideas as this is a man or that a woman do not remain at all. We have actually seen this in the life of Sri Ramakrishna. Therefore do I say that though outwardly there may be difference between men and women, in their real nature there is none. Therefore if a man can be a knower of Brahman, why cannot a woman attain to the same knowledge? Therefore I was saying that if even one amongst the women became a knower of Brahman, then by the radiance of her personality thousands of women would be inspired and awakened to truth, and great well-being of the country and society would ensure. Do you understand?

Disciple:—Sir, your teachings have opened my eyes today.

Swamiji:—Not fully yet. When you will realize that all-illumining truth of the Atman, then you will see that this idea of sex-distinction has vanished altogether, then only will you look upon all women as the veritable manifestation of the Brahman. We have seen in Sri Ramakrishna how he had this idea of divine motherhood in every woman, of whatever caste she might be, or whatever might be her worth. It is because I have seen this that I ask you all so earnestly to do likewise and open girls' schools in every village and try to uplift them. If the women are raised, then their children will by their noble actions glorify the name of the country—then will culture, knowledge, power and devotion awaken in the country.

Disciple:—But, sir, contrary results appear to have come out of the present women's education. With a smattering of education, they take merely to the Western modes of living, but it is not clear how far they are advancing in the spirit of renunciation, self-control, austerity, Brahmacharya and other qualities conducive to Brahmajnâna.

Swamiji:—In the beginning a few mistakes like that are unavoidable. When a new idea is preached in the country, some failing to grasp it properly go wrong in that way. But what matters it to the well-being of society at large? Well, those who are pioneers of the little bit of women's education that now obtains in the country, were undoubtedly very great-hearted. But the truth is that some defect or other must creep into that learning of culture which is not founded on a religious basis. But now women's education is to be spread with religion as its centre. All other training should be secondary to religion. Religious training, the formation of character and observance of the vow of celibacy—these should be attended to. In the women's education which has obtained up till now in India, it is religion that has been made a secondary concern, hence those defects you were speaking of have crept in. But no blame attaches therefore to the women. Reformers having proceeded to start women's education without being Brahmachârins themselves have stumbled like that. Founders of all good undertakings, before they launch on their desired work, must attain to the knowledge of the Atman through rigorous self-discipline. Otherwise defects are bound to occur in their work.

Disciple:—Yes, sir, it is observed that many educated women spend their time in reading novels and so on; but in East Bengal even with education women have not given up their religious observances. Is it so here in this part?

Swamiji :—In every country, nations have their good and bad sides. Ours is to do good works in our lives and hold an example before others. No work succeeds by condemnation. It only repels people. Let anybody say what he likes, don't contradict him. In this world of Mâyâ, whatever work you will take up will be attended with some defect—सर्वारम्भा हि दोषेण धूमेनाग्निरिवावृताः —"All works are covered with derects as fire is with smoke." (*Gita, xviii.* 48) Every fire has a chance of being attended with smoke. But will you, on that account, sit inactive? As far as you can, you must go on doing good work.

Disciple :—What is this good work?

Swamiji :—Whatever helps the manifestation of Brahman is good work. Any work can be done so as to help, if not directly, at least indirectly, the manifestation of the Atman. But following the path laid down by the Rishis, that knowledge of the Atman manifests quickly; on the contrary, the doing of works which have been indicated by the scriptural writers as wrong, brings only bondage of the soul and sometimes this bondage of delusion does not vanish even in many lives. But in all ages and climes, freedom is sure to be attained by Jivas ultimately. For, the Atman is the real nature of the Jiva. Can anybody give up his own nature? If you fight with your shadow for a thousand years, can you drive it away from you?—it will always remain with you.

Disciple :—But, sir, according to Shankara, Karma is antagonistic to Jnâna. He has variously refuted the intermingling of Jnana and Karma. So how can Karma be helpful to the manifestation of Jnana?

Swamiji :—Shankara after saying so has again described Karma as indirect help to the manifestation of Jnana and the means for the purification of the mind. But I do not contradict his conclusion that in transcendent knowledge there is no touch of any work whatsoever. So long as man is within the realm of the consciousness of action, agent and the result of action, he is powerless to sit idle without doing some work. So, as work is thus ingrained in the very nature of man, then why don't you go on doing such works as are helpful to the manifestation of the knowledge of the Atman? That all work is the effect of ignorance may be true from the absolute standpoint, but within the sphere of relative consciousness it has a great utility. When you will realize the Atman, the doing or non-doing of work will be within your control, and whatever you will do in that state will be good work, conducive to the well-being of Jivas and the world. With the manifestation of Brahman, even the breath you draw will be to the good of Jivas. Then you will no longer have to work by means of conscious planning. Do you understand ?

Disciple :—Yes, it is a beautiful conclusion reconciling Karma and Jnana from the Vedantic standpoint.

At this time, the bell for supper rang, and the disciple before going to partake of it, prayed with folded hands, "Bless me, sir, that I may attain to the knowledge of Brahman in this very life." Swamiji placing his hand on the disciple's head said, "Have no fear, my son. You are not like ordinary worldly men—neither householders, nor exactly Sannyâsins—but quite a new type."

XXXVI

SWAMI VIVEKANANDA'S WONDERFUL MEMORY—
HIS OPINION ABOUT BHARATCHANDRA AND MICHAEL
MADHUSUDAN DUTT, TWO BENGALI POETS.

[Place : *Belur Math*. Year : *1901*.]

Swamiji is in indifferent health. At the earnest request of Swami Niranjanananda he has been taking Kaviraji medicines for six or seven days. According to this treatment, the drinking of water is strictly forbidden. He has to appease his thirst with milk.

The disciple has come to the Math early in the day. Swamiji on seeing him spoke with affection, "Oh, you have come ? Well done, I was thinking of you."

Disciple : —I hear that you are living on milk for the last six or seven days.

Swamiji : —Yes, at the earnest entreaty of Niranjan, I had to take to this medicine! I cannot disregard their request.

Disciple : —You were in the habit of taking water too frequently. How could you give it up altogether ?

Swamiji : —When I heard that according to this treatment water had to be given up, I made a firm resolve immediately not to take water. Now the idea of drinking water does not even occur to the mind.

Disciple : —The treatment is doing you good I hope ?

Swamiji : —That I don't know. I am simply obeying the orders of my brother-disciples.

Disciple : —I think that indigenous drugs such as the Vaids use, are very well-suited to our constitution.

Swamiji :—My idea, is, that it is better even to die under the treatment of a scientific doctor than expect recovery from the treatment of laymen who know nothing of modern science, but blindly go by the ancient books, without gaining a mastery of the subject—even though they may have cured a few cases.

Swamiji cooked certain dishes, one of which was prepared with vermicelli. When the disciple, who partook of it, asked Swamiji what it was, he replied, "It is a few English earthworms which I have brought dried from London." This created a laughter among those present at the expense of the disciple. Despite his spare food and scanty sleep, Swamiji is very active. A few days ago, a new set of Encyclopedia Britannica had been bought for the Math. Seeing the new shining volumes, the disciple said to Swamiji, "It is almost impossible to read all these books in a single life-time." He was unaware that Swamiji had already finished ten volumes and had begun the eleventh.

Swamiji :—What do you say ? Ask me anything you like from these ten volumes and I will answer you all.

The disciple asked in wonder, "Have you read all these books ?"

Swamiji :—Why should I ask you to question

me otherwise?

Being examined Swamiji reproduced not only the sense, but at places the very language of the difficult topics selected from each volume. The disciple being astonished put aside the books, saying, "This is not within human power!"

Swamiji :—Do you see, simply by the observance of strict Brahmacharya (continence) all learning can be mastered in a very short time— one has an unfailing memory of what one hears or knows but once. It is owing to this want of continence that everything is on the brink of ruin in our country.

Disciple :—Whatever you may say, sir, the manifestation of such superhuman power cannot be the result of mere Brahmacharya, something else there must be.

Swamiji did not say anything in reply.

Then Swamiji began to explain lucidly to the disciple the arguments and conclusions about the difficult points in all philosophies. In course of the conversation Swami Brahmananda entered the room and said to the disciple : "You are a nice man! Swamiji is unwell. and instead of trying to keep his mind cheerful by light talk, you are making him talk incessantly, raising the most abstruse subjects!" The disciple was abashed. But Swamiji said to Swami Brahmananda : "Keep your regulation of Kaviraji treatment aside. These are my children; and if my body goes in teaching them, I don't care." After this, some light talk followed. Then arose the topic of the place of Bhâratchandra in Bengali literature. From the beginning Swamiji began to ridicule Bhâratchandra in various ways and satirised the life, manners, marriage-customs and other usages of the society at the time of Bhâratchandra, who was an advocate of child-marriage. He expressed the opinion that the poems of Bhâratchandra being full of bad taste and obscenities had not found acceptance in any cultured society except in Bengal, and said, "It should be guarded that such books do not come into the hands of boys." Then raising the topic of Michael Madhusudan Dutt he added : "That was a wonderful genius born in your province. There is not another epic in Bengali literature like the *Meghnâdbadh*, no mistake in that; and it is difficult to come across a poem like that in the whole of modern European literature."

Disciple :—But, sir, I think Michael was very fond of a bombastic style.

Swamiji :—Well, if anybody in your country does anything new, you at once hoot him. First examine well what he is saying, but instead of that, the people of the country will chase after anything which is not quite after the old modes. For example, in order to bring to ridicule this *Meghnâdbadh Kâvya* which is the gem of Bengali literature, the parody of *Chhuchhundaribadh Kâvya* (The Death of a Mole) was written. They may caricature as much as they like, it does not matter. But the *Meghnâdbadh Kâvya* still stands unshaken in its reputation like the Himalayas. While the opinions and writings of carping critics who are busy picking holes in it, have been washed away into oblivion. What will the vulgar public understand of the epic Michael has written in such a vigorous diction and an original metre? And at the present time Girish Babu is writing wonderful books in a new metre which your overwise Pandits are criticising and finding fault with. But does G. C. care for that? People will appreciate the books afterwards.

Thus speaking on the subject of Michael he said, "Go and get the *Meghnâdbadh Kâvya* from the library downstairs." On the disciple's bringing it he said, "Now read, let me see how you can read it."

The disciple read a portion, but the reading not being to the liking of Swamiji, he took the book and showed him how to read and asked him to read again. Then he asked him, "Now, can you say which portion of the Kâvya is the best?" The disciple failing to answer, Swamiji said: "That portion of the book which describes that Indrajit has been killed in battle and Mandodari, beside herself with grief, is dissuading Râvana from the battle—but Râvana casting off forcibly from his mind the grief for his son is firmly resolved on battle like a great hero, and forgetting in a fury of rage and vengeance all about his wife and children, is ready to rush out for battle—that is the most finely conceived portion of the book. Come what may, I shall not forget my duty, whether the world remains or dissolves—these are the words of a great hero. Inspired by such feelings Michael has written that portion."

Saying this Swamiji opened the particular passage and began to read it in the most impressive manner.

XXXVII

WHY ATMAN IS NOT PERCEIVED, THOUGH SO VERY NEAR—ON SELF-REALIZATION ALL QUESTIONINGS CEASE—MOTHER KALI.

[Place : *Belur Math.* Year : *1901.*]

Swamiji is much better under the Kavirâji treatment. The disciple is at the Math. While attending on Swamiji, he asked, "The Atman is all-pervading, the very life of the life of all beings and so very near, still why is It not perceived?"

Swamiji:—Do you see yourself that you have eyes? When others speak of the eyes, then you are reminded that you have got eyes. Again when dust or sand enters into them and sets up an irritation then you feel quite well that you have got eyes. Similarly the realization of this universal Atman which is inner than the innermost is not easily attained. Reading from scriptures or hearing from the lips of the preceptor, one has some idea of It, but when the hard lashes of the bitter sorrow and pain of the world make the heart sore, when on the death of one's near and dear relatives, man thinks himself helpless, when the impenetrable and insurmountable darkness about the future life agitates his mind, then does the Jiva pant for a realization of the Atman. Therefore is sorrow helpful to the knowledge of the Atman. But one should remember the bitter lessons of experience. Those who die, merely suffering the woes of life like cats and dogs, are they men? He is a man who even when agitated by the sharp interaction of pleasure and pain is discriminating, and knowing them to be of an evanescent nature, becomes passionately devoted to the Atman. This is all the difference between men and animals. That which is nearest is least observed. The Atman is the nearest of the near, therefore the careless and unsteady mind of man gets no clue to It. But the man who is alert, calm, self-restrained and discriminating, ignores the external world and diving more and more into the inner world, realizes the glory of the Atman and becomes great. Then only he attains to the knowledge of the Atman, and realizes the truth of such scriptural texts as, "I am the Atman," "Thou art That, O Svetaketu," and so on. Do you understand?

Disciple :—Yes, sir. But why this method of attaining Self-knowledge through the path of pain and suffering? Instead of all this, it would have been well if there had been no creation at all. We were all at one time identified with the Brahman. Why then this desire for creation on the part of the Brahman? Why again this going forth of the Jiva (who is no other than Brahman) along the path of birth and death, amidst the interaction of the dualities of life?

Swamiji :—When a man is intoxicated, he sees many hallucinations; but when the intoxication goes off, he understands them as the imaginations of a heated brain. Whatever you see of this creation which is without a beginning, but has an end, is only an effect of your state of intoxication; when that passes off, such questions will not arise at all.

Disciple:—Then is there no reality in the creation and preservation etc., of the Universe?

Swamiji:—Why should not there be? So long as you identify yourself with the body and have the ego-consciousness, all these will remain. But when you are bereft of the body-consciousness and devoted to the Atman and live in the Atman, then with respect to you none of these will remain, and such questions as whether there is any creation, or birth or death—will have no room. Then you will have to say,

क्व गतं केन वा नीतं कुत्र लीनमिदं जगत् ।
अधुनैव मया दृष्टं नास्ति किं महदद्भुतम् ॥

—"Where is it gone, by whom is it taken, wherein is the world merged? It was just observed by me and is it non-existent now? What a wonder!"

—*Vivekachudâmani.* 483

Disciple:—If there is no knowledge of the existence of the universe, how can it be said, "Wherein is the world merged?"

Swamiji:—Because one has to express the idea in language, therefore that mode of expression has been used. The author has tried to

TALKS WITH SWAMI VIVEKANANDA 347

express in thought and language about the state where thought or language cannot reach, and therefore he has stated the fact that the world is wholly unreal, in a relative mode like the above. The world has no absolute reality which only belongs to Brahman, which is beyond the reach of mind and speech. Say what more you have to ask. Today I will put an end to all your arguments.

The bell of evening service in the worship-room rang at the time, and everybody made for it. But the disciple stayed in Swamiji's room, noticing which Swamiji said, "Won't you go to the worship-room?"

Disciple :—I would like to stay here.

Swamiji :—All right.

After some time the disciple looking outside of the room said, "It is the new-moon night and all the quarters are overspread with darkness. It is the night for the worship of Mother Kâli."

Swamiji without saying anything gazed at the eastern sky for some time and said, "Do you see what a mysterious and solemn beauty there is in this darkness!" Saying this and continuing to look at the dense mass of darkness he stood enwrapt. After some minutes had passed, Swamiji slowly began to sing a Bengali song, "O Mother, in deep darkness flashes Thy formless beauty," etc. After the song Swamiji entered his room and sat down with an occasional word like "Mother," "Mother," or "Kâli," "Kâli," on his lips.

Uneasy at Swamiji's profoundly abstracted mood, the disciple said, "Now, sir, please speak with me."

Swamiji smilingly said, "Can you fathom the beauty and profundity of the Atman, whose eternal manifestation is so sweet and beautiful?". The disciple wished for a change of topic, noticing which Swamiji began another song of Kâli : "O Mother, Thou flowing stream of nectar, in how many forms and aspects dost Thou play in manifestation!" After the song he said, "This Kâli is the Brahman in manifestation. Haven't you heard Sri Ramakrishna's illustration of the 'snake moving and the snake at rest' (representing the dynamic and static aspects of the same thing)?"

Disciple :—Yes, sir.

Swamiji :—This time, when I get well, I shall worship the Mother with my heart's blood, then only will She be pleased. Your Raghunandan also says like that. The Mother's child shall be a hero, a Mahâvira. In unhappiness, sorrow, death and desolation, the Mother's child shall always remain fearless.

XXXVIII

WANTED A STURDY BAND OF YOUNG MEN READY TO SACRIFICE ALL FOR OTHERS—MANLINESS SHOULD BE THE IDEAL—REMEDY AGAINST LOW SPIRITS AND WEAKNESS OF MIND—WORK FOR OTHERS—NO INDIVIDUAL LIBERATION BEFORE THE SALVATION OF ALL—INFLUENCE OF THOUGHTS.

[Place : *Belur Math.* Year : *1901.*]

Swamiji is staying at the Math nowadays. His health is not very good—but he goes out for a walk in the mornings and evenings. The disciple, after bowing at the feet of Swamiji, enquired about his health.

Swamiji :—Well, this body is in such a pitiable condition, but none of you are stepping forward to help in my work! What shall I do single-handed? This time the body has come out of the soil of Bengal, so can it bear the strain of much work? You who come here are pure souls and if you do not be my helpers in this work, what shall I do alone?

Disciple :—Sir, these self-sacrificing Brahmachârins and Sannyâsins are standing behind you, and I think that each one of them can devote his life to your work—still why do you say so?

Swamiji :—Well, I want a band of young Bengal who alone are the hope of the country.

My hope of the future lies in the youths of character—intelligent, renouncing all for the service of others, and obedient—who can sacrifice their lives in working out my ideas and thereby do good to themselves and the country at large. Otherwise, boys of the common run are coming in groups and will come. Dullness is written on their face—their heart is devoid of energy, their body feeble and unfit for work, and mind devoid of courage. What work will be done by these? If I get ten or twelve boys with the faith of Nachiketa, I can turn the thoughts and pursuits of this country in a new channel.

Disciple :—Sir, so many young men are coming to you, and do you find none among them of such a nature?

Swamiji :—Among those who appear to me to be of good calibre, some have bound themselves by matrimony, some have sold themselves for the acquisition of worldly name, fame or wealth, while some are of feeble bodies. The rest who form the majority, are unable to receive any high idea. You are no doubt fit to receive my high ideas, but you are not able to work them out in the practical field. For these reasons sometimes an anguish comes into the mind and I think that taking this human body through untowardness of fortune, I could not do much work. Of course, I have not yet wholly given up hopes, for, by the will of God, from among these very boys may arise in time great heroes of action and spirituality who will in future work out my ideas

Disciple :—It is my firm belief that your broad and liberal ideas must find universal acceptance some day or other. For I see, they are all-sided and infusing vigour into every department of thought and activity. And the people of the country are accepting, either overtly or covertly your ideas, and teaching them to the people.

Swamiji :—What matters it if they acknowledge my name or not ? It is enough if they accept my ideas. Ninety-nine per cent. of the Sâdhus, even after renouncing lust and wealth, get bound at last by the desire of name and fame. "Fame...that last infirmity of noble mind"—haven't you read ? We shall have to work, giving up altogether all desire for results. People will call us both good and bad. But we shall have to work like lions, keeping the ideal before us, without caring whether "the wise ones praise or blame us."

Disciple :—What ideal should we follow now ?

Swamiji:—You have now to make the character of Mahâvira your ideal. See how at the command of Râmachandra he crossed the ocean! He had no care for life or death! He was a perfect master of his senses and wonderfully sagacious. You have now to build your life on this great ideal of personal service. Through that all the other ideals will gradually manifest in life. Obedience to the Guru without questioning, and strict observance of Brahmacharya—this is the secret of success. As on the one hand Hanumân represents the ideal of service, so on the other he represents leonine courage, striking the whole world with awe. He has not the least hesitation in sacrificing his life for the good of Râma. A supreme indifference to everything except the service of Râma, even to the attainment of the status of Brahmâ and Shiva, the great World-Gods! Only the carrying out of Sri Râma's behest is the one vow of his life! Such whole-hearted devotion is wanted. Playing on the Khol and Kartâl and dancing in the frenzy of Kirtana has degenerated the whole people. They are, in the first place, a race of dyspeptics—and if in addition to this they dance and jump in that way, how can they bear the strain? In trying to imitate the highest Sâdhanâ the preliminary qualification for which is absolute purity, they have been swallowed in dire Tamas. In every district and village you may visit, you will find only the sound of the Khol and Kartal! Are not drums made in the country? Are not trumpets and kettle-drums available in India? Make the boys hear the deep-toned sound of these instruments. Hearing from boyhood the sound of these effeminate forms of music and listening to the Kirtan, the country is well-nigh converted into a country of women. What more degradation can you expect? Even the poet's imagination fails to draw this picture! The Damaru* and horn have to be sounded, drums are to be beaten so as to raise the deep and martial notes and with "Mahâvira, Mahâvira" on our lips and shouting "Hara, Hara, Vyom, Vyom," the quarters are to be reverberated. The music which awakens only the softer feelings of man is to be stopped now for some time. Stopping the light tunes such as Kheâl and Tappâ for some time, the people are to be accustomed to hear the Dhrupad music. Through the thunder-roll of the dignified Vedic hymns, life is to be brought back into the country. In everything the austere spirit of heroic manhood is to be revived. In following such an ideal lies the good of the

* An hour-glass-shaped drum, held in Shiva's hand.

people and the country. If you can build your character after such an ideal, then a thousand others will follow. But take care that you do not swerve an inch from the ideal. Never lose heart. In eating, dressing or lying, in singing or playing, in enjoyment or disease, always manifest the highest moral courage. Then only will you attain the grace of Mahâshakti, the Divine Mother.

Disciple :—Sir, at times I am overcome by low spirits, I don't know how.

Swamiji :—Then think like this : "Whose child am I ? I associate with him and shall I have such weak-mindedness and lowness of spirits ?" Stamping down such weakness of mind and heart, stand up saying, "I am possessed of heroism—I am possessed of a steady intellect—I am a knower of Brahman, a man of illumination." Be fully conscious of your dignity by remembering, "I am the disciple of such and such who is the companion-in-life of Sri Ramakrishna, the conqueror of lust and wealth." This will produce a good effect. He who has not this pride, has no awakening of the Brahman within him. Haven't you heard Ramprasâd's song ? He used to say, "Whom do I fear in the world, whose sovereign is the Divine Mother!"

Keep such a pride always awake in the mind. Then weakness of mind and heart will no longer be able to approach you. Never allow weakness to overtake your mind. Remember Mahâvira, remember the Divine Mother! And you will see that all weakness, all cowardice will vanish at once.

Saying these words, Swamiji came downstairs and took his accustomed seat on a cot in the courtyard. Then addressing the assembled Sannyâsins and Brahmachârins he said : "Here is the unveiled presence of the Brahman. Fie upon those who disregarding It set their mind on other things! Ah! here is the Brahman as palpable as a fruit in one's palm. Don't you see ? Here!"

These words were spoken in such an appealing way, that every one stood motionless like a figure painted on canvas—and felt as if he were suddenly drawn into the depth of meditation....After some time that tension of feeling passed and they regained their normal consciousness.

Next in the course of a walk Swamiji spoke to the disciple : "Did you see how everybody had to become concentrated today ? These are all children of Sri Ramakrishna, and on the very uttering of the words, they felt the truth."

Disciple :—Sir, not to speak of them, even my heart was overflowing with an unearthly bliss! But now it appears like a vanished dream.

Swamiji :—Everything will come in time. Now, go on working. Set yourself to some work for the good of men sunk in ignorance and delusion. You will see that such experiences will come of themselves.

Disciple :—I feel nervous to enter into its labyrinths—neither have I the strength. The scriptures also say, "Impenetrable is the path of Karma."

Swamiji :—What do you like to do then ?

Disciple :—To live and hold discussion with one like you, who has realized the truth of all scriptures and through hearing, thinking and meditating on the Truth to realize the Brahman in this very life. I have no enthusiasm nor perhaps the strength for anything else.

Swamiji :—If you love that, well, you can go on doing it. And speak your thoughts and conclusions about the Shâstras to others, it will benefit them. So long as there is the body, one cannot live without doing some work or other ; therefore one should do such work as is conducive to the good of others. Your own realizations and conclusions about scriptural truths may benefit many a seeker after Truth. Put them into writing which may help many others.

Disciple :—First let me realize the Truth, then I shall write. Sri Ramakrishna used to say : "Without the badge of authority, none will listen to you."

Swamiji :—There may be many in the world who have got stuck in that stage of spiritual discipline and reasoning through which you are passing, without being able to pass beyond that stage. Your experience and way of thinking if recorded, may be of benefit to them at least. If you put down in easy language the substance of the discussions which you hold with the Sâdhus of this Math, it may help many.

Disciple :—Since you are wishing it, I shall try to do it.

Swamiji :—What is the good of that spiritual practice or realization which does not benefit others, does not conduce to the well-being of people sunk in ignorance and delusion, does not help in rescuing them from the clutches of lust and wealth ? Do you think, so long as one Jiva endures in bondage, you will have any liberation ? So long as he is not liberated—it may take several life-times—you will have to be born to help him, to make him realize the Brahman. Every Jiva is part of yourself—which is the *rationale* of all work for others. As you desire the whole-hearted good of your wife and children, knowing them to be your own, so when a like amount of love and attraction for every Jiva will awaken in you, then I shall know that the Brahman is awakening in you, not a moment before. When this feeling of the all-round good of all without respect to caste or colour will awaken in your heart, then I shall know you are advancing towards the ideal.

Disciple :—Sir. it is a most tremendous statement that without the salvation of all, there shall be no salvation for an individual! I have never heard of such a wonderful proposition.

Swamiji :—There is a class of Vedantists who hold such a view. They say that individual liberation is not the real and perfect form of liberation, but universal and collective liberation is true Mukti. Of course, both merits and defects can be pointed out in that view.

Disciple :—According to Vedanta, the state of individualized existence is the root of bondage, and the Infinite Intelligence, through desires and effects of works, appears bound in that limiting condition. When by means of discrimination that limiting condition vanishes and the Jiva is bereft of all adjuncts, then how can there be bondage for the Atman which is of the essence of transcendent Intelligence? He for whom the idea of the Jiva and the world is a persisting reality may think that without the liberation of all he has no liberation. But when the mind becomes bereft of all limiting adjuncts and is merged in the Brahman, where is there any differentiation for him? So nothing can operate as a bar to his Mukti.

Swamiji:—Yes, what you say is right, and most Vedantins hold that view, which is also flawless. In that view, individual liberation is not barred. But just consider the greatness of his heart who thinks that he will take the whole universe with him to liberation!

Disciple:—Sir, it may indicate boldness of heart but it is not supported by the scriptures.

Swamiji was in an abstracted mood and did not listen to the words. After some time he said, "Day and night think and meditate on the Brahman, meditate with great one-pointedness of mind. And during the time of awakeness to outward life, either do some work for the sake of others or repeat in your mind, "Let good happen to Jivas and the world"—"Let the mind of all flow in the direction of Brahman!" Even by such a continuous current of thought world will be benefited. Nothing good in the world becomes fruitless, be it work or thought.

Your thought-currents will perhaps rouse the religious feeling of someone in America.

Disciple :—Sir, please bless me that my mind may be concentrated on the Truth.

Swamiji :—So it will be. If you have earnestness of desire, it will certainly be.

XXXIX

SWAMI VIVEKANANDA'S PLAN TO CELEBRATE DURGA PUJA AT BELUR MATH—HIS VISIT TO THE TEMPLE AT KALIGHAT.

[Place : *The Math, Belur.* Year : 1901.]

At the time the Belur Math was established, many among the orthodox Hindus were wont to make sharp criticism of the ways of life in the Math. Hearing the report of such criticism from the disciple, Swamiji would say : (in the words of the couplet of Tulsidâs) "The elephant passes through the market-place, and a thousand curs begin barking after him; so the Sâdhus have no ill-feeling when worldly people slander them." Or again he would say, "Without persecution no beneficent idea can enter into the heart of a society." He would exhort everybody, "Go on working without an eye to results. One day you are sure to reap the fruits of it."

Again, on the lips of Swamiji were very often heard the words of the Gita, "A doer of good never comes to grief, my son."

In May or June, 1901, seeing the disciple at the Math, Swamiji said, "Bring me a copy of *Ashtâvimshati-tattwa* (Twenty-eight Categories) of Raghunandan at an early date."

Disciple :—Yes, sir, but what will you do with the Raghunandan Smriti—which the present educated India calls a heap of superstition ?

Swamiji :—Why ? Raghunandan was a wonderful scholar of his time. Collecting the ancient Smritis he codified the customs and observances of the Hindus, adapting them to the needs of the changed times and circumstances. All Bengal is following the rules laid down by him. But in the iron grip of his rules regulating the life of a Hindu from conception to death, the Hindu society was much oppressed. In matters of eating and sleeping, in even the ordinary functions of life, not to speak of the important ones, he tried to regulate every one by rules. In the altered circumstances of the times that did not last long. At all times in all countries the Karmakânda, comprising the social customs and observances, changes forms. Only the Jnânakânda endures. Even in the Vedic age you find that the rituals gradually changed in form. But the philosophic portion of the Upanishads has remained unchanged up till now —only there have been many interpreters, that is all.

Disciple :—What will you do with the Smriti of Raghunandan ?

Swamiji :—This time I have a desire to celebrate the Durgâ Pujâ. If the expenses are forthcoming I shall worship the Mahâmâyâ. Therefore I have a mind to read the ceremonial forms of that worship. When you come to the Math next Sunday, you must get a copy of the book with you.

Disciple :—All right, sir.

Next Saturday the disciple brought a copy of the book, and Swamiji was much pleased to get it. Meeting the disciple a week after this he said, "I have finished the Raghunandan Smriti presented by you. If possible, I shall celebrate the Puja of the Divine Mother."

The Durga Puja took place with great *éclat* at the proper time.

*

Shortly after this Swamiji performed a Homa before the Mother Kali at Kalighat. Referring to this incident he spoke to the disciple, "Well,

I was glad to see that there was yet a liberality of view at Kalighat. The temple authorities did not object in the least to my entering the temple, though they knew that I was a man who had returned from the West. On the contrary, they very cordially took me into the holy precints and helped me to worship the Mother to my heart's content."

XL

THE LAST BIRTHDAY ANNIVERSARY OF SRI RAMAKRISHNA THAT SWAMI VIVEKANANDA SAW—SWAMI VIVEKANANDA'S IDEA AS TO HOW THE CELEBRATION SHOULD TAKE PLACE—HOW FAR A GURU CAN HELP —WHAT IS MEANT BY GRACE—SWAMI VIVEKANANDA'S VISION OF SRI RAMAKRISHNA.

[Place : *The Math, Belur,* Year : 1902.]

Today is the anniversary celebration of Sri Ramakrishna—the last that Swamiji ever saw. The disciple presented an invocatory hymn on Sri Ramakrishna to Swamiji. He then proceeded to rub Swamiji's feet gently. Swamiji before starting to read the poem spoke to him, "Do it very gently as the feet have become very tender."

After reading the poem Swamiji said : "It is well done."

Swamiji's illness had increased so much that the disciple observing it felt sore at heart. Swamiji understanding his inner feelings said : "What are you thinking? This body is born and it will die. If I have been able to instil a few of my ideas into you all, then I shall know that my birth has not been in vain."

Disciple :—Are we fit objects of your grace? If you without taking my fitness into consideration bless me, then I will consider myself blessed.

Swamiji :—Always remember that renunciation is the root idea. Unless one is initiated into this idea, not even Brahmâ and the World-Gods have the power to attain Mukti.

Disciple :—It is a matter of deep regret that even hearing this from you almost every day, I have not been able to realize it.

Swamiji :—Renunciation must come, but in the fulness of time. कालेनात्मनि विन्दति—"In the fulness of time one attains to knowledge within himself." When the few Samskâras of previous life are spent, then renunciation sprouts up in the heart.

After some time he said : "Why should you go outside and see the big concourse of people?

Stay with me now. And ask Niranjan to sit at the door, so that nobody may disturb me today."

Then the following conversation took place between Swamiji and the disciple :

Swamiji :—I think that it will be better if from now the anniversary is celebrated in a different way. The celebration should extend to four or five days instead of one. On the first day, there may be study and interpretation of scriptures ; on the second, discussion on the Vedas and the Vedanta and solution of the problems in connection with them ; on the third day, there may be a question class. The fourth day may be fixed for lectures. On the last day, there will be a festival on the present lines. This will be like the Durgâ Pujâ extends for four or five days. Of course if the celebration is on the above lines none except the devotees of Sri Ramakrishna will be able to attend on the other days except the last. But that does not matter. A large promiscuous crowd of people does not mean a great propagation of the message of Sri Ramakrishna.

Disciple :—Sir, it is a beautiful idea. Next time it may be done according to your wishes.

Swamiji :—Now, my son, you all will carry them out. I have no more inclination for these things.

Disciple :—Sir, this year many Kirtan parties have come.

Hearing these words Swamiji stood up holding the iron bars of the window and looked at the assembled crowd of devotees. After some time he sat down.

Swamiji :—You are the actors in the Divine Lilâ of Sri Ramakrishna. After this, not to speak of ours, people will take your names also. These hymns which you are writing will afterwards be read by people for the acquirement of love and knowledge. Know that the attainment of the knowledge of the Atman is the highest object of life. If you have devotion for the Avatâras who are the world-teachers, that knowledge will manifest of itself in time.

Disciple :—Sir, shall I attain to such knowledge?

Swamiji :—By the blessings of Sri Ramakrishna you shall attain to divine love and knowledge. You will not find much happiness in the worldly life.

Disciple :—Sir, if you condescend to destroy the weaknesses of my mind, then only there is hope for me.

Swamiji :—What fear! When you have chanced to come here, you shall be free.

Disciple (with great entreaty):—You must

save me and lift me from ignorance in this very life.

Swamiji :—Say, who can save anybody ? The Guru can only take away some covering veils. When these veils are removed the Atman shines in Its own glory and manifests like the sun.

Disciple :—Then why do we find mention of grace in the scriptures ?

Swamiji :—Grace means this. He who has realized the Atman becomes a store-house of great power. Making him the centre and with a certain radius a circle is formed, and whoever comes within the circle becomes animated with the ideas of that saint, i.e., they are overwhelmed by his ideas. Thus without much religious striving they inherit the results of his wonderful spirituality. If you call this a grace, you may do it.

Disciple :—Is there no other grace than this ?

Swamiji :—Yes, there is. When the Avatâra comes, then with him are born liberated persons as helpers in his world-play. Only the Avatâra has the power to dispel the darkness of a million souls and give them salvation in one life. This is known as grace. Do you understand ?

Disciple :—Yes, sir. But what is the way

for those who have not been blessed with the sight of him?

Swamiji:—The way for them is to call on him. Calling on him, many are blessed with his vision—can see him in a human form just like ours and obtain his grace.

Disciple:—Have you ever had a vision of Sri Ramakrishna after his passing away?

Swamiji:—After his leaving the body, I associated for some time with Pâvhâri Bâbâ of Ghazipur. There was a garden not far distant from his Ashrama where I lived. People used to say it was a haunted garden, but as you know, I am a sort of demon myself and have not much fear of ghosts. In that garden there were many lemon trees which bore numerous fruits. At that time I was suffering from diarrhoea, and there no food could be had except bread. So, to increase the digestive powers I used to take plenty of lemons. Mixing with Pâvhâri Bâba, I liked him very much, and he also came to love me deeply. One day I thought that I did not learn any art for making this weak body strong, after living with Sri Ramakrishna for so many years. I had heard that Pâvhâri Bâba knew the science of Hatha-Yoga. So I thought I would learn the practices of Hatha-Yoga from him, and through them strengthen the body. You know,

I have a dogged resolution and whatever I set my heart on, I always carry out. On the eve of the day on which I was to take initiation, I was lying on a cot thinking, and just then I saw the form of Sri Ramakrishna standing on my right side, looking steadfastly at me, as if very much grieved. I had dedicated myself to him and at the thought that I was taking another Guru I was much ashamed and kept looking at him. Thus perhaps two or three hours passed, but no words escaped from my mouth. Then he disappeared all on a sudden. My mind became upset seeing Sri Ramakrishna that night, so I postponed the idea of initiation from Pâvhâri Bâba for the day. After a day or two again the idea of initiation from Pâvhâri Bâbâ arose in the mind—and again in the night there was the appearance of Sri Ramakrishna as on the previous occasion. Thus when for several nights in succession I got the vision of Sri Ramakrishna, I gave up the idea of initiation altogether, thinking that as every time I resolved on it, I was getting such a vision, then no good but harm would come from it.

After some time he addressed the disciple, saying : "Those who have seen Sri Ramakrishna are really blessed. Their family and birth have become purified by it. All of you will also get his vision. The very fact that you have come here, shows that you are very near to him. Nobody has been able to understand who came on earth as Sri Ramakrishna. Even his own nearest devotees have got no real clue to it. Only some have got a little inkling of it. All will understand it afterwards."

The conversation was thus going on when Swami Niranjanananda knocked at the door. The disciple rose and enquired, "Who has come?" Swami Niranjanananda said, "Sister Nivedita and some other English ladies." They were admitted into the room, sat on the floor and enquired about the health of Swamiji. After a few more words they went away. Then Swamiji said to the disciple, "See how cultured they are! If they were Bengalees, they would have made me talk, at least for half an hour, though they find me unwell."

It is about half past two now, and there is a great gathering of people on the outside. Swamiji understanding the disciple's mind, said, "Just go and have a look round—but come back soon."

XLI

SWAMI VIVEKANANDA'S LOVE AND SYMPATHY FOR THE POOR—"DON'T-TOUCHISM"—WHO SERVES JIVA, SERVES GOD INDEED.

[Place : *The Math, Belur.* Year : *1902.*]

After returning from East Bengal Swamiji stayed in the Math and lived a simple childlike life. Every year some Santal labourers used to work in the Math. Swamiji would joke and make fun with them and loved to hear their tales of weal and woe. One day several noted gentlemen of Calcutta came to visit Swamiji in the Math. That day Swamiji had started such a warm talk with the Santals, that when he was informed of the arrival of those gentlemen, he said, "I shan't be able to go now. I am happy with these men." Really that day Swamiji did not leave the poor Santals to see those visitors.

One among the Santals was named "Keshta". Swamiji loved Keshta very much. Whenever Swamiji came to talk with them, Keshta used to say to Swamiji, "O my Swami, do not come to us when we are working, for while talking with you our work stops and the supervising Swami rebukes us afterwards." Swamiji would be touched by these words and say, "No, no, he will not say anything; tell me a little about your part of the country,"—saying which he used to introduce the topic of their worldly affairs.

One day Swamiji said to Keshta, "Well, will you take food here one day?" Keshta said, "We do not take food touched by you; if you put salt in our food and we eat it, we shall lose our caste." Swamiji said, "Why should you take salt? We will prepare curry for you without salt, will you then take it?" Keshta agreed to it. Then at the orders of Swamiji, roti, curry, sweets, curds, etc., were arranged for the Santals and he made them sit before him to eat. While eating, Keshta said, "Whence have you got such a thing? We have never tasted anything like this." Swamiji feeding them sumptuously said, "You are Nârâyanas, God manifest; today I have offered food to Nârâyana." The service of "Daridra Nârâyana"—God in the poor—about which Swamiji spoke, he himself performed one day like this.

After meals, the Santals went for rest and Swamiji addressing the disciple said, "I found them the veritable embodiment of God—such simplicity, such sincere guileless love I have seen nowhere else." Then addressing the Sannyâsins of the Math he said: "See how simple they are, can you mitigate their misery a little ? Otherwise of what good is the wearing of the Geruâ robe ? Sacrifice of everything for the good of others is real Sannyâsa. They have never enjoyed any good thing in life. Sometimes I feel a desire to sell the Math and everything, and distribute the money to the poor and destitute. We have made the tree our shelter! Alas! the people of the country cannot get anything to eat, and how can we have the heart to raise food to our mouths ? When I was in the Western countries, I prayed to the Divine Mother, 'People here are sleeping on a bed of flowers, they eat all kinds of delicacies, and what do they not enjoy, While people in our country are dying of starvation. Mother, will there be no way for them!' One of the objects of my going to the West to preach religion was to see if I could find any means for feeding the people of this country.

"Seeing the poor people of our country starving for food a desire comes to me to overthrow all ceremonial worship and learning, and go round from village to village collecting money from the rich by convincing them through force of character and Sâdhanâ, and to spend the whole life in serving the poor.

"Alas! nobody thinks of the poor of the country. They are the backbone of the country, who by their labour are producing food—these poor people, the sweepers and labourers, who if they stop work for one day will create a panic in the town. But there is none to sympathise with them, none to console them in their misery. Just see, for want of sympathy from the Hindus thousands of Pariahs in Madras are turning Christians. Don't think this is simply due to the pinch of hunger; it is because they do not get any sympathy from us. We are day and night calling out to them, 'Don't touch us! Don't touch us!' Is there any compassion or kindliness of heart in the country? Only a class of 'Don't-touchists'; kick such customs out! I sometimes feel the urge to break the barriers of 'Don't-touchism,' go at once and call out, 'Come all who are poor, miserable, wretched and down-trodden,' and to bring them all together in the name of Sri Ramakrishna. Unless they rise, the Mother won't awaken. We could not make any provision for food and clothes for these—what have we done then? Alas! they know nothing of worldliness, and therefore even after working day and night cannot provide themselves with food and clothes. Let us open their eyes—I see clear as daylight that there is the one Brahman in all, in them and me—one Shakti dwells in all. The only difference is of manifestation. Unless the blood circulates over the whole body, has any country risen at any time? If one limb is paralysed, then even with the other limbs whole, not much can be done with that body—know this for certain."

Disciple:—Sir, there is such a diversity of religions and ideas among the people of this country, that it is a difficult affair to bring harmony among them.

Swamiji (in anger):—If you think any work difficult, then do not come here. Through the grace of God all paths become easy. Your work is to serve the poor and miserable, without distinction of caste or colour, and you have no need to think about the results. Your duty is to go on working, and then everything will follow of itself. My method of work is to construct and not to pull down. Read the history of the world and you will find that a great soul stood as the central figure in a certain period of a country. Animated by his ideas, hundreds of people did good to the world. You are all intelligent boys, and are coming here for a long time, say, what have you done? Couldn't you give one life for the service of others? Next life you may read Vedanta and other philosophies. Give this life for the service of others, then I shall know that your coming here has not been in vain.

Saying these words, Swamiji sat silent, wrapt in deep thought. After some time he said: "After so much austerity I have understood this as the real truth—God is present in every Jiva; there is no other God besides that. 'Who serves Jiva, serves God indeed.'" After some pause Swamiji addressing the disciple said, "What I have told you today, inscribe in your heart. See that you do not forget it."

XLII

LIFE AT THE BELUR MATH IN EARLY DAYS—
SWAMI VIVEKANANDA'S REMINISCENCE OF BARANA-
GORE MATH—RIGOURS OF MONASTIC VOW.

[Place : *The Math, Belur.* Year : *1902 (beginning).*]

It was Saturday and the disciple came to the Math just before evening. An austere routine was being followed now at the Math regarding spiritual practices. Swamiji had issued an order that all Brahmachârins and Sannyâsins should get up very early in the morning and practise Japam and meditation in the worship-room. Swamiji was having little sleep during these days, and would rise from bed at 3 in the morning.

On the disciple saluting Swamiji just after his appearance at the Math, he said : "Well, see how they are practising religious exercises here nowadays. Everyone passes a considerable time in Japam and meditation on mornings and evenings. Look there—a bell has been procured, which is used for rousing all from sleep. Everyone has to get up before dawn. Sri Ramakrishna used to say, 'In the morning and evening the mind remains highly imbued with Sattva ideas; those are the times when one should meditate with earnestness.'

"After the passing away of Sri Ramakrishna we underwent a lot of religious practice at the Baranagore Math. We used to get up at three A.M., and after washing our face etc.—some after bath, and others without it—we would sit in the worship-room and become absorbed in Japam and meditation. What a strong spirit of dispassion we had in those days! We had no thought even as to whether the world existed or not. Ramakrishnananda busied himself day and night with the duties pertaining to Sri Ramakrishna's worship and service, and occupied the same position in the Math as the mistress of the house does in a family. It was he who would procure, mostly by begging, the requisite articles for Sri Ramakrishna's worship and our subsistence. There have been days when the Japam and meditation continued from morning till 4 or 5 in the afternoon. Ramakrishnananda waited and waited with our meals ready, till at last he would come and snatch us from our meditation by sheer force. Oh, what a wonderful constancy of devotion we have noticed in him!"

Disciple :—Sir, how did you use to meet the Math expenses then?

Swamiji :—What a question! Well, we were Sâdhus, and what would come by begging and such other means, would be utilised for defraying the Math expenses. Today both Suresh Babu and Balaram Babu are no more; had they been alive they would have been exceedingly glad to see this Math. You have doubtless heard Suresh Babu's name. He was in a way the founder of this Math. It was he who used to bear all the expenses of the Baranagore Math. It was this Suresh Mitra who used to think most for us in those days. His devotion and faith have no parallel!

Disciple :—Sir, I have heard that you did not see him very often at his deathbed.

Swamiji :—We could only do it if we were

allowed (by his relatives)! Well, it is a long tale. But know this for certain that among worldly people it is of little count to you relatives and kinsmen whether you live or die. If you succeed in leaving some property, you will find even in your life-time that there has been set up a brawl over it in your household. You will have no one to console you in your deathbed—not even your wife and sons! Such is the way of the world!

Referring to the past condition of the Math, Swamiji went on: "Owing to want of funds I would sometimes fight for abolishing the Math altogether. But I could never induce Ramakrishnananda to accede to the proposal. Know Ramakrishnananda to be the central figure of the Math. There have been days when the Math was without a grain of food. If some rice was collected by begging, there was no salt to take it with! On some days there would be only rice and salt, but nobody cared for it in the least. We were then being carried away by a tidal wave of spiritual practice. Boiled *Bimba* leaves, rice and salt—this was the menu for a month at a stretch. Oh, those wonderful days! The austerities of that period were enough to dismay supernatural beings, not to speak of men. But it is a tremendous truth that if there be real worth in you, the more are circumstances against you, the more will that inner power manifest itself. But the reason why I have provided for beds and a tolerable living in the Math is, that the Sannyâsins that are enrolling themselves nowadays will not be able to bear so much strain as we did. There was life of Sri Ramakrishna before us, and that was why we did not care much for privations and hardships. Boys of this generation will not be able to undergo so much hardship. Hence it is that I have provided for some sort of habitation and a bare subsistence for them. If they get just enough food and clothing, the boys will devote themselves to religious practice, and will learn to sacrifice their lives for the good of humanity."

Disciple :—Sir, outside people say a good deal against this sort of bedding and furniture.

Swamiji :—Let them say. Even in jest they will at least once think of this Math. And they say, it is easier to attain liberation through cherishing a hostile spirit. Sri Ramakrishna used to say, "Men should be counted as worms." Do you mean we have to conduct ourselves according to the chance opinion of others? Pshaw!

Disciple :—Sir, you sometimes say, "All are Nârâyanas, the poor and the needy are my

Nârâyanas," and again you say, "Men should be counted as worms." What do you really mean?

Swamiji:—Well, there is not the least doubt that all are Nârâyanas. But all Nârâyanas do not criticize the furniture of the Math. I shall go on working for the good of men, without caring in the least for the criticisms of others—it is in this sense that the expression, "Men are to be counted as worms," has been used. He who has a dogged determination like that shall have everything. Only some may have it sooner, and others a little later, that is all. But one is bound to reach the goal. It is because we had such a determination that we have attained the little that we have. Otherwise, what dire days of privation we have had to pass through! One day, for want of food I fainted in the outer platform of a house on the roadside, and quite a shower of rain had passed over my head before I recovered my senses! Another day, I had to do odd jobs in Calcutta for the whole day without food, and had my meal on my return to the Math at ten or eleven in the night. And these were not solitary instances.

Saying these words Swamiji sat for a while pursuing some trend of thought. Then he resumed:

"Real monasticism is not easy to attain.

There is no order of life so rigorous as this. If you stumble ever so little, you are hurled down a precipice—and are smashed to pieces. One day I was travelling on foot from Agra to Brindaban. There was not a farthing with me. I was about a couple of miles from Brindaban when I found a man smoking on the roadside, and I was seized with a desire to smoke. I said to the man, 'Hallo, will you let me have a puff at your chillum?' He seemed to be hesitating greatly and said, 'Sire, I am a sweeper.' Well, there was the influence of old Samskâras, and I immediately stepped back and resumed my journey without smoking. I had gone a short distance when the thought occurred to me that I was a Sannyâsin, who had renounced caste, family, prestige and everything—and still I drew back as soon as the man gave himself out as a sweeper, and could not smoke at the chillum touched by him! The thought made me restless at heart; then I had walked on half a mile. Again I retraced my steps and came to the sweeper, whom I found still sitting there. I hastened to tell him, 'Do prepare a chillum of tobacco for me, dear friend.' I paid no heed to his objections and insisted on having it. So the man was complelled to prepare a chillum for me. Then I gladly had a puff at it and proceeded to Brindaban. When one has embraced the monastic life, one has to test whether one has gone beyond the prestige of caste and birth etc. It is so difficult to observe the monastic vow in right earnest! There must not be the slightest divergence between one's words and action."

Disciple :—Sir, you sometimes hold before us the householder's ideal and sometimes the ideal of the Sannyâsin. Which one are we to adopt?

Swamiji :—Well, go on listening to all. Then stick to that one which appeals to you—grip it hard like a bull-dog.

Swamiji came downstairs accompanied by the disciple, while speaking these words, and began to pace to and fro, uttering now and then the name of Shiva, or humming a song on the Divine Mother, such as, "Who knows how diversely Thou playest, O Mother, Thou flowing stream of nectar,"—and so on.

XLIII

ON MEDITATION—HOW TO AWAKEN THE KUNDA-
LINI—HOW TO HAVE CONCENTRATION—DIRECTIONS
ABOUT SPIRITUAL PRACTICE.

[Place : *The Math, Belur.* Year : 1902.]

The disciple passed the preceding night in Swamiji's room. At 4 A.M. Swamiji roused him and said, "Go and knock up the Sâdhus and Brahmachârins from sleep with the bell." In pursuance of the order the disciple rang the bell near the Sâdhus who slept. The monastic inmates hastened to go to the worship-room for meditation.

According to Swamiji's instructions the disciple rang the bell lustily near Swami Brahmananda's bed, which made the latter exclaim, "Good heavens! The Bângâl* has made it too hot for us to stay in the Math!" On the disciple's communicating this to Swamiji he burst out into a hearty laugh, saying "Well done!"

Then Swamiji, too, washed his face and entered the chapel accompanied by the disciple.

The Sannyâsins—Swami Brahmananda and others—had been already seated for medita-

---

* Meaning an East Bengal man, used as a term of endearing reproach for the disciple.

tion. A separate seat was kept for Swamiji, on which he sat facing the east, and pointing to a seat in front to the disciple, said, "Go and meditate, sitting there."

Shortly after taking his seat Swamiji became perfectly calm and motionless, like a statue, and his breathing became very slow. Everyone else kept his seat.

After about an hour and a half Swamiji rose from meditation with the words "Shiva, Shiva." His eyes were flushed, the expression placid, calm and grave. Bowing before Sri Ramakrishna he came downstairs and paced on the courtyard of the Math. After a while he said to the disciple : "Do you see how the Sâdhus are practising meditation etc. nowadays? When the meditation is deep, one sees many wonderful things. While meditating at the Baranagore Math, one day I saw the nerves Idâ and Pingalâ. One can see them with a little effort. Then, when one has a vision of the Sushumnâ, one can see anything one likes. If a man has unflinching devotion to the Guru, spiritual practices—meditation and Japam etc.—come quite naturally; one need not struggle for them. 'The Guru is Brahmâ, the Guru is Vishnu, and the Guru is Shiva Himself!'"

Then the disciple prepared tobacco for

Swamiji and when he returned with it, Swamiji spoke as he puffed at it : "Within there is the lion—the eternally pure, illumined and ever free Atman; and directly one realizes Him through meditation and concentration, this world of Mâyâ vanishes. He is equally present in all; and the more one practises, the quicker does the Kundalini (the 'coiled-up' power) awaken in him. When this power reaches the head, one's vision is unobstructed—one realizes the Atman."

Disciple :—Sir, I have only read of these things in the scriptures, but nothing has been realized as yet.

Swamiji :— कालेनात्मनि विन्दति—It is bound to come in time. But some attain this early, and others are a little late. One must stick to it—determined never to let it go. This is true manliness. You must keep the mind fixed on one object, like an unbroken stream of oil. The ordinary man's mind is scattered on different objects, and at the time of meditation, too, the mind is at first apt to wander. But let any desire whatever arise in the mind, you must sit calmly and watch what sort of ideas are coming. By continuing to watch in that way, the mind becomes calm, and there are no more thought-waves in it. These waves represent the thought-activity of the mind. Those things that you have previously thought too deeply, have transformed themselves into a subconscious current, and therefore these come up in the mind in meditation. The rise of these waves, or thoughts, during meditation is an evidence that your mind is tending towards concentration. Sometimes the mind is concentrated on a set of ideas—this is called meditation with Vikalpa or oscillation. But when the mind becomes almost free from all activities, it melts in the inner Self, which is the essence of infinite Knowledge, One, and Itself Its own support. This is what is called Nirvikalpa Samâdhi, free from all activities. In Sri Ramakrishna we have again and again noticed both these forms of Samâdhi. He had not to struggle to get these states. They came to him spontaneously, then and there. It was a wonderful phenomenon! It was by seeing him that we could rightly understand these things. Meditate everyday alone. Everything will open up of itself. Now the Divine Mother —the embodiment of Illumination—is sleeping within, hence you do not understand this. She is the Kundalini. When, before meditating, you proceed to "purify the nerves," you must mentally strike hard on the Kundalini in the Mulâdhâra (sacral plexus), and repeat, "Arise, Mother, arise!" One must practise these slowly. During meditation, suppress the emotional side altogether. That is a great source of danger. Those that are very emotional, have no doubt their Kundalini rushing quickly upwards, but it is as quick to come down as to go up. And when it does come down, it leaves the devote in a state of utter ruin. It is for this reason that *kirtanas* and other auxiliaries to emotional development have a great drawback. It is true that by dancing and jumping etc., through a momentary impulse, that power is made to course upwards, but it is never enduring. On the contrary when it traces back its course, it rouses violent lust in the individual. Listening to my lectures in America, through temporary excitement many among the audience used to get into an ecstatic state, and some would even become motionless like statues. But on inquiry I afterwards found that many of them had an excess of the carnal instinct immediately after that state. But this happens simply owing to a lack of steady practice in meditation and concentration.

Disciple :—Sir, in no scripture have I ever read these secrets of spiritual practice. Today I have heard quite new things.

Swamiji :—Do you think the scriptures contain all the secrets of spiritual practice? These are being handed down secretly through a succession of Gurus and disciples. Practise meditation and concentration with the utmost care. Place fragrant flowers in front and burn incense. At the outset take such external help as will make the mind pure. As you repeat the name of your Guru and Ishtam, say—Peace be to all creatures and the universe! First send impulses of these good wishes to the north, south, east, west, above, below—in all directions, and then sit down to meditate. One has to do like this during the early stages. Then sitting still (you may face in any direction), meditate in the way I have taught you while initiating. Don't leave out a single day. If you have too much pressing work, go through the spiritual exercises for at least a quarter of an hour. Can you reach the goal without a steadfast devotion, my son?

Now Swamiji went upstairs, and as he did so, he said: "You people will have your spiritual insight opened without much trouble. Now, that you have chanced to come here, well, you have liberation and all under your thumb. Now, besides practising meditation etc., set yourselves heart and soul to remove to a certain extent the miseries of the world so full of wails. Through hard austerities I have almost ruined this body. There is hardly any energy left in this pack of bones and flesh. You set yourselves to work now, and let me rest a while. If you fail to do anything else, well, you can tell the world at large about the scriptural truths you have studied so long. There is no higher gift than this, for the gift of knowledge is the highest gift in the world."

XLIV

ABOUT THE DISCIPLES OF SRI RAMAKRISHNA.

[Place : *The Math, Belur.* Year : *1902.*]

Swamiji was now staying at the Math. The disciple came to the Math and towards the evening accompanied Swamiji and Swami Premananda for a walk. Finding Swamiji absorbed in thought the disciple entered into a conversation with Swami Premananda on what Sri Ramakrishna used to say of Swamiji's greatness. After walking some distance Swamiji turned to go back to the Math. Seeing Swami Premananda and the disciple near by he said, "Well, what were you talking ?" Swamiji only heard the reply, but again lapsed into thought and walking by the road returned to the Math. He sat on the camp-cot placed under the mango-tree and resting there some time, washed his face and while pacing the upper verandah spoke to the disciple thus: "Why do you not set about propagating Vedanta in your part of the country? There Tântrikism prevails to a fearful extent. Rouse and agitate the country with the lion-roar of Advaitavâda. Then I shall know you to be a Vedantist. First open a Tol there and teach the Upanishads, and the *Brahmasutras*. Teach the boys the system of Brahmacharya. I have heard that in your country there is much logic-chopping of the Nyâya school. What is there in it? Only Vyâpti (pervasiveness) and Anumâna (inference)—on these subjects the Naiyâyika Pandits discuss for months. What does it help towards the Knowledge of the Atman? Either in your village or Nâg Mahâshaya's, open a Chaushpâthi (indigenous school) in which the scriptures will be studied and also the life and teachings of Sri Ramakrishna. In this way you will advance your own good as well as the good of the people, and your fame will endure.

Disciple:—Sir, I cherish no desire for name or fame. Only, sometimes I feel a desire to do as you are saying. But by marriage I have got so entangled in the world that I fear my desire will always remain in the mind only.

Swamiji:—What if you have married? As you are maintaining your parents and brothers with food and clothing, so do your wife likewise, and by giving her religious instruction draw her to your path. Think her to be a partner and helper in the living of your religious life. At other times look upon her with an even eye with others. Thinking thus all the unsteadiness of the mind will die out. What fear?

The disciple felt assured by these words. After meals Swamiji sat on his own bed and the disciple got an opportunity of doing some personal service to him.

Swamiji began to speak to the disciple, enjoining him to be reverential to the Math members: "These children of Sri Ramakrishna whom you see, are wonderful Tyâgis (selfless souls), and by service to them you will attain to the purification of mind and be blessed with the vision of the Atman. You remember the words of the Gitâ,—'by interrogation and service to the great souls'. Therefore you must serve them, by which you will attain your goal, and you know how much they love you."

Disciple:—But I find it very difficult to understand them. Each one seems to be of a different type.

Swamiji:—Sri Ramakrishna was a wonderful gardener. Therefore he has made a bouquet of different flowers and formed his Order. All different types and ideas have come into it and many more will come. Sri Ramakrishna used to say, "Whoever has prayed to God sincerely for one day, must come here." Know each of those who are here, to be of great spiritual power. Because they remain shrivelled before me, do not think them to be ordinary souls. When they will go out they will be the cause of the awakening of spirituality in people. Know them to be part of the spiritual body of Sri Ramakrishna, who was the embodiment of infinite religious ideas. I look upon them with that eye. See, for instance, Brahmananda, who is here—even I have not the spirituality which he has. Sri Ramakrishna looked upon him as his spiritual son and he lived and walked, ate and slept with him. He is the ornament of our Math our king. Similarly, Premananda, Turiyananda, Trigunatita, Akhandananda, Saradananda, Ramakrishnananda, Subodhananda and others—you may go round the world, but it is doubtful if you will find men of such spirituality and faith in God like them. They are each a centre of religious power and in time that power will manifest.

The disciple listened in wonder, and Swamiji said again: "But from your part of the country, except Nag Mahashaya none came to Sri Ramakrishna. A few others who saw Sri Ramakrishna, could not appreciate him." At the thought of Nag Mahashaya, Swamiji kept silent for some time. It was only four or five months since he had passed away. Swamiji had heard that on one occasion a spring of Ganga water rose in the house of Nag Mahashaya, and remembering it he asked the disciple, "Well, how did that event take place ? Tell me about it."

Disciple :—I have only heard about it but not seen it with my own eyes. I have heard that in a Mahâvâruni Yoga Nag Mahashaya started with his father for Calcutta. But not getting any accommodation in the railway train he stayed for three or four days at Narayangunge in vain and returned home. Then Nag Mahashaya said to his father, "If the mind is pure, then the Mother Ganga will appear here." Then at the auspicious hour of the holy bath, a jet of water rose, piercing the ground of his courtyard. Many of those who saw it, are living today. But that was many years before I met him.

Swamiji :—There is nothing strange in it. He was a saint of unfalsified determination. I do not consider such a phenomenon at all strange in his case.

Saying this Swamiji felt sleepy and lay on

his side. At this the disciple came down to take his supper.

XLV

DIFFERENT GRADES OF DEVOTEES OF SRI RAMAKRISHNA—DIFFERENT INTERPRETATION OF THE TEACHINGS OF SRI RAMAKRISHNA—FUTURE OF THE MESSAGE OF SRI RAMAKRISHNA.

[Place : *From Calcutta to the Math on a boat.* Year : *1902.*]

While walking on the banks of the Ganga at Calcutta one afternoon, the disciple saw a Sannyâsin at a distance approaching towards Aheereetolâ Ghât. When he came near, the disciple found the Sannyâsin to be no other than his Guru, Swami Vivekananda. In his left hand he had a leaf receptacle containing fried grams which he was eating like a boy. and was walking his way in great joy. When he stood before him the disciple fell at his feet and asked the reason of his coming to Calcutta unexpectedly.

Swamiji :—I came on a business. Come, will you go to the Math ? Eat a little of the fried grams. It has a nice saline and pungent taste.

The disciple took the food with gladness and

agreed to go to the Math with him.

Swamiji :—Then look for a boat.

The disciple hurried to hire a boat. He was settling the amount of the boat-hire with the boatman who demanded eight annas, when Swamiji also appeared on the scene and stopped the disciple saying, "Why are you higgling with them?" and said to the boatman, "Very well, I will give you eight annas," and got into the boat. The boat proceeded slowly against the current and took nearly an hour and a half to reach the Math. Getting Swamiji alone in the boat, the disciple got an opportunity of asking him freely about all subjects. Raising the topic of the glorificatory poem which the disciple had recently composed singing of the greatness of the devotees of Sri Ramakrishna, Swamiji asked him : "How do you know that those whom you have named in your hymn are the near and intimate disciples of Sri Ramakrishna ?"

Disciple :—Sir, I have associated with the Sannyâsin and householder disciples of Sri Ramakrishna for so many years; I have heard from them that they are all devotees of Sri Ramakrishna.

Swamiji :—Yes, they are devotees of Sri Ramakrishna. But all devotees do not belong to the group of his most intimate and nearest disciples. Staying in the Cossipore Garden Sri Ramakrishna said to us, "The Divine Mother showed me that all of these are not my inner devotees." Sri Ramakrishna said so that day with respect to both his men and women devotees.

Then speaking on the way Sri Ramakrishna would indicate different grades among devotees, high and low, Swamiji began to explain to the disciple at length the great difference there is between the householder's and the Sannyâsin's life.

Swamiji :—Is it possible that one would serve the path of lust and wealth and understand Sri Ramakrishna aright at the same time? Or will it ever be possible? Never put your faith in such words. Many among the devotees of Sri Ramakrishna are now proclaiming themselves as "Ishwara-koti," "Antaranga," etc. They could not imbibe his great renunciation or dispassion, yet they say they are his intimate devotees! Sweep away all such words. He was a prince of Tyâgis (self-renouncers), and obtaining his grace can anybody spend his life in the enjoyment of lust and wealth?

Disciple :—Is it then, sir, that those who came to him at Dakshineshwar were not his devotees?

Swamiji :—Who says that? Everybody who has gone to Sri Ramakrishna has advanced in spirituality, is advancing and will advance. Sri Ramakrishna used to say that the perfected Rishis of a previous Kalpa (cycle) take human bodies and come on earth with the Avatâras. They are the associates of the Lord. God works through them and propagates His religion. Know this for a truth that they alone are the associates of the Avatâra who have renounced all self for the sake of others, who giving up all sense enjoyment with repugnance spend their lives for the good of the world, for the welfare of the Jivas. The disciples of Jesus were all Sannyâsins. The direct recipients of the grace of Shankara, Râmânuja, Sri Chaitanya and Buddha were the all-renouncing Sannyâsins. It is men of this stamp who have been through a succession of disciples spreading the Brahma-vidyâ in the world. Where and when have you heard that a man being the slave of lust and wealth has been able to liberate another or to show the path of God to him? Without himself being free, how can he make others free? In Veda, Vedanta, Itihâsa (history), Purâna (ancient tradition), you will find everywhere that the Sannyâsins have been the teachers of religion in all ages and climes. History repeats itself. It will also be likewise now. The capable Sannyâsin children of Sri Ramakrishna, the teacher of the great synthesis of religions, will be honoured everywhere as the teachers of men. The words of others will dissipate in the air like an empty sound. The real self-sacrificing Sannyâsins of the Math will be the centre of the preservation and spread of religious ideas. Do you understand?

Disciple :—Then is it not true—what the householder devotees of Sri Ramakrishna are preaching about him in diverse ways?

Swamiji :—It can't be said that they are altogether false; but what they are saying about Sri Ramakrishna are all partial truths. According to one's own capacity, one has understood Sri Ramakrishna and so is discussing about him. It is not bad either to do so. But if any of his devotees has concluded, that what he has understood of him is the only truth, then he is an object of pity. Some are saying that Sri Ramakrishna was a Tântrika and Kaula, some that he was Sri Chaitanya born on earth to preach "Nâradiya Bhakti", some again that to undertake spiritual practices is opposed to faith in him as an Avatâra, while some are opining that it is not agreeable to his teachings to take to Sannyâsa. You will hear such words from the householder devotees, but do not listen to such one-sided estimates. What he was, the concentrated embodiment of how many previous Avatâras —we could not understand a bit even spending the whole life in religious austerity. Therefore one has to speak about him with caution and restraint. As are one's capacities, to that extent has he filled him with ideas. One spray from the full ocean of his spirituality, if realized, will make gods of men. Such a synthesis of universal ideas you will not find in the history of the world again. Understand from this who was born in the person of Sri Ramakrishna. When he used to instruct his Sannyâsin disciples, he would rise from his seat and look about if any householder was coming that way or not. If he found none, then in glowing words he would depict the glory of renunciation and Tapasyâ. As a result of the rousing power of that fiery dispassion, we have renounced the world and become averse to worldliness.

Disciple :—He used to make such distinctions between householders and Sannyâsins!

Swamiji :—Ask and learn from the householder devotees themselves about it. And you yourself can think and know which are greater —those of his children who for the realization of God have renounced all enjoyments of the worldly life and are spending themselves in the practice of austerities on hills and forests, Tirthas and Ashramas (holy places), or those who are praising and glorifying his name and practising his remembrance, but are not able to rise above the delusion and bondage of the world ? Which are greater—those who are coming forward in the service of humanity, regarding them as the Atman, those who are continent since early age, who are the moving embodiments of renunciation and dispassion,—or those who like flies are at one time sitting on a flower, and at the next moment on a dung heap ? You can yourself think and come to a conclusion.

Disciple :—But, sir, what does the world really means to those who have obtained his grace ? Whether they remain in the householder's life or take to Sannyâsa, it is immaterial —so it appears to me.

Swamiji :—The mind of those who have truly received his grace cannot be attached to wordliness. The test of his grace is—unattachment to lust or wealth. If that has not come in anyone's life, then he has not truly received his grace.

When the above discussion ended thus, the disciple raising another topic asked Swamiji,

"Sir, what is the outcome of all your labours here and in foreign countries?"

Swamiji:—You will see only a little manifestation of what has been done. In time the whole world must accept the universal and catholic ideas of Sri Ramakrishna and of this, only the beginning has been made. Before this flood everybody will be swept off.

Disciple:—Please tell me more about Sri Ramakrishna. I like very much to hear of him from your mouth.

Swamiji:—You are hearing so much about him all the time, what more? He himself is his own parallel. Has he any exemplar?

Disciple:—What is the way for us who have not seen him?

Swamiji:—You have been blessed with the company of these Sâdhus who are the direct recipients of his grace. How then can you say you have not seen him? He is present among his Sannyâsin disciples. By service to them, he will in time be revealed in your heart. In time you will realize everything.

Disciple:—But, sir, you speak about others who have received his grace, but never about what he used to say about yourself.

Swamiji:—What shall I say about myself? You see, I must be one of his demons. In his presence even, I would sometimes speak ill of him, hearing which he would laugh.

Saying thus Swamiji's face assumed a grave aspect, and he looked towards the river with an absent mind and sat still for some time. Within a short time the evening fell and the boat also reached the Math. Swamiji was then humming a tune to himself, "Now in the evening of life, take the child back to his home."

When the song was finished, Swamiji said, "In your part of the country (East Bengal) sweet-voiced singers are not born. Without drinking the water of mother Ganga, a sweet, musical voice is not acquired."

After paying the hire, Swamiji descended from the boat and taking off his coat sat in the western verandah of the Math. His fair complexion and ochre robe presented a beautiful sight.

XLVI

DENATIONALIZATION AND NATIONAL DEGRADATION —DIRECTIONS ABOUT SPIRITUAL PRACTICE.

[Place : *Belur Math.* Year : *1902.*]

Today is the first of Asârh. The disciple has come to the Math before dusk from Bally, with his office-dress on, as he has not found time to change it. Coming to the Math, he prostrated himself at the feet of Swamiji and enquired about his health. Swamiji replied that he was well, but looking at his dress, he said, "You put on coat and trousers, why don't you put on collars?" Saying this, he called Swami Saradananda who was near and said, "Give him tomorrow two collars from my stock." Swami Saradananda bowed assent to his order.

The disciple then changed his office dress and came to Swamiji, who addressing him said: "By giving up one's national costume and ways of eating and living, one gets denationalized. One can learn from all, but that learning which leads to denationalization does not help one's uplift but becomes the cause of degradation."

Disciple:—Sir, one cannot do without putting on dress approved by superior European officers in official quarters.

Swamiji:—No one prevents that. In the interests of your service, you put on official dress in official quarters. But on returning home you should be a regular Bengalee Babu—with flowing cloth, a native shirt and with the Chudder on the shoulder. Do you understand?

Disciple:—Yes, sir.

Swamiji:—You go about from house to house only with the European shirt on. In the

West, to go about visiting people with simply the shirt on is ungentlemanly—one is considered naked. Without putting on a coat over the shirt, you will not be welcomed in a gentleman's house. What nonsense have you learnt to imitate in the matter of dress! Boys and young men nowadays adopt a peculiar mode of dress which is neither Indian nor Western, but a queer combination.

After such talk Swamiji began to pace the banks of the river, and the disciple was alone with him. He was hesitating to ask Swamiji a question about religious practices.

Swamiji :—What are you thinking of ? Out with it.

The disciple with great delicacy said : "Sir, I have been thinking that if you can teach me some method by which the mind becomes calm within a short time, by which I may be immersed in meditation quickly, I shall feel much benefited. In the round of worldly duties, I feel it difficult to make the mind steady in meditation at the time of spiritual practice."

Swamiji seemed delighted at this humility and earnestness of the disciple. In reply he affectionately said, "After some time come to me when I am alone upstairs, I will talk to you about it."

Coming up shortly after, the disciple found that Swamiji was sitting in meditation, facing the west. His face wore a wonderful expression, and his whole body was completely motionless. The disciple stood by, looking with speechless wonder on the figure of Swamiji in meditation, and when even after standing long he found no sign of external conciousness in Swamiji, he sat noiselessly by. After half an hour, Swamiji seemed to show signs of a return to external consciousness. The disciple found that his folded hands began to quiver and a few minutes later Swamiji opened his eyes and looking at the disciple said, "When did you come ?"

Disciple :—A short while ago.

Swamiji :—Very well, get me a glass of water.

The disciple hurriedly brought a glass of water and Swamiji drinking a little asked the disciple to put the glass back in its proper place. The disciple did so and again sat by Swamiji.

Swamiji :—Today I had a very deep meditation.

Disciple :—Sir, please teach me so that my mind also may get absorbed in meditation.

Swamiji :—I have already told you all the methods. Meditate every day accordingly and in the fulness of time you will feel like that.

Now tell me what form of Sâdhanâ appeals to you most.

Disciple : —Sir, I practise every day as you have told me, still I don't get a deep meditation. Sometimes I think it is useless for me to practise meditation. So I feel that I shall not fare well in it, and therefore now desire only eternal companionship with you.

Swamiji : —Those are weaknesses of the mind. Always try to get absorbed in the eternally present Atman. If once you get the vision of the Atman, you get everything—the bonds of birth and death will be broken.

Disciple : —You bless me to attain to it. You asked me to come alone today, so I have come. By some means, do please make my mind steady.

Swamiji : —Meditate whenever you get time. If the mind once enters the path of Sushumnâ, everything will get right. You will not have to do much after that.

Disciple : —You encourage me in many ways. But shall I be blessed with a vision of the Truth ? Shall I get freedom by attaining true knowledge ?

Swamiji : —Yes, of course. Everybody will attain Mukti, from a worm up to Brahmâ, and shall you alone fail ? These are weaknesses of the mind; never think of such things.

After this he said again: "Be possessed of Shraddhâ (faith), of Virya (courage), attain to the knowledge of the Atman, and sacrifice your life for the good of others—this is my wish and blessing."

The bell for the meal ringing at this moment, Swamiji asked the disciple to go and partake of it. The disciple, prostrating at the feet of Swamiji, prayed for his blessings. Swamiji putting his hand on his head blessed him and said: "If my blessings be of any good to you, I say— may Bhagavân Sri Ramakrishna give you his grace! I know of no blessing higher than this." After meals, the disciple did not go upstairs to Swamiji, who had retired early that night. Next morning the disciple, having to return to Calcutta in the interests of his business, appeared before Swamiji upstairs.

Swamiji:—Will you go immediately?

Disciple:—Yes, sir.

Swamiji:—Come again next Sunday, won't you?

Disciple:—Yes, certainly.

Swamiji:—All right, there is a boat coming.

The disciple took leave of Swamiji. He did not know that this was to be his last meeting with his Ishtadeva (chosen Ideal) in the physical body. Swamiji with a glad heart bade him farewell and said, "Come on Sunday." The disciple replied, "Yes, I will," and got downstairs.

The boatmen were calling for him, so he ran for the boat. Boarding it he saw Swamiji pacing the upper verandah, and saluting him he entered the boat.

Seven days after this, Swamiji passed away from mortal life. The disciple had got no knowledge of the impending catastrophe. Getting the news on the second day of Swamiji's passing away he came to the Math, and therefore he had not the good fortune to see his physical form again!

CHAPTER II

[Priya Nath Sinha]

I

EDUCATIVE VALUE OF ROYAL DURBARS—FREEDOM AND DISCIPLINE—SWAMI VIVEKANANDA'S CATHOLICITY—TEST OF CIVILIZATION.

We evince a sad lack of restraint in conversation or any conjoint action such as music and so on. Everyone tries to put himself foremost. The jostling at railway or steamer stations is another illustration of this. A friend of Swamiji had a talk with him one day at the Math on this subject. Swamiji remarked: "You see, we have an old adage—'If your son is not inclined to study, put him in the Durbars (Sabhâ).' The word Sabha here does not mean social meetings, such as take place occasionally at people's houses—it means royal Durbars. In the days of the independent kings of Bengal, they used to hold their courts mornings and evenings. There, all the affairs of the State were discussed in the morning—and as there were no newspapers at that time, the king used to converse with the leading gentry of the capital and gather from them all information regarding the people and the State. These gentlemen had to attend these meetings, for if they did not do so, the king would inquire into the reason of their non-attendance. Such Durbars were the centres of civilization in every country and not merely in ours. In the present day, the western parts of India, especially Rajputana, are much better off in this respect than Bengal, as something similar to these old Durbars still obtains there."

Q :—Then, Mahârâj,* have our people lost their good manners because we have no kings of our own ?

Swamiji :—It is all a degeneration which has its root in selfishness. That in boarding a steamer one follows the vulgar maxim—"Uncle, save thy own precious skin," and in music and moments of recreation everyone tries to make a display of himself, is a typical picture of their mental state. Only a little training in self-sacrifice would take it away. It is the fault of the parents, who do not teach their children even good manners. Self-sacrifice, indeed, is the basis of all civilization.

On the other hand, owing to the undue domination exercised by the parents, our boys

* The form of addressing a Sâdhu.

do not get free scope for growth. The parents consider singing as improper. But the son, when he hears a fine piece of music, at once sets his whole mind on how to learn it, and naturally he must look out for an *âddâ*† Then again, "It is a sin to smoke!"—So what else can the young man do than mix with the servants of the house, to indulge in this habit in secret? In everyone there are infinite tendencies, which require proper scope for satisfaction. But in our country that is not allowed; and to bring about a different order of things would require a fresh training of the parents. Such is the condition! What a pity! We have not yet developed a high grade of civilization, and in spite of this our educated Babus want the British to hand over the government to them to manage! It makes me laugh and cry as well. Well, where is that martial spirit which, at the very outset, requires one to know how to serve and obey, and to practise self-restraint! The martial spirit is not self-assertion but self-sacrifice. One must be ready to advance and lay down one's life at the word of command, before he can command the hearts and lives of others. One must sacrifice himself first.

† Something like a club. The word has got a bad odour about it in Bengali.

A devotee of Sri Ramakrishna once passed some servere remarks, in a book written by him, against those who did not believe in Sri Ramakrishna as an Incarnation of God. Swamiji summoned the writer to his presence and addressed him thus in a spirited manner :

What right had you to write like that, abusing others ? What matters it if they do not believe in your Lord ? Have we created a sect ? Are we Ramakrishnites, that we should look upon anyone who will not worship him, as our enemy ? By your bigotry you have only lowered him, and made him small. If your lord is God Himself, then you ought to know that in whatsoever name one is calling upon him, it is *his* worship only—and who are you to abuse others ? Do you think they will hear you if you inveigh against them ? How foolish! You can only win others' hearts when you have sacrificed yourself to them, otherwise why should they hear you?

Regaining his natural composure after a short while, Swamiji spoke in a sorrowful tone :

Can anyone, my dear friend, have faith or resignation in the Lord, unless he himself is a hero ? Never can hatred and malice vanish from one's heart unless one becomes a hero, and unless one is free from these, how can one become truly civilized? Where in this country is that sturdy manliness, that spirit of heroism? Alas, nowhere! Often have I looked for that and I found only one instance of it, and only one.

Q :—In whom have you found it, Swamiji?

Swamiji :—In G. C.[*] alone I have seen that true resignation—that true spirit of a servant of the Lord. And was it not because he was ever ready to sacrifice himself that Sri Ramakrishna took upon himself all his responsibility? What a unique spirit of resignation to the Lord! I have not met his parallel. From him have I learned the lesson of self-surrender.

So saying, Swamiji raised his folded hands to his head out of respect for him.

II

THE PICTURE OF SRI KRISHNA, THE PREACHER OF THE GITA—WHAT IS MEANT BY 'KARMA' IN THE GITA—EGOISM AND SELF-SURRENDER—PROBLEM OF EVIL—THE VALUE OF SINCERITY—ORIGIN OF IMAGE WORSHIP—TANTRIKISM—HARMONY OF YOGAS—REVERENCE FOR WOMEN.

Arrangements were being made for Swamiji's leaving India for America for the second time

[*] Babu Girish Chandra Ghosh.

(1899 A. D.). He had gone to Calcutta to see one of his friends, and returning from there stopped for a few minutes at Balaram Babu's house at Baghbazar. He then sent for another friend to accompany him to the Math. The friend came, and the following conversation took place between him and Swamiji.

Swamiji :—A very funny thing happened today. I went to a friend's house. He has had a picture painted, the subject of which is "Sri Krishna addressing Arjuna on the battlefield of Kurukshetra."—Sri Krishna is standing in the chariot, holding the reins in His hand, and preaching the Gita to Arjuna. He showed me the picture and asked me how I liked it. "Fairly well," I said. But as he insisted on having my criticism on it, I had to give my honest opinion by saying, "There is nothing in it to commend itself to me; first, because the chariot of the time of Sri Krishna was not like the modern pagoda-shaped car, and also, there is no expression in the figure of Sri Krishna."

Q :—Was not the pagoda-chariot in use then ?

Swamiji :—Don't you know that since the Buddhistic era, there has been a great confusion in everything in our country ? The kings never used to fight in pagoda-chariots. There are chariots even today in Rajputana that greatly resemble the chariots of old. Have you seen the chariots in the pictures of Grecian mythology? They have two wheels, and one mounts them from behind; we had that sort of chariot. What good it is to paint a picture if the details are wrong? An historical picture comes up to a standard of excellence when, after making proper study and research, things are portrayed exactly as they were at that period. The truth must be represented, otherwise the picture is nothing. In these days, our young men who go in for painting, are generally those who were unsuccessful at school, and who have been given up at home as good-for-nothing—what work of art can you expect from them? To paint a really good picture requires as much talent as to produce a perfect drama.

Q:—How then should Sri Krishna be represented in the picture in question?

Swamiji:—Sri Krishna ought to be painted as He really was, the Gita personified; and the central idea of the Gita should radiate from His whole form as He was teaching the path of Dharma to Arjuna, who had been overcome by infatuation and cowardice.

So saying Swamiji posed himself in the way in which Sri Krishna should be portrayed, and continued: "Look here, thus does he hold the bridle of the horses—so tight that they are brought to their haunches, with their forelegs fighting the air, and their mouths gaping. This will show a tremendous play of action in the figure of Sri Krishna. His friend, the world-renowned hero, casting aside his bow and arrows, has sunk down like a coward on the chariot, in the midst of the two armies. And Sri Krishna, whip in one hand and tightening the reins with the other, has turned Himself towards Arjuna, with His child-like face beaming with unworldly love and sympathy, and calm and serene looks—and is delivering the message of the Gita to His beloved comrade. Now, tell me what idea this picture of the Preacher of the Gitâ conveys to you."

The friend:—Activity combined with firmness and serenity.

Swamiji:—Aye, that's it!—Intense action in the whole body, and withal a face expressing the profound calmness and serenity of the blue sky! This is the central idea of the Gitâ—to be calm and steadfast in all circumstances, with one's body, mind and soul centred at His hallowed Feet!

कर्मण्यकर्म यः पश्येदकर्मणि च कर्म यः ।
स बुद्धिमान्मनुष्येषु स युक्तः कृत्स्नकर्मकृत् ॥ (Gita, iv. 18).

"He who even while doing action can keep his mind calm, and in whom, even when not doing any outward action, flows the current of activity in the form of the contemplation on Brahman, is the intelligent one among men, he indeed is the Yogi, he indeed is the perfect worker."

At this moment, the man who had been sent to arrange a boat returned, and said that it was ready; so Swamiji told his friend, "Now let us go to the Math. You must have left word at home that you were going there with me?"

They continued their talk as they walked to the boat.

Swamiji :—This idea must be preached to every one—work—work—endless work; without looking at results, and always keeping the whole mind and soul steadfast at the lotus Feet of the Lord!

Q :—But is this not Karma-Yoga?

Swamiji :—Yes, this is Karma-Yoga—but without spiritual practices you will never be able to do this Karma-Yoga. You must harmonise the four different Yogas—otherwise how can you always keep your mind and heart wholly on the Lord?

Q :—It is generally said that work according to the Gitâ means the performance of Vedic sacrifices, and religious exercises; any other kind of work is futile.

Swamiji :—All right; but you must make it more comprehensive. Who is responsible for every action you do, every breath you take, and every thought you think? Isn't it you yourself?

The friend :—Yes and no. I cannot solve this clearly. The truth about it is that man is the instrument and the Lord is the agent. So, when I am directed by His will, I am not at all responsible for my actions.

Swamiji :—Well, that can be said only in the highest state of realization. When the mind will be purified by work and you will *see* that it is He who is causing all to work, then only you will have a right to speak like that. Otherwise it is all bosh, a mere cant.

Q :—Why so ?—If one is truly convinced by reasoning that the Lord alone is causing all actions to be done ?

Swamiji :—It may hold good when one *has been* so convinced. But it only lasts for that moment, and not a whit afterwards. Well, consider this thoroughly, whether all that you do in your everyday life, you are not doing with an egoistic idea that you yourself are the agent. How long do you remember that it is the Lord who is making you work? But then, by repeatedly analysing like that, you will come to a state when the ego will vanish, and in its place the Lord will come in. Then you will be able to say with justice—Thou, Lord, art guarding all my actions from within. But, my friend, if the ego occupies all the space in your heart, where forsooth will there be room enough for the Lord to come in? Then the Lord is verily absent!

Q:—But is it He who is giving me the wicked impulse?

Swamiji:—No, by no means. It would be blaspheming the Lord to think in that way. He is not inciting you to evil action, it is all the creation of your desire for self-gratification. If one says the Lord is causing everything to be done, and wilfully persists in wrong-doing, it only brings ruin on him. That is the origin of self-deception. Don't you feel an elation after you have done a good deed? You then give yourself the credit of doing something good—you can't help it, is very human. But how absurd to take the credit of doing the good act on oneself, and lay the blame for the evil act on the Lord! It is a most dangerous idea—the effect of ill-digested Gitâ and Vedanta. Never hold that view. Rather say that He is causing the good work to be done, while you are responsible for the evil action. That will bring on devotion and faith, and you will see His grace manifested at every step. The truth about it is that no one has created you—you have created yourself. This is discrimination, this is Vedanta. But one does not understand it before realization. Therefore the aspirant should begin with the dualistic standpoint, that the Lord is causing the good actions, while he is doing the evil. This is the easiest way to the purification of the mind. Hence you find dualism so strong among the Vaishnavas. It is very difficult to entertain Advaitic ideas at the outset. But the dualistic standpoint gradually leads to the realization of the Advaita.

Hypocrisy is always a dangerous thing. If there is no wilful self-deception, that is to say, if one sincerely believes that the most wicked impulse is also prompted by the Lord, rest assured that one will not have to do those mean acts for long. All the impurities of his mind are quickly destroyed. Our ancient scriptural writers understood this well. And I think that the Tântrika form of worship originated from the time that Buddhism began to decline, and through the oppression of the Buddhists people began to perform their Vedic sacrifices in secret. They had no more opportunity to conduct them for two months at a stretch so they made clay images, worshipped them, and consigned them to the water—finishing everything in one night, without leaving the least trace! Man longs for a concrete symbol, otherwise his heart is not satisfied. So in every home that one-night sacrifice began to take place. But then the tendencies of men had become sensual. As Sri Ramakrishna used to say, "Some enter the house by the scavenger's entrance," so the spiritual teachers of that time saw that those who could not perform any religious rite owing to their evil propensities, also needed some way of coming round by degrees to the path of virtue. For them those queer Tantrika rites came to be invented.

Q :—They went on doing evil actions knowing them to be good, so how could this remove their evil tendencies?

Swamiji :—Why, they gave a different direction to their propensities—they did them but with the object of realizing the Lord.

Q :—Can this really be done?

Swamiji :—It comes to the same thing. The motive must be all right. And what should prevent them from succeeding?

Q :—But many are caught in the temptation

for wine, meat, etc., in trying to get along with such means.

Swamiji:—It was therefore that Sri Ramakrishna came. The days of practising the Tantra in that fashion are gone. He, too, practised the Tantra, but not in that way. Where there is the injunction of drinking wine, he would simply touch his forehead with a drop of it. The Tantrika form of worship is a very slippery ground. Hence I say that this province has had enough of the Tantra. Now it must go beyond. The Vedas should be studied. A harmony of the four kinds of Yoga must be practised, and absolute chastity must be preserved.

Q:—What do you mean by the harmony of the four Yogas?

Swamiji:—Discrimination between the real and the unreal, dispassion and devotion, work, and practices in concentration, and along with these there must be a reverential attitude towards women.

Q:—How can one look with reverence on the women?

Swamiji:—Well, they are the representations of the Divine Mother. And real well-being of India will commence from the day the worship of the Divine Mother will truly begin, and every man will sacrifice himself at the altar of the Mother.

* * *

Q :—Swamiji, in your boyhood, when we asked you to marry, you would reply, "I won't, but you will see what I shall become." You have actually verified your words.

Swamiji :—Yes, dear brother, you saw how I was in want of food, and had to work hard besides. Oh, the tremendous labour! Today the Americans out of love have given me this nice bed, and I have something to eat also. But, alas, I have not been destined to enjoy physically —and lying on the mattress only aggravates my illness, I feel suffocated, as it were. I have to come down and lie on the floor for relief!

III

REMINISCENCES—THE PROBLEM OF FAMINES IN INDIA AND SELF-SACRIFICING WORKERS—EAST AND WEST—IS IT SATTVA OR TAMAS—A NATION OF MENDICANTS—THE "GIVE AND TAKE" POLICY—TELL A MAN HIS DEFECTS DIRECTLY BUT PRAISE HIS VIRTUES BEFORE OTHERS—VIVEKANANDA EVERYONE MAY BECOME—UNBROKEN BRAHMACHARYA IS THE SECRET OF POWER—SAMADHI AND WORK.

Our house was very close to Swamiji's, and

since we were boys of the same section of the town, I often used to play with him. From my boyhood I had a special attraction for him, and I had a sincere belief that he would become a great man. When he became a Sannyâsin we thought that the promise of a brilliant career for such a man was all in vain.

Afterwards, when he went to America, I read in newspapers reports of his lectures at the Chicago Parliament of Religions and others delivered in various places of America, and I thought that fire can never remain hidden under a cloth; the fire that was within Swamiji had now burst into a flame; the bud after so many years had blossomed.

After a time I came to know that he had returned to India, and had been delivering fiery lectures at Madras. I read them and wondered that such sublime truths existed in the Hindu religion and that they could be explained so lucidly. What an extraordinary power he had! Was he a man or a god?

A great enthusiasm prevailed when Swamiji came to Calcutta, and we followed him to the Sil's garden-house, on the Ganga, at Cossipore. A few days later, at the residence of Raja Radhakanta Dev, the "Calcutta boy" delivered an inspiring lecture to a huge concourse of people in reply to an address of welcome, and Calcutta heard him for the first time and was lost in admiration. But these are facts known to all.

After his coming to Calcutta, I was very anxious to see him once alone and be able to talk freely with him as in our boyhood. But there was always a gathering of eager inquirers about him, and conversations were going on without a break; so I did not get an opportunity for some time, until one day when we went out for a walk in the garden on the Ganga side. He at once began to talk, as of old, to me, the playmate of his boyhood. No sooner had a few words passed between us than repeated calls came, informing him that many gentlemen had come to see him. He became a little impatient at last and told the messenger, "Give me a little respite, my son; let me speak a few words with this companion of my boyhood; let me stay in the open air for a while. Go and give a welcome to those who have come, ask them to sit down, offer them tobacco and request them to wait a little."

When we were alone again I asked him, "Well, Swamiji, you are a Sâdhu. Money was raised by subscription for your reception here, and I thought, in view of the famine in this country, that you would wire, before arriving in

Calcutta, saying, 'Don't spend a single pice on my reception, rather contribute the whole sum to the famine relief fund'; but I found that you did nothing of the kind. How was that?"

Swamiji:—Why, I wished rather that a great enthusiasm should be stirred up. Don't you see, without some such thing how would the people be drawn towards Sri Ramakrishna and be fired in his name? Was this ovation done for me personally, or was not his name glorified by this? See, how much thirst has been created in the minds of men to know about him! Now they will come to know of him gradually, and will not that be conducive to the good of the country? If the people do not know him who came for the welfare of the country, how can good befall them? When they know what he really was, then *men*—real men—will be made, and when there be such *men*, how long will it take to drive away famines etc., from the land? So I say that I rather desired that there should be some bustle and stir in Calcutta, so that the public might be inclined to believe in the mission of Sri Ramakrishna; otherwise what was the use of making so much fuss for my sake? What do I care for it? Have I become any greater now than when I used to play with you at your house?

I am the same now as I was before. Tell me, do you find any change in me?

Though I said, "No, I do not find much change to speak of," yet in my mind I thought, "You have now, indeed, become a god."

Swamiji continued : "Famine has come to be a constant quantity in our country, and now it is, as it were, a sort of blight upon us. Do you find in any other country such frequent ravages of famine? No, because there are *men* in other countries, while in ours, men have become akin to dead matter, quite inert. Let the people first learn to renounce their selfish nature by studying Sri Ramakrishna, by knowing him as he really was, and then will proceed from them real efforts trying to stop the frequently recurring famines. By and by I shall make efforts in that direction too; you will see."

Myself :—That will be good. Then you are going to deliver many lectures here, I presume; otherwise, how will his name be preached?

Swamiji :—What nonsense! Nothing of the kind! Has anything been left undone by which his name can be known? Enough has been done in that line. Lectures won't do any good in this country. Our educated countrymen would hear them and, at best, would cheer and clap their hands, saying "Well done"; that is all. Then they would go home and digest, as we say, everything they had heard, with their meal! What good will hammering do on a piece of rusty old iron? It will only crumble into pieces. First, it should be made red-hot, and then it can be moulded into any shape by hammering. Nothing will avail in our country without setting a glowing and living example before the people. What we want are some young men who will renounce everything and sacrifice their lives for their country's sake. We should first form their lives and then some real work can be expected.

Myself :—Well, Swamiji, it has always puzzled me that, while men of our country, unable to understand their own religion, were embracing alien religions, such as Christianity, Mohammedanism, etc., you, instead of doing anything for them, went over to England and America to preach Hinduism.

Swamiji :—Don't you see that circumstances have changed now? Have the men of our country the power left in them to take up and practise true religion? What they have is only pride in themselves that they are very Sâttvika. Time was when they were Sâttvika, no doubt, but now they have fallen very low. The fall from Sattva brings one down headlong into Tamas! That is what has happened to them. Do you think that a man who does not exert himself at all, who only takes the name of Hari, shutting himself up in a room, who remains quiet and indifferent even when seeing a huge amount of wrong and violence done to others before his very eyes, possesses the quality of Sattva? Nothing of the kind, he is only enshrouded in dark Tamas. How can the people of a country practise religion, who do not get even sufficient food to appease their hunger? How can renunciation come to the people of a country, in whose minds the desires for Bhoga (enjoyment) have not been in the least satisfied? For this reason, find out, first of all, the ways and means by which men may get enough to eat and have enough luxuries to enable them to enjoy life a little; and then gradually, true Vairâgya (dispassion) will come, and they will be fit and ready to realize religion in life. The people of England and America, how full of Rajas they are! They have become satiated with all sorts of worldly enjoyment. Moreover, Christianity, being a religion of faith and superstition, occupies the same rank as our religion of the Purânas. With the spread of education and culture, the people of the West can no more find peace in that. Their present condition is such that, giving them one lift will make them reach the Sattva. Then again, in these days, would you accept the words of a Sannyâsin, clad in rags, in the same degree as you would the words of a white-face (Westerner), who might come and speak to you on your own religion?

Myself:—Just so, Swamiji! Mr. N. N. Ghose* also speaks exactly to the same effect.

Swamiji:—Yes, when my Western disciples after acquiring proper training and illumination will come in numbers here and ask you: "What are you all doing? Why are you of so little faith? How are your rites and religion, manners, customs and morals in any way inferior? We even regard your religion to be the highest!"—then, you will see that lots of our big and influential folk will hear them. Thus they will be able to do immense good to this country. Do not think for a moment that they will come to take up the position of teachers of religion to you. They will, no doubt, be your Guru regarding practical sciences etc., for the improvement of material conditions, and the people of our country will be their Guru in

* A celebrated barrister, journalist and educationist of Calcutta, Since dead.

everything pertaining to religion. This relation of Guru and disciple in the domain of religion will for ever exist between India and the rest of the world.

Myself :—How can that be, Swamiji ? Considering the feeling of hatred with which they look upon us, it does not seem probable that they will ever do good to us, purely from an unselfish motive.

Swamiji :—They find many reasons to hate us, and so they may justify themselves in doing so. In the first place, we are a conquered race, and moreover there is nowhere in the world such a nation of mendicants as we are! The masses who comprise the lowest castes, through ages of constant tyranny of the higher castes and by being treated by them with blows and kicks at every step they took, have totally lost their manliness and become like professional beggars; and those who are removed one stage higher than this, having read a few pages of English, hang about the thresholds of public offices with petitions in their hands. In the case of a post of twenty or thirty rupees falling vacant, five hundred B.A.'s and M.A.'s will apply for it! And, dear me! how curiously worded these petitions are! "I have nothing to eat at home, sir, my wife and children are starving; I most humbly implore you, sir, to give me some means to provide for myself and my family, or we shall die of starvation!" Even when they enter into service, they cast all self-respect to the winds, and servitude in its worst form is what they practise. Such is the condition, then, of the masses. The highly-educated, prominent men among you form themselves into societies and clamour at the top of their voices: "Alas, India is going to ruin, day by day! O English rulers, admit our countrymen to the higher offices of the State, relieve us from famines," and so on, thus rending the air, day and night, with the eternal cry of "Give" and "Give"! The burden of all their speech is, "Give to us, give more to us, O Englishmen!" Dear me! what more will they give to you? They have given railway, telegraphs, well-ordered administration to the country—have almost entirely suppressed robbers, have given education in science—what more will they give? What does anyone give to others with perfect unselfishness? Well, they have given you so much; let me ask, what have you given to them in return?

Myself :—What have we to give, Swamiji? We pay taxes.

Swamiji :—Do you, really? Do you give taxes to them of your own will, or do they exact them by compulsion because they keep peace in the country? Tell me plainly, what do you give them in return for all that they have done for you? You also have something to give them that they have not. You go to England, but that is also in the garb of a beggar—praying for education. Some go, and what they do there at the most is, perchance, to applaud the Westerner's religion in some speeches and then come back. What an achievement, indeed! Why, have you nothing to give them? An inestimable treasure you have, which you can give—give them your religion, give them your philosophy! Study the history of the whole world, and you will see that every high ideal you meet with anywhere had its origin in India. From time immemorial India ha[s] been the mine of precious ideas to human society; giving birth to high ideas herself, she ha[s] freely distributed them broadcast over the whol[e] world. The English are in India today, t[o] gather those higher ideals, to acquire a knov[v]ledge of the Vedanta, to penetrate into the dee[p] mysteries of that eternal religion which is you[r]. Give those invaluable gems in exchange for wh[at] you receive from them. The Lord took me [to] their country to remove this opprobrium of t[he] beggar that is attributed by them to us. It not right to go to England for the purpose of begging only. Why should they always give us alms? Does anyone do so for ever? It is not the law of nature to be always taking gifts with outstretched hands like beggars. To give and take is the law of nature. Any individual or class or nation that does not obey this law never prospers in life. We also must follow that law. That is why I went to America. So great is now the thirst for religion in the people there that there is room enough even if thousands of men like me go. They have been for a long time giving you of what wealth they possess, and now is the time for you to share your priceless treasure with them. And you will see how their feelings of hatred will be quickly replaced by those of faith, devotion and reverence towards you, and how they will do good to your country even unasked. They are a nation of heroes—never do they forget any good done to them.

Myself:—Well, Swamiji, in your lectures in the West you have frequently and eloquently dwelt on our characteristic talents and virtues, and many convincing proofs you have put forward to show our whole-souled love of religion; but now you say that we have become full of Tamas; and at the same time you are accrediting us as the teachers of the eternal religion of the Rishis, to the world! How is that?

Swamiji:—Do you mean to say that I should go about from country to country, expatiating on your failings before the public? Should I not rather hold up before them the characteristic virtues that mark you as a nation? It is always good to tell a man his defects in a direct way and in a friendly spirit to make him convinced of them, so that he may correct himself—but you should trumpet forth his virtues before others. Sri Ramakrishna used to say that if you repeatedly tell a bad man that he is good, he turns in time to be good; similarly, a good man becomes bad if he is incessantly called so. There in the West, I have said enough to the peopl[e] of their shortcomings. Mind, up to my time all who went over to the West from our countr[y] have sung paeans to them in praise of their vi[r]tues and have trumpeted out only our blemish[es] to their ears. Consequently, it is no wond[er] that they have learnt to hate us. For this reas[on] I have laid before them your virtues, and poin[t]ed out to them their vices, just as I am n[ow] telling you of your weaknesses and their go[od] points. However full of Tamas you may ha[ve] become, something of the nature of the anci[ent]

Rishis, however little it may be, is undoubtedly in you still—at least the framework of it. But that does not show that one should be in a hurry to take up at once the role of a teacher of religion and go over to the West to preach it. First of all, one must completely mould one's religious life in solitude, must be perfect in renunciation and must preserve Brahmacharya without a break. The Tamas has entered into you—what of that? Cannot the Tamas be destroyed? It can be done in less than no time! It was for the destruction of this Tamas that Bhagavân Sri Ramakrishna came to us.

Myself:—But who can aspire to be like you, Swamiji?

Swamiji:—Do you think that there will be no more Vivekanandas after I die! That batch of young men who came and played music before me a little while ago, whom you all despise for being addicted to intoxicating drugs and look upon as worthless fellows, if the Lord wishes, each and everyone of them may become a Vivekananda! There will be no lack of Vivekanandas, if the world needs them—thousands and millions of Vivekanandas will appear —from where, who knows! Know for certain that the work done by me is not the work of Vivekananda, it is His work—the Lord's own work! If one governor-general retires, another is sure to be sent in his place by the Emperor. Enveloped in Tamas however much you may be, know all that will clear away if you take refuge in Him by being sincere to the core of your heart. The time is opportune now, as the physician of the world-disease has come. Taking His name, if you set yourself to work, He will accomplish everything Himself through you. Tamas itself will be transformed into the highest Sattva!

Myself :—Whatever you may say, I cannot bring myself to believe in these words. Who can come by that oratorical power of expounding philosophy which you have?

Swamiji :—You don't know! That power may come to all. That power comes to him who observes unbroken Brahmacharya for a period of twelve years, with the sole object of realizing God. I have practised that kind of Brahmacharya myself, and so a screen has been removed, as it were, from my brain. For that reason, I need not any more think over or prepare myself for any lectures on such a subtle subject as philosophy. Suppose I have to lecture tomorrow; all that I shall speak about will pass tonight before my eyes like so many pictures; and the next day I put into words during my lecture all those things that I saw. So you will understand now that it is not any power which is exclusively my own. Whoever will practise unbroken Brahmacharya for twelve years will surely have it. If you do so, you too will get it. Our Shâstras do not say that only such and such a person will get it and not others!

Myself :—Do you remember, Swamiji, one day, before you took Sannyâsa, we were sitting in the house of—, and you were trying to explain the mystery of Samâdhi to us? And when I called in question the truth of your words, saying that Samâdhi was not possible in this Kali Yuga, you emphatically demanded : "Do you want to see Samâdhi or to have it youself ? I get Samâdhi myself, and I can make you have it!" No sooner had you finished saying so than a stranger came up and we did not pursue that subject any further.

Swamiji :—Yes, I remember the occasion.

Later, on my pressing him to make me get Samâdhi, he said, "You see, having continually lectured and worked hard for several years, the quality of Rajas has become too predominant in me. Hence that power is lying covered, as it were, in me now. If I leave all work and go to the Himalayas and meditate in solitude for some time, then that power will again come out in me."

IV

REMINISCENCES—PRANAYAMA—THOUGHT-READING—KNOWLEDGE OF PREVIOUS BIRTHS.

A day or two later, as I was coming out of my house intending to pay a visit to Swamiji, I met two of my friends who expressed a wish to accompany me, as they wanted to ask Swamiji something about Prânâyâma. As I had heard that one should not visit a temple or a Sannyâsin without taking something as an offering, we took some fruits and sweets with us, and placed them before him. Swamiji took them in his hands, raised them to his head and bowed to us before even we made our obeisance to him. One of the two friends with me had been a fellow-student of his. Swamiji recognised him at once and asked about his health and welfare. Then he made us sit down by him. There were many others there who had come to see and hear him. After replying to a few questions put by some of the gentlemen, Swamiji, in the course of his conversation, began to speak about Prânâyâma. First of all he explained through modern science the origin of matter from the mind, and then went on to show what Prânâyama is. All three of us had carefully read beforehand his book called Râja-Yoga. But from what we heard from him that day about Prânâyama, it seemed to me that very little of the knowledge that was in him had been recorded in that book. I understand also that what he said was not mere book-learning, for who could explain so lucidly and elaborately all the intricate problems of religion, even with the help of science, without himself realizing the Truth?

His conversation on Prânâyama went on from half-past three o'clock till half-past seven in the evening. When the meeting dissolved and we came away, my companions asked me how Swamiji could have known the questions that were in their hearts, and whether I had communicated to him their desire for asking those questions.

A few days after this occasion, I saw Swamiji in the house of the late Priya Nath Mukherjee, at Baghbazar. There were present Swami Brahmananda, Swami Yogananda, Mr. G. C. Ghosh, Atul Babu and one or two other friends. I said:—"Well, Swamiji, the two gentlemen who went to see you the other day wanted to ask you some questions about Prânâyama, which had been raised in their minds by reading your book on Raja-Yoga some time before you returned to this country, and they had then told me of them. But that day, before they asked you anything, you yourself raised those doubts that had occurred to them and solved them! They were very much surprised and inquired of me if I had let you know of their doubts beforehand." Swamiji replied : "Similar occurrences having come to pass many times in the West, people often used to ask me, 'How could you know the questions that were agitating our minds ?' This knowledge does not happen to me so often, but with Sri Ramakrishna it was almost always there."

In this connection Atul Babu asked him : "You have said in "Raja-Yoga" that one can come to know all about one's previous births. Do you know them yourself ?"

Swamiji :—Yes, I do.

Atul Babu :—What do you know ? Have you any objection to tell ?

Swamiji :—I can know them—I do know them—but I prefer not to say anything in detail.

V

THE ART AND SCIENCE OF MUSIC, EASTERN AND WESTERN.

It was an evening in July, 1898, at the Math, in Nilambar Mukherjee's garden-house, Belur. Swamiji with all his disciples had been meditating, and at the close of the meditation came out and sat in one of the rooms. As it was raining hard and a cold wind was blowing, he shut the door and began to sing to the accompaniment of *tânpurâ*. The singing being over, a long conversation on music followed. Swami Shivananda asked him, "What is Western music like?"

Swamiji:—Oh, it is very good; there is in it a perfection of harmony, which we have not attained. Only, to our untrained ears it does not sound well, hence we do not like it, and we think that the singers howl like jackals. I also had the same sort of impression, but when I began to listen to the music with attention and study it minutely, I came more and more to understand it, and I was lost in admiration. Such is the case with every art. In glancing at a highly finished painting we cannot understand where its beauty lies. Moreover, unless the eye is, to a certain extent, trained, one cannot appreciate the subtle touches and blendings, the inner genius of a work of art. What real music we have, lies in Kirtan and Dhrupad; the rest has been spoiled by being modulated according to the Islamic methods. Do you think that singing the short and light airs of *tappâ* songs in a nasal voice and flitting like lightning from one note to another by fits and starts are the best things in the world of music? Not so. Unless each note is given full play in every scale, all the science of music is marred. In painting, by keeping in touch with Nature you can make it as artistic as you like; there is no harm in doing that, and the result will be nothing but good. Similarly, in music, you can display any amount of skill by keeping to science, and it will be pleasing to the ear. The Mohammedans took up the different Râgs and Râginis after coming into India. But they put such a stamp of their own colouring on the art of *tappâ* songs that all the science in music was destroyed.

Q :—Why, Mahârâj? Who has not a liking for music in *tappâ*?

Swamiji :—The chirping of crickets sounds very good to some. The Santâls think their music also to be the best of all. You do not seem to understand that when one note comes upon another in such quick succession, it not only robs music of all grace but, on the other hand, creates discordance rather. Do not the permutation and combination of the seven keynotes form one or other of the different melodies of music, known as Râgs and Râginis? Now, in *tappâ*, if one slurs over a whole melody (rag) and creates a new tune, and over and above that, if the voice is raised to the highest pitch by tremulous modulation, say, how can the Rag be kept intact? Again, the poetry of music is completely destroyed if there be in it such profuse use of light and short strains just for effect. To sing by keeping to the idea meant to be conveyed by a song totally disappeared from our country when *tappas* came into vogue. Nowadays, it seems, the true art is reviving a little, with the improvement in theatres, but, on the other hand, all regard for Râgs and Râginis is being more and more flung to the winds.

Accordingly, to those who are past-masters in the art of singing Dhrupad, it is painful to hear *tappas*. But in our music the cadence, or a duly regulated rise and fall of voice or sound, is very good. The French detected and appreciated this trait first, and tried to adapt and introduce it in their music. After their doing this, the whole of Europe has now thoroughly mastered it.

Q :—Maharaj, their music seems to be pre-eminently martial, whereas that element appears to be altogether absent in ours.

Swamiji :—Oh, no, we have it also. In martial music, harmony is greatly needed. We sadly lack harmony, hence it does not show itself so much. Our music was improving steadily. But when the Mohammedans came, they took possession of it in such a way that the tree of music could grow no further. The music of the Westerners is much advanced. They have the sentiment of pathos as well as of heroism in their music, which is as it should be. But our antique musical instrument made from the gourd has been no further improved.

Q :—Which of the Râgs and Râginis are martial in tune ?

Swamiji :—Every Rag may be made martial, if it is set in harmony and the instruments are tuned accordingly. Some of the Raginis can also become martial.

The conversation was then closed, as it was time for supper. After supper, Swamiji enquired as to the sleeping arrangements for the guests who had come from Calcutta to the Math

TALKS WITH SWAMI VIVEKANANDA 447

to pass the night, and he then retired to his bed-room.

VI

THE OLD INSTITUTION OF LIVING WITH THE GURU—THE PRESENT UNIVERSITY SYSTEM—LACK OF SHRADDHA—WE HAVE A NATIONAL HISTORY—WESTERN SCIENCE COUPLED WITH VEDANTA—THE SO-CALLED HIGHER EDUCATION—THE NEED OF TECHNICAL EDUCATION AND EDUCATION ON NATIONAL LINES—THE STORY OF SATYAKAMA—MERE BOOK-LEARNING AND EDUCATION UNDER TYAGIS—SRI RAMAKRISHNA AND THE PANDITS—ESTABLISHMENT OF MATHS WITH SADHUS IN CHARGE OF COLLEGES—TEXT-BOOKS FOR BOYS TO BE COMPILED—STOP EARLY MARRIAGE—PLAN OF SENDING UNMARRIED GRADUATES TO JAPAN—THE SECRET OF JAPAN'S GREATNESS—ART, ASIATIC AND EUROPEAN—ART AND UTILITY—STYLES OF DRESS—THE FOOD QUESTION AND POVERTY.

It was about two years after the new Math had been constructed and while all the Swamis were living there that I came one morning to pay a visit to my Guru. Seeing me, Swamiji smiled and after inquiring of my welfare etc., said, "You are going to stay today, are you not?"

"Certainly," I said, and after various inquiries

I asked, "Well, Mahârâj, what is your idea of educating our boys?"

Swamiji :—गुरुगृहवास:—Living with the Guru.

Q :—How?

Swamiji :—In the same way as of old. But with this education has to be combined modern Western science. Both these are necessary.

Q :—Why, what is the defect in the present university system?

Swamiji :—It is almost wholly one of defects. Why, it is nothing but a perfect machine for turning out clerks. I would even thank my stars if that were all. But no! See how men are becoming destitute of Shraddhâ and faith. They assert that the Gitâ was only an interpolation, and that the Vedas were but rustic songs! They like to master every detail concerning things and nations outside of India, but if you ask them they do not know even the names of their own forefathers up to the seventh generation, not to speak of the fourteenth!

Q :—But what does that matter? What if they do not know the names of their forefathers?

Swamiji :—Don't think so. A nation that has no history of its own has nothing in this world. Do you believe that one who has such faith and pride as to feel, "I come of noble descent," can ever turn out to be bad? How could that be? That faith in himself would curb his actions and feelings, so much so that he would rather die than commit wrong. So, a national history keeps a nation well-restrained and does not allow it to sink so low. Oh, I know you will say, "But we have not such a history!" No, there is not any, according to those who think like you. Neither is there any, according to your big university scholars; and so also think those who, having travelled through the West in one great rush, come back dressed in European style and assert, "We have nothing, we are barbarians." Of course, we have no history exactly like that of other countries. Suppose we take rice, and the Englishmen do not. Would you for that reason imagine that they all die of starvation, and are going to be exterminated? They live quite well on what they can easily procure or produce in their own country and is suited to them. Similarly, we have our own history exactly as it ought to have been for us. Will that history be made extinct by shutting your eyes and crying, "Alas! we have no history!" Those who have eyes to see, find a luminous history there, and by the strength of that they know the nation is still alive. But that history has to be rewritten. It should be restated and suited to the understanding and ways of thinking, which our men have acquired in the present age, through Western education.

Q :—How has that to be done?

Swamiji :—That is too big a subject for a talk now. However, to bring that about, the old institution of "living with the Guru" and similar systems of imparting education are needed. What we want are Western science coupled with Vedanta, Brahmacharya as the guiding motto, and also Shraddhâ and faith in one's own self. Another thing that we want is the abolition of that system which aims at educating our boys in the same manner as that of the man who battered his ass, being advised that it could thereby be turned into a horse.

Q :—What do you mean by that?

Swamiji :—You see, no one can teach anybody. The teacher spoils everything by thinking that he is teaching. Thus Vedanta says that within man is all knowledge—even in a boy it is so—and it requires only an awakening, and that much is the work of a teacher. We have to do only so much for the boys that they may learn to apply their own intellect to the proper use of their hands, legs, ears, eyes, etc., and finally everything will become easy. But the root is religion. Religion is as the rice, and everything else, like the curries. Taking only curries causes indigestion, and so is the case with taking rice alone. Our pedagogues are making parrots of our boys, and ruining their brains by cramming a lot of subjects into them. Looking from one standpoint, you should rather be grateful to the Viceroy* for his proposal of reforming the university system, which means practically abolishing the higher education—the country will, at least, feel some relief by having breathing time. Goodness gracious! what a fuss and fury about graduating, and after a few days all cooled down! And after all that, what is it they learn but that what religion and customs we have are all bad, and what the Westerners have are all good! At last, they cannot keep the wolf from the door! What does it matter if this higher education remains or goes? It would be better if the people got a little technical education so that they might find work and earn their bread, instead of dawdling about and crying for service.

Q :—Yes, the Marwaris are wiser as they do not accept service and most of them engage

---

* Lord Curzon, who took steps to raise the standard of University education so high, as to make it very expensive and hence almost inaccessible to boys of the middle classes.

themselves in some trade.

Swamiji :—Nonsense! They are on the way to bring ruin to the country. They have little understanding of their own interests. You are much better, because you have more of an eye towards manufactures. If the money that they lay out in their business and with which they made only a small percentage of profit were utilized in conducting a few factories and workshops, instead of filling the pockets of Europeans by letting them reap the benefit of most of the transactions, then it would not only conduce to the well-being of the country but bring far greater amount of profit to them, as well. It is only the Cabulis who do not care for service—the spirit of independence is in their very bone and marrow. Propose to anyone of them to take service, and you will see what follows!

Q :—Well, Maharaj, in case the higher education is abolished, will not the men become as stupid as they were before?

Swamiji :—What nonsense! Can ever a lion become a jackal? What do you mean? Is it ever possible for the sons of the land that has nourished the whole world with knowledge from time immemorial to turn stupid, because of the abolition of higher education by Lord Curzon ?

Q : —But think what our people were before the advent of the English, and what they are now.

Swamiji : —Does higher education mean mere study of material sciences and turning out things of everyday use by machinery ? The use of higher education is to find out how to solve the problems of life, and this is what is engaging the profound thought of the modern civilized world, but it was solved in our country thousands of years ago.

Q : —But your Vedanta also was about to disappear ?

Swamiji : —It might be so. In the efflux of time the light of Vedanta now and then seems as if about to be extinguished, and when that happens, the Lord has to incarnate Himself in this human body ; He then infuses such life and strength into religion that it goes on again for some time with irresistible vigour. That life and strength has come into it again.

Q : —What proof is there, Maharaj, that India has freely contributed her knowledge to the rest of the world ?

Swamiji : —History itself bears testimony to the fact. All the soul-elevating ideas and the different branches of knowledge that exist in the world are found out by proper investigation to have their roots in India.

Aglow with enthusiasm Swamiji dwelt at length on this topic. His health was very bad at the time, and moreover owing to the intense heat of summer he was feeling thirsty and drinking water too often. At last he said, "Dear Singhi, get a glass of iced water for me please, I shall explain everything to you clearly." After drinking the iced water he began afresh.

Swamiji :—What we need, you know, is to study, independent of foreign control, different branches of the knowledge that is our own, and with it the English language, and Western science; we need technical education and all else which may develop industries, so that men, instead of seeking for service, may earn enough to provide for themselves, and save something against a rainy day.

Q :—What were you going to say the other day about the Tol (Sanskrit boarding school) system ?

Swamiji :—Haven't you read the stories from the Upanishads ? I will tell you one. Satyakâma went to live the life of a Brahmachârin with his Guru. The Guru gave into his charge some cows and sent him away to the forest with them. Many months passed by, and when Satyakâma saw that the number of cows was doubled he thought of returning to his Guru. On his way back, one of the bulls, the fire, and some other animals gave him instructions about the Highest Brahman. When the disciple came back, the Guru at once saw by a mere glance at his face that the disciple had learnt the knowledge of the Supreme Brahman. Now, the moral this story is meant to teach is that true education is gained by constant living in communion with Nature.

Knowledge should be acquired in that way, otherwise by educating yourself in the Tol of a Pandit you will be only a human ape all your life. One should live from his very boyhood with one whose character is like a blazing fire, and should have before him a living example of the highest teaching. Mere reading that it is a sin to tell a lie will be of no use. Every boy should be trained to practise absolute Brahmacharya, and then, and then only, faith and Shraddhâ will come. Otherwise, why will not one who has no Shraddhâ and faith speak an untruth? In our country, the imparting of knowledge has always been through men of renunciation. Later, the Pandits, by monopolizing all knowledge and restricting it to the Tols, have only brought the country to the brink of ruin. India had all good prospects so long as Tyâgis (men of renunciation) used to impart knowledge.

Q :—What do you mean, Maharaj ? There are no Sannyâsins in other countries, but see how by dint of their knowledge India is laid prostrate under their feet!

Swamiji :—Don't talk nonsense, my dear, hear what I say. India will have to carry other's shoes for ever on her head if the charge of imparting knowledge to her sons does not again fall upon the shoulders of Tyagis. Don't you know how an illiterate boy, possessed of renunciation, turned the heads of your great old Pandits ? Once at the Dakshineswar Temple the Brâhmana who was in charge of the worship of Vishnu broke a leg of the image. Pandits were brought together at a meeting to give their opinions, and they, after consulting old books and manuscripts, declared that the worship of this broken image could not be sanctioned according to the Shâstras and a new image would have to be consecrated. There was, consequently, a great stir. Sri Ramakrishna was called at last. He heard and asked, "Does a wife forsake her husband in case he becomes lame ?" What followed ? The Pandits were struck dumb, all their Shâstric commentaries and learned comments could not withstand the force of this simple statement. If that was true, why should Sri Ramakrishna come down to this earth, and why should he discourage mere book-learning so much? That new life-force which he brought with him has to be instilled into learning and education, and then the real work will be done.

Q :—But that is easier said than done.

Swamiji :—Had it been easy, it would not have been necessary for him to come. What you have to do now is to establish a Math in every town and in every village. Can you do that? Do something at least. Start a big Math in the heart of Calcutta. A well-educated Sâdhu should be at the head of that centre and under him there should be departments for teaching practical science and arts, with a specialist Sannyâsin in charge of each of these departments.

Q :—Where will you get such Sâdhus?

Swamiji :—We have to make and manufacture them. So, I always say that some young men with burning patriotism and renunciation are needed. None can master a thing perfectly in so short a time as the Tyâgis will.

After a short silence Swamiji said, "Singhi,

there are so many things left to be done for our country that thousands like you and me are needed. What will mere talk do ? See to what a miserable condition the country is reduced ; now do something! We haven't even got a single book well suited for the little boys.

Q :—Why, there are so many books of Ishwar Chandra Vidyâsâgar for the boys!

No sooner had I said this than he laughed out and said : Yes, there you read "Ishwar Nirâkâr Chaitanya Svarup"—(God is without form and of the essence of pure knowledge); Subal ati subodh bâlak"—Subal is a very good, intelligent boy, and so on—that won't do. We must compile some books in Bengali as well as in English with short stories from the Râmâyaṅa, the Mahâbhârata, and the Upanishads, etc., in very easy and simple language, and these are to be given to our little boys to read.

It was about eleven o'clock by this time. The sky became suddenly overcast, and a cold wind began to blow. Swamiji was greatly delighted at the prospect of rain. He got up and said, "Let us, Singhi, have a stroll by the side of the Ganga." We did so, and he recited many stanzas from *Meghadutam* of Kâlidâsa, but the one undercurrent of thought that was all the time running through his mind was, the good of

India. He exclaimed, "Look here, Singhi, can you do one thing? Can you put a stop to the marriage of our boys for some time?"

I said, "Well, Maharaj, how can we think of that, when the Bâbus are trying, on the other hand, all sorts of means to make marriage cheaper?"

Swamiji:—Don't trouble your head on that score; who can stem the tide of time! All such agitations will end in empty sound, that is all. The dearer the marriages become, the better for the country. What a hurry scurry of passing examinations and marrying right off! It seems as if no one is to be left a bachelor, but it is just the same thing again, next year!

After a short silence, Swamiji again said, "If I can get some unmarried graduates, I may try to send them over to Japan and make arrangements for their technical education there, so that when they come back, they may turn their knowledge to the best account for India. What a good thing that would be!

Q:—Why, Maharaj, is it better for us to go to Japan than to England?

Swamiji:—Certainly! In my opinion, if all our rich and educated men once go and see Japan, their eyes will be opened.

Q:—How?

Swamiji :—There, in Japan, you find a fine assimilation of knowledge, and not its indigestion as we have here. They have taken everything from the Europeans, but they remain Japanese all the same, and have not turned European; while in our country the terrible mania of becoming Westernised has seized upon us like a plague.

I said : "Maharaj, I have seen some Japanese paintings; one cannot but marvel at their art. Its inspiration seems to be something which is their own and beyond imitation."

Swamiji :—Quite so. They are great as a nation because of their art. Don't you see they are Asiatics, as we are? And though we have lost almost everything, yet what we still have is wonderful. The very soul of the Asiatic is interwoven with art. The Asiatic never uses a thing unless there be art in it. Don't you know that art is, with us, a part of religion? How greatly is a-lady admired among us, who can nicely paint the floors and walls, on auspicious occasions, with the paste of rice-powder! How great an artist was Sri Ramakrishna himself!

Q :—The English art is also good, is it not?

Swamiji :—What a stupid fool you are! But what is the use of blaming you, when that seems to be the prevailing way of thinking!

Alas, to such a state is our country reduced! The people will look upon their own gold as brass, while the brass of the foreigner is gold to them! This is, indeed, the magic wrought by modern education! Know, that since the time the Europeans have come into contact with Asia, they are trying to infuse art into their own life.

Myself :—If others hear you talk like this, Maharaj, they will think that you take a pessimistic view of things.

Swamiji :—Naturally! What else can they think, who move in a rut! How I wish I could show you everything through my eyes! Look at their buildings, how common-place, how meaningless, they are! Look at those big government buildings; can you, just by seeing their outsides, make out any meaning for which each of them stands? No, because they are all so unsymbolical. Take again the dress of Westerners : their stiff coats and straight pants, fitting almost tightly to the body, are, in our estimation, hardly decent, is it not so? And, oh, what beauty, indeed, in that! Now, go all over our motherland and see if you cannot read aright, from their very appearance, the meaning for which our buildings stand, and how much art there is in them!

The glass is their drinking vessel, and ours is the metal *ghati* (pitcher-shaped); which of the two is artistic? Have you seen the farmers' homes in our villages?

Myself:—Yes, I have, of course.

Swamiji:—What have you seen of them?

I did not know what to say. However, I replied, "Maharaj, they are faultlessly neat and clean, the yards and floors being daily well plastered over."

Swamiji:—Have you seen their granaries for keeping paddy? What an art is there in them! What a variety of paintings even on their mud walls! And then, if you go and see how the lower classes live in the West, you would at once mark the difference. Their ideal is utility, ours, art. The Westerner looks for utility in everything, whereas with us art is everywhere. With the Western education, those beautiful *ghatis* of ours have been discarded, and enamel glasses have usurped their place in our homes! Thus, the ideal of utility has been imbibed by us to such an extent as to make it look little short of the ridiculous. Now what we need is the combination of art and utility. Japan has done that very quickly, and so she has advanced by giant strides. Now, in their turn, the Japanese are going to teach the Westerners.

Q : —Maharaj, which nation in the world dresses best ?

Swamiji : —The Aryans do; even the Europeans admit that. How picturesquely their dresses hang in folds! The royal constumes of most nations are, to some extent, a sort of imitation of the Aryans—the same attempt is made there to keep them in folds, and those costumes bear a marked difference to their national style.

By the by, Singhi, leave off that wretched habit of wearing those European shirts.

Q : —Why, Maharaj ?

Swamiji : —For the reason that they are used by the Westerners only as underwear. They never like to see them worn outside. How mistaken of the Bengalees to do so! As if one should wear anything and everything, as if there is no unwritten Law about dress, as if there is no ancestral style to follow! Our people are outcasted by taking the food touched by the lower classes ; it would have been very well if the same law applied to their wearing any irregular style of dress. Why can't you adapt your dress in some way to our own style ? What sense is there for your going in for European shirts and coats ?

It began to rain now, and the dinner-bell also rang. So we went in to partake of the

Prasâda with others. During the meal Swamiji said, addressing me: "Concentrated food should be taken. To fill the stomach with a large quantity of rice is the root of laziness." A little while after he said again: "Look at the Japanese, they take rice with the soup of split-pulses, twice or thrice a day. But even the strongly-built take little at a time, though the number of meals may be more. Those who are well-to-do among them take meat daily. Twice a day we stuff ourselves up to the throat, as it were, and the whole of our energy is exhausted in digesting such a quantity of rice!"

Q :—Is it feasible for us Bengalees, poor as we are, to take meat?

Swamiji :—Why not? You can afford to have it in small quantities. Half a pound a day is quite enough. The real evil is idleness, which is the principal cause of our poverty. Suppose the head of a firm gets displeased with someone and decreases his pay; or, out of three or four bread-winning sons in a family one suddenly dies; what do they do? Why, they at once curtail the quantity of milk for the children, or live on one meal a day, having a little popped-rice or so at night!

Q :—But what else can they do under the circumstances?

Swamiji :—Why can they not exert themselves and earn more, to keep up their standard of food? But no! They must go to their local *âddâs* (rendezvous) and idle hours away! Oh, if they did but know how they waste their time!

VII

THE DISCRIMINATION OF THE FOUR CASTES ACCORDING TO JATI AND GUNA—BRAHMANAS AND KSHATRIYAS IN THE WEST—THE KULA-GURU SYSTEM IN BENGAL.

Once I went to see Swamiji while he was staying in Calcutta at the house of the late Balaram Basu. After a long conversation about Japan and America, I asked him, "Well, Swamiji, how many disciples have you in the West?"

Swamiji :—A good many.

Q :—Two or three thousand?

Swamiji :—Maybe more than that.

Q :—Are they all initiated by you with Mantras?

Swamiji :—Yes.

Q :—Did you give them permission to utter Pranava (Om)?

Swamiji :—Yes.

Q :—How did you, Mahârâj? They say

that the Shudras have no right to Pranava, and none has except the Brâhmanas. Moreover, the Westerners are Mlechchhas, not even Shudras.

Swamiji :—How do you know that those whom I have initiated are not Brâhmanas ?

Myself :—Where could you get Brâhmanas outside India, in the lands of the Yavanas and Mlechchhas ?

Swamiji :—My disciples are all Brâhmanas! I quite admit the truth of the words that none except the Brâhmanas has the right to Pranava. But the son of a Brâhmana is not necessarily always a Brâhmana ; though there is every possibility of his being one, he may not become so. Did you not hear that the nephew of Aghore Chakravarti of Baghbazar became a sweeper and actually used to do all the menial services of his adopted caste ? Was he not the son of a Brâhmana ?

The Brâhmana caste and the Brâhmanya qualities are two distinct things. In India, one is held to be a Brâhmana by one's caste, but in the West, one should be known as such by one's Brâhmanya qualities. As there are three Gunas—Sattva, Rajas and Tamas—so there are Gunas which show a man to be a Brâhmana, Kshatriya, Vaishya or a Shudra. The qualities of being a Brâhmana or a Kshatriya are dying out from the country, but in the West they have now attained to Kshatriyahood, from which the next step is Brâhmanahood, and many there are who have qualified themselves for that.

Q :—Then you call those Brâhmanas who are Sâttvika by nature ?

Swamiji :—Quite so. As there are Sattva, Rajas and Tamas—one or other of these Gunas more or less—in every man, so the qualities which make a Brâhmana, Kshatriya, Vaishya or a Shudra are inherent in every man, more or less. But at times one or other of these qualities predominates in him in varying degrees and is manifested accordingly. Take a man in his different pursuits, for example : when he is engaged in serving another for pay, he is in Shudrahood; when he is busy transacting some piece of business for profit, on his own account he is a Vaisya, where he fights to right wrongs, then the qualities of a Kshatriya come out in him ; and when he meditates on God, or passes his time in conversation about Him, then he is a Brâhmana. Naturally, it is quite possible for one to be changed from one caste into another. Otherwise, how did Vishvâmitra become a Brâhmana and Parashurâma a Kshatriya ?

Q :—What you say seems to be quite right,

but why then do not our Pandits and family-Gurus teach us the same thing?

Swamiji :—That is one of the great evils of our country. But let the matter rest now.

Swamiji here spoke highly of the Westerners' spirit of practicality, and how, when they take up religion also, that spirit shows itself.

Myself :—True, Maharaj, I have heard that their spiritual and psychic powers are very quickly developed when they practise religion. The other day Swami Saradananda showed me a letter written by one of his Western disciples, describing the spiritual powers highly developed in the writer through the Sâdhanâs practised for only four months.

Swamiji :—So you see! Now you understand whether there are Brâhmanas in the West or not. You have Brâhmanas here also, but they are bringing the country down to the verge of ruin by their awful tyranny, and consequently what they have naturally is vanishing away by degrees. The Guru initiates his disciple with a Mantra, but that has come to be a trade with him. And then, how wonderful is the relation nowadays between a Guru and his disciple! Perchance, the Guru has nothing to eat at home, and his wife brings the matter to his notice and says : "Pray, go once again to your disciples, dear. Will your playing at dice all day long save us from hunger?" The Brâhmana in reply says: "Very well, remind me of it tomorrow morning. I have come to hear tnat my disciple so-and-so is having a run of luck, and moreover, I have not been to him for a long time." This is what your Kula-Guru system has come to be in Bengal! Priestcraft in the West is not so degenerated, as yet; it is on the whole better than your kind!

CHAPTER III
[SURENDRA NATH SEN]

I

THE LOSS OF SHRADDHA IN INDIA AND NEED OF ITS REVIVAL—MEN WE WANT—REAL SOCIAL REFORM.

[*Saturday, the 22nd January, 1898.*]

Early in the morning I came to Swamiji who was then staying in the house of Balaram Babu, at 57, Ramkanta Bose Street, Calcutta. The room was packed full with listeners. Swamiji was saying, "We want Shraddhâ, we want faith in our own selves. Strength is life, weakness is death. 'We are the Atman, deathless and free; pure, pure by nature. Can we ever commit any sin? Impossible!'—such a faith is needed. Such a faith makes men of us, makes gods of us. It is by losing this idea of Shraddhâ that the country has gone to ruin."

Question :—How did we come to lose this Shraddhâ?

Swamiji :—We have had a negative education all along from our boyhood. We have only learnt that we are nobodies. Seldom are we given to understand that great men were ever born in our country. Nothing positive has been taught to us. We do not even know how to use our hands and feet! We master all the facts and figures concerning the ancestors of the English, but we are sadly unmindful about our own. We have learnt only weakness. Being a conquered race, we have brought ourselves to believe that we are weak and have no independence in anything. So, how can it be but that the Shraddhâ is lost? The idea of true Shraddhâ must be brought back once more to us, the faith in our own selves must be reawakened, and, then only, all the problems which face our country will gradually be solved by ourselves.

Q :—How can that ever be? How will Shraddhâ alone remedy the innumerable evils with which our society is beset? Besides, there are so many crying evils in the country, to remove which the Indian National Congress and other partriotic associations are carrying on a strenuous agitation and petitioning the British Government. How better can their wants be made known? What has Shraddhâ to do with the matter?

Swamiji :—Tell me, whose wants are those

—yours or the ruler's? If yours, will the ruler supply them for you, or will you have to do that for yourselves?

Q :—But it is the ruler's duty to see to the wants of the subject people. Whom should we look up to for everything, if not to the King?

Swamiji :—Never are the wants of a beggar fulfilled. Suppose the Government give you all you need, where are the men who are able to keep up the things demanded? So *make men* first. *Men* we want, and how can men be made unless Shraddhâ is there?

Q :—But such is not the view of the majority, sir.

Swamiji :—What you call majority is mainly composed of fools and men of common intellect. Men who have brains to think for themselves are few, everywhere. These few men with brains are the real leaders in everything and in every department of work; the majority are guided by them as with a string, and that is good, for everything goes all right when they follow in the footsteps of these leaders. Those are only fools who think themselves too high to bend their heads to anyone, and they bring on their own ruin by acting on their own judgment. You talk of social reform? But what do you do? All that you mean by your social reform is either widow remarriage or female emancipation, or something of that sort. Do you not? And these again are directed within the confines of a few of the castes only. Such a scheme of reform may do good to a few no doubt, but of what avail is that to the whole nation? Is that reform or only a form of selfishness—somehow to cleanse your own room and keep it tidy and let others go from bad to worse!

Q :—Then, you mean to say that there is no need of social reform at all?

Swamiji :—Who says so? Of course there is need of it. Most of what you talk of as social reform does not touch the poor masses; they have already those things—the widow remarriage, female emancipation, etc.,—which you cry for. For this reason they will not think of those things as reforms at all. What I mean to say is that want of Shraddhâ has brought in all the evils among us, and is bringing in more and more. My method of treatment is to take out by the roots the very causes of the diseases and not to keep them merely suppressed. Reforms we should have in many ways; who will be so foolish as to deny it? There is, for example, a good reason for inter-marriage in India, in the absence of which the race is becoming physically weaker day by day.

Since it was a day of a solar eclipse, the gentleman who was asking these questions saluted Swamiji and left, saying, "I must go now for a bath in the Ganga. I shall, however, come another day."

II

RECONCILIATION OF JNANA YOGA AND BHAKTI YOGA—GOD IN GOOD AND IN EVIL TOO—USE MAKES A THING GOOD OR EVIL—KARMA—CREATION—GOD —MAYA.

[*Sunday, the 23rd January, 1898.*]

It was evening and the occasion of the weekly meeting of the Ramakrishna Mission, at the house of Balaram Babu of Baghbazar. Swami Turiyananda, Swami Yogananda, Swami Premananda and others had come from the Math. Swamiji was seated in the verandah to the east, which was now full of people, as were the northern and the southern section of the verandah. But such used to be the case every day when Swamiji stayed in Calcutta.

Many of the people who came to the meeting had heard that Swamiji could sing well, and so were desirous of hearing him. Knowing this, Master Mahâshaya (M.) whispered to a few gentlemen near him to request Swamiji to sing; but he saw through their intention and playfully asked, "Master Mahâshaya, what are you talking about among yourselves in whispers? Do speak out." At the request of Master Mahâshaya, Swamiji now began in his charming voice the song—"Keep with loving care the darling Mother Shyâmâ in thy heart..." It seemed as if a Vinâ was playing. At its close, he said to Master Mahâshaya, "Well, are you now satisfied? But no more singing! Otherwise, being in the swing of it, I shall be carried away by its intoxication. Moreover, my voice is now spoilt by frequent lecturing in the West. My voice trembles a great deal...."

Swamiji then asked one of his Brahmachârin disciples to speak on the real nature of Mukti. So, the Brahmachârin stood up and spoke at some length. A few others followed him. Swamiji then invited a discussion on the subject of the discourse, and called upon one of his householder disciples to lead it; but as the latter tried to advocate the Advaita and Jnâna and assign a lower place to Dualism and Bhakti, he met with a protest from one of the audience. As each of the two opponents tried to establish his own view-point, a lively word-fight ensued. Swamiji watched them for a while but, seeing that they were getting excited, silenced them with the following words : —

Why do you get excited in argument and spoil everything? Listen! Sri Ramakrishna used to say that pure Knowledge and pure Bhakti are one and the same. According to the doctrine of Bhakti, God is held to be 'All-Love.' One cannot even say, 'I love Him,' for the reason that He is All-Love. There is no love outside of Himself; the love that is in the heart with which you love Him is even He Himself. In a similar way, whatever attractions or inclinations one feels drawn by, are all He Himself. The thief steals, the harlot sells her body to prostitution, the mother loves her child—in each of these too is He! One world system attracts another—there also is He. Everywhere is He. According to the doctrine of Jnana also, He is realized by one everywhere. Here lies the reconciliation of Jnana and Bhakti. When one is immersed in the hightest ecstasy of Divine Vision (Bhâva), or is in the state of Samâdhi, then alone the idea of duality ceases, and the distinction between the devotee and his God vanishes. In the scriptures on Bhakti, five different paths of relationship are mentioned, by any of which one can attain to God; but another one can very well be added to them, viz,—the path of meditation on the nonseparateness, or oneness with God. Thus the Bhaktas can call the Advaitins Bhaktas as well, but of the non-differentiating type. As long as one is within the region of Mâyâ, so long the idea of duality will no doubt remain. Space-time-causation, or name-and-form, is what is called Mâyâ. When one goes beyond this Mâyâ, then only the Oneness is realized, and then man is neither a Dualist nor an Advaitist—to him all is One. All this difference that you notice between a Bhakta and a Jnânin is in the preparatory stage—one sees God outside, and the other sees Him within. But there is another point : Sri Ramakrishna used to say that there is another stage of Bhakti which is called the Supreme Devotion (Parâ-bhakti), i.e., to love Him after becoming established in the consciousness of Advaita and after having attained Mukti. It may seem paradoxical, and the question may be raised here why such a one who has already attained Mukti should be desirous of retaining the spirit of Bhakti ? The answer is—the Mukta, or the Free, is beyond all law; no law applies in his case, and hence no question can be asked regarding him. Even becoming Mukta, some, out of their own free will, retain Bhakti to taste of its sweetness.

Q :—God may be in the love of the mother for her child, but, sir, this idea is really perplexing that God is even in the thieves and the harlots in the form of their natural inclinations to sin! It follows then that God is as responsible for the sin as for all the virtue in this world.

Swamiji :—That consciousness comes in a stage of highest realization, when one sees that whatever is of the nature of love or attraction is God. But one has to reach that state to see and realize that idea for oneself in actual life.

Q :—But still one has to admit that God is also in the sin!

Swamiji :—You see, there are, in reality, no such different things as good and evil. They are mere conventional terms. The same thing we call bad, and again another time we call good, according to the way we make use of it. Take for example this lamplight; because of its burning, we are able to see and do various works of utility; this is one mode of using the light. Again, if you put your fingers in it, they will be burnt; that is another mode of using the same light. So we should know that a thing becomes good or bad according to the way we use it. Similarly with virtue and vice. Broadly speaking, the proper use of any of the faculties of our mind and body is termed virtue, and its improper application or waste is called vice.

Thus questions after questions were put and answered. Someone remarked, "The theory that God is even there, where one heavenly body attracts another, may or may not be true as a fact, but there is no denying the exquisite poetry the idea conveys."

Swamiji :—No, my dear sir, that is not poetry. One can see for oneself its truth when one attains Knowledge.

From what Swamiji further said on this point, I understood him to mean that matter and spirit, though to all appearances they seem to be two distinct things, are really two different forms of one substance; and similarly, all the different forces that are known to us, whether in the material or in the internal world, are but varying forms of the manifestation of one Force. We call a thing matter, where that spirit force is manifested less; and living, where it shows itself more; but there is nothing which is absolutely matter at all times and in all conditions. The same Force which presents itself in the material world as attraction or gravitation is felt in its finer and subtler state as love and the like, in the higher spiritual stages of realization.

Q :—Why should there be even this difference relating to individual use? Why should there be at all this tendency in man to make bad or improper use of any of his faculties?

Swamiji:—That tendency comes as a result of one's own past actions (Karma); everything one has is of his own doing. Hence it follows that it is solely in the hands of every individual to control his tendencies and to guide them properly.

Q:—Even if everything is the result of our Karma, still it must have had a beginning, and why should our tendencies have been good or bad at the beginning?

Swamiji:—How do you know that there is a beginning? The Srishti (Creation) is without beginning—this is the doctrine of the Vedas. So long as there is God, there is Creation as well.

Q:—Well, sir, why is this Mâyâ here, and whence has it come?

Swamiji:—It is a mistake to ask "why" with respect to God; we can only do so regarding one who has wants or imperfections. How can there be any "why" concerning Him who has no wants, and who is the One Whole? No such question as "Whence has Mâyâ come?" can be asked. Time-space-causation is what is called Mâyâ. You, I and everyone else are within this Mâyâ, and you are asking about what is beyond Mâyâ! How can you do so while living within Mâyâ?

Again, many questions followed. The conversation turned on the philosophies of Mill, Hamilton, Herbert Spencer, etc., and Swamiji dwelt on them to the satisfaction of all. Everyone wondered at the vastness of his Western philosophical scholarship and the promptness of his replies.

The meeting dispersed after a short conversation on miscellaneous subjects.

III

INTERMARRIAGE AMONG SUBDIVISIONS OF A VARNA—AGAINST EARLY MARRIAGE—THE EDUCATION THAT INDIA NEEDS—BRAHMACHARYA.

[Monday, the 24th January, 1898.]

The same gentleman who was asking questions of Swamiji on Saturday last came again. He raised again the topic on intermarriage and enquired, "How should intermarriage be introduced between different nationalities?"

Swamiji:—I do not advise our intermarriage with nations professing an alien religion. At least for the present, that will, of a certainty, slacken the ties of society and be a cause of manifold mischief. It is the intermarriage between people of the same religion that I advocate

Q :—Even then, it will involve much perplexity. Suppose I have a daughter who is born and brought up in Bengal, and I marry her to a Maharatti or a Madrasi. Neither will the girl understand her husband's language nor the husband the girl's. Again, the difference in their individual habits and customs is so great. Such are a few of the troubles in the case of the married couple. Then as regards society, it will make confusion worse confounded.

Swamiji :—The time is yet very long in coming when marriages of that kind will be widely possible. Besides, it is not judicious now to go in for that all of a sudden. One of the secrets of work is to go by the way of the least possible resistance. So, first of all, let there be marriages within the sphere of one's own caste-people. Take for instance, the Kâyasthas of Bengal. They have several subdivisions amongst them, such as, the Uttar-rârhi, Dakshin-rârhi, Bangaja, etc., and they do not intermarry with each other. Now, let there be intermarriages between the Uttar-rarhis and the Dakshin-rarhis, and if that is not possible at present, let it be between the Bangajas and the Dakshin-rarhis. Thus we are to build up that which is already existing, and which is in our hands to reduce into practice—reform does not mean wholesale breaking down.

Q :—Very well, let it be as you say; but what corresponding good can come of it?

Swamiji :—Don't you see how in our society, marriage being restricted for several hundreds of years within the same subdivisions of each caste, has come to such a pass nowadays as virtually to mean marital alliance between cousins and near relations; and how for this very reason the race is getting deteriorated physically, and consequently all sorts of disease and other evils are finding a ready entrance into it? The blood having had to circulate within the narrow circle of a limited number of individauls has become vitiated; so the new-born children inherit from their very birth the constitutional diseases of their fathers. Thus, born with poor blood, their bodies have very little power to resist the microbes of any disease, which are ever ready to prey upon them. It is only by widening the circle of marriage that we can infuse a new and a different kind of blood into our progeny, so that they may be saved from the clutches of many of our present-day diseases and other consequent evils.

Q :—May I ask you, sir, what is your opinion about early marriage?

Swamiji :—Amongst the educated classes in Bengal, the custom of marrying their boys too early is dying out gradually. The girls are also given in marriage a year or two older than before, but that has been under compulsion—from pecuniary want. Whatever might be the reason for it, the age of marrying girls should be raised still higher. But what will the poor father do? As soon as the girl grows up a little, every one of the female sex. beginning with the mother down to the relatives and neighbours even, will begin to cry out that he must find a bridegroom for her, and will not leave him in peace until he does so! And, about your religious hypocrites, the less said the better. In these days no one hears them, but still they will take up the role of leaders themselves. The rulers passed the Age of Consent Bill prohibiting a man under the threat of penalty to live with a girl of twelve years, and at once all these socalled leaders of your religion raised a tremendous hue and cry against it, sounding the alarm, "Alas, our religion is lost!" As if religion consists in making a girl a mother at the age of twelve or thirteen! So the rulers also naturally think, "Goodness gracious! What a religion is theirs!

And these people lead political agitations and demand political rights!"

Q :—Then, in your opinion, both men and women should be married at an advanced age?

Swamiji :—Certainly. But education should be imparted along with it, otherwise irregularity and corruption will ensue. By education I do not mean the present system, but something in the line of positive teaching. Mere book-learning won't do. We want that education by which character is formed, strength of mind is increased, the intellect is expanded, and by which one can stand on one's own feet.

Q :—We have to reform our women in many ways.

Swamiji :—With such an education women will solve their own problems. They have all the time been trained in helplessness, servile dependence on others, and so they are good only to weep their eyes out at the slightest approach of a mishap or danger. Along with other things they should acquire the spirit of valour and heroism. In the present-day it has become necessary for them also to learn self-defence. See how grand was the Queen of Jhansi!

Q :—What you advise is quite a new departure, and it will, I am afraid, take a very long time yet to train our women in that way.

Swamiji :—Anyhow, we have to try our best. We have not only to teach them but to teach ourselves also. Mere begetting children does not make a father; a great many responsibilities have to be taken upon one's shoulders as well. To make a beginning in women's education: our Hindu women easily understand what chastity means, because it is their heritage. Now, first of all, intensify that ideal within them above everything else, so that they may develop a strong character by the force of which, in every stage of their lives, whether married, or single if they prefer to remain so, they will not be in the least afraid even to give up their lives rather than flinch an inch from their chastity. Is it little heroism to be able to sacrifice one's life for the sake of one's ideal, whatever that ideal may be? Studying the present needs of the age, it seems imperative to train some of them up in the ideals of renunciation, so that they will take up the vow of lifelong virginity, fired with the strength of that virtue of chastity which is innate in their life-blood, from hoary antiquity. Along with that they should be taught sciences and other things which would be of benefit, not only to them but to others as well, and knowing this they would easily learn these things and feel pleasure in doing so. Our motherland requires for her well-being some of her children to become such pure-souled Brahmachârins and Brahmachârinis.

Q :—In what way will that conduce to her well-being ?

Swamiji :—By their example and through their endeavours to hold the national ideal before the eyes of the people, a revolution in thoughts and aspirations will take place. How do matters stand now ? Somehow, the parents must dispose of a girl in marriage, if she be nine or ten years of age! And what a rejoicing of the whole family if a child is born to her at the age of thirteen! If the trend of such ideas is reversed, then there is some hope for the ancient Shraddhâ to return. And what to talk of those who will practise Brahmacharya as defined above—think how much Shraddhâ and faith in themselves will be theirs! And what a power for good will they be!

The questioner now saluted Swamiji and was ready to take leave. Swamiji asked him to come now and then. "Certainly, sir," replied the gentleman. "I feel so much benefited; I have heard many new things from you, which I have not been told anywhere before." I also went home, as it was about time for dinner.

IV

MADHURA-BHAVA—PREMA—NAMAKIRTANA—ITS DANGER—BHAKTI TEMPERED WITH JNANA—A CURIOUS DREAM.

[*Monday, the 24th January, 1898.*]

In the afternoon I came again to Swamiji and saw quite a good gathering round him. The topic was the Madhura-Bhâva or the way of worshipping God as husband, as in vogue with the followers of Sri Chaitanya. His occasional *bons mot* were raising laughter, when someone remarked, "What is there to make so much fun of about the Lord's doings ? Do you think that he was not a great saint, and that he did not do everything for the good of humanity ?"

Swamiji :—Who is that! Should I poke fun at *you* then, my dear is! You only see the fun of it, do you ? And you, sir, do not see the lifelong struggle through which I have passed to mould this life after his burning ideal of renunciation of wealth and lust, and my endeavours to infuse that ideal into the people at large! Sri Chaitanya was a man of tremendous renunciation and had nothing to do with woman and carnal appetites. But, in later times, his disciples admitted women into their order, mixed indiscriminately with them in his name, and made an awful mess of the whole thing. And the ideal of love which the Lord exemplified in his life was perfectly selfless and bereft of any vestige of lust; that sexless love can never be the property of the masses. But the subsequent Vaishnava Gurus, instead of laying particular stress first on the aspect of renunciation in the Master's life, bestowed all their zeal on preaching and infusing his ideal of love among the masses, and the consequence was that the common people could not grasp and assimilate that high ideal of divine love, and naturally made of it the worst form of love between man and woman.

Q :—But, sir, he preached the name of the Lord Hari to all, even to the Chandâlas; so why should not the common masses have a right to it?

Swamiji :—I am talking not of his preaching, but of his great ideal of love—the Râdhâ-prema,* with which he used to remain intoxicated day and night, losing his individuality in Radha.

Q :—Why may not that be made the common property of all?

Swamiji :—Look at this nation and see what

---

* The divine love which Râdha had towards Sri Krishna as the Lord of the universe.

has been the outcome of such an attempt. Through the preaching of that love broadcast, the whole nation has become effeminate—a race of women! The whole of Orissa has been turned into a land of cowards; and Bengal, running after that Radha-prema, these past four hundred years, has almost lost all sense of manliness! The people are very good only at crying and weeping; that has become their national trait. Look at their literature, the sure index of a nation's thoughts and ideas. Why, the refrain of the Bengali literature for these four hundred years is strung to that same tune of moaning and crying. It has failed to give birth to any poetry which breathes a true heroic spirit!

Q :—Who are then truly entitled to possess that Prema (love)?

Swamiji :—There can be no love so long as there is lust—even a speck of it, as it were, in the heart. None but men of great renunciation, none but mighty giants among men, have a right to that Love Divine. If that highest ideal of love is held out to the masses, it will indirectly tend to stimulate its worldly prototype which dominates the heart of man—for, meditating on love to God by thinking of oneself as His wife or beloved, one would very likely be thinking most of the time of one's own wife—the result is too obvious to point out.

Q :—Then is it impossible for householders to realize God through that path of love, worshipping God as one's husband or lover and considering oneself as His spouse ?

Swamiji :—With a few exceptions; for ordinary householders it is impossible no doubt. And why lay so much stress on this delicate path, above all others ? Are there no other relationships by which to worship God, except this Madhura idea of love ? Why not follow the four other paths, and take the name of the Lord with all your heart ? Let the heart be opened first, and all else will follow of itself. But know this for certain, that Prema cannot come while there is lust. Why not try first to get rid of carnal desires ? You will say—"How is that possible ?—I am a householder." Nonsense! Because one is a householder, does it mean that one should be a personification of incontinence, or that one has to live in marital relations all one's life ? And, after all, how unbecoming of a man to make of himself a woman, so that he may practise this Madhura love!

Q :—True, sir. Singing God's name in a party (Nâmakirtana) is an excellent help and gives one a joyous feeling. So say our scriptures, and so did Sri Chaitanya Deva also preach to the masses. When the Khole (drum) is played upon, it makes the heart leap with such a transport that one feels inclined to dance.

Swamiji :—That is all right, but don't think that Kirtana means dancing only. It means singing the glories of God, in whatever way that suits you. That vehement stirring up of feeling and that dancing of the Vaishnavas are good and very catching no doubt, but there is also a danger in practising them, from which you must save yourself. The danger lies here—in the reaction. On the one hand, the feelings are at once roused to the highest pitch, tears flow from the eyes, the head reels as it were under intoxication—on the other hand, as soon as the Sankirtana stops, that mass of feeling sinks down as precipitately as it rose. The higher the wave rises on the ocean, the lower it falls, with equal force. It is very difficult at that stage to contain oneself against the shock of reaction; unless one has proper discrimination, one is likely to succumb to the lower propensities of lust etc. I have noticed the same thing in America also. Many would go to church, pray with much devotion, sing with great feeling, and even burst into tears when hearing the sermons; but after coming out of church, they would have a great reaction and succumb to carnal tendencies.

Q :—Then, sir, do instruct us which of the ideas preached by Sri Chaitanya we should take up as well-suited to us, so that we may not fall into errors.

Swamiji :—Worship God with Bhakti tempered with Jnâna. Keep the spirit of discrimination along with Bhakti. Besides this, gather from Sri Chaitanya his heart, his loving-kindness to all beings, his burning passion for God, and make his renunciation the ideal of your life.

The questioner now addressed the Swamiji with folded hands. "I beg your pardon, sir. Now I come to see you are right. Seeing you criticize in a playful mood the Madhura love of the Vaishnavas, I could not at first understand the drift of your remarks; hence I took exception to them."

Swamiji :—Well, look here, if we are to criticize at all, it is better to criticize God or God-men. If you abuse me I shall very likely get angry with you, and if I abuse you, you will try to retaliate. Isn't it so ? But God or God-men will never return evil for evil.

The gentleman now left, after bowing down at the feet of Swamiji. I have already said that such a gathering was an everyday occurrence when Swamiji used to stay in Calcutta. From early in the morning till eight or nine at night, men would flock to him at every hour of the day. This naturally occasioned much irregularity in the time of his taking his meals; so, many desiring to put a stop to this state of things, strongly advised Swamiji not to receive visitors except at appointed hours. But the loving heart of Swamiji, ever ready to go to any length to help others, was so melted with compassion at the sight of such a thirst for religion in the people, that in spite of ill health he did not comply with any request of the kind. His only reply was, "They take so much trouble to come walking all the way from their homes, and can I, for the consideration of risking my health a little, sit here and not speak a few words to them?"

At about 4 P.M. the general conversation came to a close, and the gathering dispersed, except for a few gentlemen with whom Swamiji continued his talk on different subjects, such as England and America, and so on. In the course of conversation he said:

"I had a curious dream on my return voyage from England. While our ship was passing through the Mediterranean Sea, in my sleep, a very old and venerable-looking person, Rishi-like in appearance, stood before me and said: 'Do ye come and effect our restoration. I am one of that ancient order of Theraputtas which had its origin in the teachings of the Indian Rishis. The truths and ideals preached by us have been given out by Christians as taught by Jesus; but for the matter of that, there was no such personality by the name of Jesus ever born. Various evidences testifying to this fact will be brought to light by excavating here.' 'By excavating which place can those proofs and relics you speak of be found?' I asked. The hoary-headed one, pointing to a locality in the vicinity of Turkey, said, 'See here.' Immediately after, I woke up, and at once rushed to the upper deck and asked the Captain, 'What neighbourhood is the ship in just now?' 'Look yonder,' the Captain replied, 'there is Turkey and the Island of Crete.'"

Was it but a dream, or is there anything in the above vision? Who knows!

CHAPTER IV

[SURENDRA NATH DAS GUPTA]

THINK OF DEATH ALWAYS AND NEW LIFE WILL COME WITHIN—WORK FOR OTHERS—GOD THE LAST REFUGE.

One day, with some of my young friends belonging to different colleges, I went to the Belur Math to see Swamiji. We sat round him; talks on various subjects were going on. No sooner was any question put to him than he gave the most conclusive answer to it. Suddenly he exclaimed, pointing to us, "You are all studying different schools of European philosophy and metaphysics and learning new facts about nationalities and countries; can you tell me what is the grandest of all the truths in life?"

We began to think, but could not make out what he wanted us to say. As none put forth any reply, he exclaimed in his inspiring language :

"Look here—we shall all die! Bear this in mind always, and then the spirit within will wake up. Then, only, meanness will vanish from you, practicality in work will come, you will get new vigour in mind and body, and those who come in contact with you will also feel that they have really got something uplifting, from you."

Then the following conversation took place between him and myself:

Myself:—But, Swamiji, will not the spirit break down at the thought of death and the heart be overpowered by despondency?

Swamiji:—Quite so. At first, the heart will break down, and despondency and gloomy thoughts will occupy your mind. But persist, let days pass like that—and then? Then you will see that new strength has come into the heart, that the constant thought of death is giving you a new life, and is making you more and more thoughtful by bringing every moment before your mind's eve the truth of the saying, "Vanity of vanities, all is vanity." Wait! Let days, months and years pass, and you will feel that the spirit within is waking up with the strength of a lion, that the little power within has transformed itself into a mighty power! Think of death always and you will realize the truth of every word I say. What more shall I say in words!

One of my friends was praising Swamiji in a low voice.

Swamiji :—Do not praise me. Praise and censure have no value in this world of ours. They only rock a man as if in a swing. Praise I have had enough of; showers of censure I have also had to bear; but what avails thinking of them! Let everyone go on doing his own duty, unconcerned. When the last moment arrives, praise and blame will be the same to you, to me, and to others. We are here to work, and will have to leave all when the call comes.

Myself :—How little we are, Swamiji!

Swamiji :—True! You have well said! Think of this infinite universe with its millions and millions of solar systems, and think with what an infinite, incomprehensible power they are impelled, running as if to touch the Feet of the One Unknown—and how little we are! Where then is room here to allow ourselves to indulge in vileness and mean-mindedness? What should we gain here by fostering mutual enmity and party-spirit? Take my advice: Set yourselves wholly to the service of others, when you come from your colleges. Believe me, far greater happiness would then be yours than if you had had a whole treasury full of money and other valuables at your command. As you go on your way serving others you will, on a parallel line, advance in the path of knowledge.

Myself :—But we are so very poor, Swamiji!

Swamiji :—Leave aside your thoughts of poverty! In what respect are you poor? Do you feel regret because you have not a coach and pair or a retinue of servants at your back and call? What of that? You little know how nothing would be impossible for you in life if you labour day and night for others with your heart's blood! And lo and behold! the other side of the hallowed river of life stands revealed before your eyes—the screen of Death has vanished, and you are the inheritors of the wondrous realm of immortality!

Myself :—Oh, how we enjoy sitting before you, Swamiji, and hearing your life-giving words!

Swamiji :—You see, in my travels throughout India all these years, I have come across many a great soul, many a heart overflowing with loving-kindness, sitting at whose feet I used to feel a mighty current of strength coursing into my heart, and the few words I speak to you are only through the force of that current gained by coming in contact with them! Do not think I am myself something great!

Myself :—But we look upon you, Swamiji, as one who has realized God!

No sooner did I say these words than those fascinating eyes of his were filled with tears (Oh, how vividly I see that scene before my eyes even now), and he with a heart overflowing with love, softly and gently spoke : "At those Blessed Feet is the perfection of Knowledge sought by the Jnânis! At those Blessed Feet also is the fulfilment of Love sought by the Lovers! Oh, say, where else will men and women go for refuge but to those Blessed Feet!"

After a while he again said, "Alas! what folly for men in this world to spend their days fighting and quarrelling with one another as they do! But how long can they go on in that way? In the evening of life* they must all come home, to the arms of the Mother."

* At the end of one's whole course of transmigratory existence.